Praise for STOP

"We need to change the way we think about our customers (and our business). Traditional Marketing methods aren't wrong, just outdated. They do not help us create loyal, raving fans who want to help us grow our businesses. In "STOP Marketing – Your Customers are Dying To Do It For You," Blaine Millet takes a quantum leap ahead of traditional marketing methods and serving customers. He provides a revolutionary yet straightforward approach to become unique and completely differentiated in our customers' eyes. Customers are motivated and excited to go out of their way to tell others and do our marketing for us. The author shows us why, and crucially how, to rethink our entire customer interaction process by creating a culture of customer obsession. This game-changing model changes and revolutionizes the most critical of all decisions, which is how we find, treat, and retain loyal customers who use the power of their microphone to sing our praises and literally do our marketing for us. This book is a must-read for any business leader who wants to grow and scale their business faster and more profitably."

Michael Langhout, Founder & Managing Partner Langhout International LLC

"Blaine's concept of becoming "REMARK"able by being Customer Obsessed connects directly with Alta's core Guiding Principle of "Customers for Life." Focusing on The "REMARK"able Triangle cornerstones of Trust, Customer Experience, and Supporting our customers and local communities are critically essential as we strive to be the differentiated leader in our industry."

Brian McKenzie, General Manager Chicago Industrial Group Alta Equipment Company®

"We have enjoyed working with Blaine at MHEDA because we share the same belief system in that being Customer Obsessed is the only way to serve our members and provide them with the value they expect and deserve. We look forward to continuing to differentiate our organization by improving our practices and focusing on his unique model, The "REMARK"able Triangle, so we can continue to build more Trust, improve our Customer Experience, and always be Helping Others."

Liz Richards, CEO Material Handling Equipment Distributors Association

"Blaine Millet brings simple AND meaningful right to your fingertips in this book. I love "How to become "REMARK"able by being Customer Obsessed" simply because it changed our business. It will change yours too. The impact you feel is two-fold: your team will become "driven to serve," and your customers will recognize that experience. I owe a profound 'debt' of gratitude to Blaine for writing this book and sharing it with me."

Dave Carroll, VP Banner Bank Retail Banking and Founder of Cantillon

"Blaine has nailed it and is right on the money in his book, "STOP Marketing – Your Customers are Dying to Do it For You." Traditional marketing is not only dead, it is a thing of the past! Being "Customer Obsessed" is the only way your business will not only succeed but thrive in today's world. The game has changed! Before selling my company, we were using Blaine's model of being "Customer Obsessed" and it not only worked externally and internally, but it changed our business! We were growing at an astounding rate and succeeding and winning every day! The "customer experience" is what your business will be judged on. If that customer experience is remarkable, then you will exceed expectations! This book is a must-read for all employees within your organization!"

Rick Smith, Former CEO EJ Bartells

STOP

Marketing

Your Customers Are
DYING TO DO IT FOR YOU!

How To Become
"*REMARK*"able™

Blaine W. Millet

Author of "*Creating and Delivering Totally Awesome Customer Experiences*"

Copyright

For general or additional information about this book, please contact Blaine W. Millet at WOM10.com and direct all inquiries to StopMarketing@WOM10.com.

This book is also available in other formats.

Library of Congress Control Number: 2020923519

Millet, Blaine W.

Stop Marketing - Your Customers Are Dying To Do It For You...How to Become "*REMARK*" able™

by Blaine W. Millet – First Edition.

p. cm.

Includes index.

This book will let you create a truly differentiated business your customers love and your competitors hate! It shows you how to turn your audience into your Advocates and Marketing Agents™ who are anxious to tell others how incredibly awesome and amazing you are and literally Do Your Marketing For You. You get the recipe and formula to become "*REMARK*"able by being Customer Obsessed...changing your business forever!

ISBN: 978-1-7362218-0-8

First Edition – Printed in the United States of America.

ATTENTION CORPORATIONS, COLLEGES, PROFESSIONAL ORGANIZATIONS AND ASSOCIATIONS:

Quantity discounts (rebates) are available on bulk purchases of this book. For information, please contact WOM10 at StopMarketing@WOM10.com, or visit our website at WOM10.com

Book Cover design by Bravoboy

Dedication

This book is dedicated to...

First would be God. Without his guidance, this would never have seen the light of day. It is for the Glory of God this book exists.

Second is my wife, Lorrie. She is my rock. She is the driving force behind everything I do. She is the love of my life and my biggest cheerleader...I am truly blessed to have her by my side.

Third is my family and extended family. Without them encouraging me and showing their love and support, this would not have been possible. A big thank you to Krystal, JB, Katrina, Tyler, Kyle, Jackson, Ollie, and Harley. And to my brother Gary, sister Joyce, and all the members of our extended families.

Finally, this is dedicated to YOU...the reader. To all the business owners, CEOs, and leaders out there who picked up this book for the sheer purpose of wanting to be a better company and organization. Having this book says a lot about who you are...you want something more, better, and different. I applaud you. And for the thousands of people I have met through speaking and consulting, I hope this continues to guide you to becoming "*REMARK*" able™!! You truly can be different, unique, and get the very best people telling others about how awesome you truly are. You can become *"REMARK"* able™...now let's go make it happen!

Preface

During a recent business trip, I rented a car. I stopped by the airport rental counter and found the desk unoccupied. A prominently placed sign redirected me to the car lot for pickup. At the lot, I noticed an exceptionally long line waiting to check-in. I felt sorry for the lone associate tasked with looking after each frustrated customer. After two long hours of waiting, it was my turn. I soon discovered the car I had reserved had already been rented to someone else. It wasn't going well, and I was tired.

The counter representative was visibly agitated. Not because I didn't get the car I reserved, but because of the long line facing her and her inability to take a break. I was just another number-an obstacle in her day, an interruption, and perhaps even a nuisance. The only option she gave me was to upgrade at a higher cost, which I had little choice but to accept. It was an unpleasant experience and likely will be the last time I rent from that company. The second time in two weeks, I had experienced this type of treatment from the same company in two different locations. This company had significant issues around training, staffing, and attitude and lacked the culture I desired as a customer.

Contrast this experience with another experience I had when traveling to Japan. My wife joined me on this trip, and I booked our hotel reservations with the same chain in Osaka and Tokyo. Our customer experience was outstanding at both locations. Days before our arrival, I received several welcoming emails from them. They recommended things to do while visiting, arranged a car for transport, arranged translation services, and recommended restaurants. In addition to the basics, they also offered assistance in helping make this an enjoyable trip for my wife, such as spa treatments, local shops, and other points of interest such as historical temples in Kyoto, Japanese gardens, and a guided tour of the grounds at the Imperial Palace in Tokyo.

Upon arrival, we were greeted by name as we stepped out of our taxi. We were ushered into the lobby and met by a personal concierge. We were given water and a light snack and asked about our trip and if we needed anything. The concierge explained the amenities available and confirmed our evening dinner reservations we had planned with a colleague. We were 'enveloped' into their way of treating people that was incredibly warm and welcoming. Our family had a similar experience with the same hotel chain in another country. The staff was passionate about delivering experiences like no other, regardless of the location. They anticipated, personalized, and always exceeded our expectations. Every time. We were grateful and pleased and will return many times to any of their properties.

This experience didn't 'just happen.' It happened because it was integral to the training given to each and every employee. It went beyond their product or service and extended into the very culture of the company. It was an effortless experience that made us feel like a part of their family. They were Customer Obsessed!

In *'STOP Marketing...Your Customers are DYING to DO IT FOR YOU,'* Blaine Millet lays out the case for a different approach and gives us the key to the ultimate differentiator. He gives us a simple yet incredibly powerful recipe (or formula) to create this ultimate differentiation. Something every CEO and business leader strives for in their career and company. He redirects our thinking from exclusively optimizing our product or service and offers an alternate approach that every leader should adopt. This approach goes well beyond traditional marketing. It embraces a change in company processes, training, and attitudes about the customer, putting them at the very center of company culture. In this new and revolutionary approach, the company literally becomes the product. A new culture is created that 'obsesses' over the customers' well-being. So much so that we, as customers, will go to great lengths to tell others about how famously and incredibly we are treated.

Examples are in abundance of transactions among consumers doing business in a B2B relationship, purchasing products or services, a B2C retail setting, a restaurant or dry goods store, or an online purchase, which have been disappointing and fallen far short of meeting their needs. Consumers are highly selective, and good companies are continually identifying ways to meet each consumer's needs. Excellent companies seek to differentiate their products or services such that their ideal or core customer will consistently return to them. Customers choose companies that deliver an outstanding experience, have earned their trust, and are continually trying to improve their lives.

Companies worldwide are rethinking their customer relationships, how they interact with customers, and anticipating their needs and desires, all to be different, unique, and endearing to anyone coming across their path. Their obsession with their customers is so evident that the customer will gladly retell their experiences to others. The reverse is also true. Customers will describe, in painstaking detail, their bad experiences with unfriendly companies as well. Achieving this utopia of getting others to tell your story and encouraging others to buy from you is the ultimate differentiator. It is what Blaine has given us in this book. It is the magic and answer to what has been elusive to most of us throughout our leadership careers. Now, the answer, and formula, is in front of us with this book.

CEOs that I coach reflect vastly different views on this subject. Invariably, when asked how their company treats or feels about their customers, they answer something like this, 'We love our customers and will do almost anything for them.' However, upon closer evaluation, an inconsistent picture of 'customer satisfaction' emerges, which often cannot be measured or tracked in any meaningfully growth-centric way. 'Customer satisfaction' is measured by the number of rejected products or the number of complaints received from dissatisfied customers. They will try hard to please but leave it up to those who deal directly with the customer to do what they think is best. There is little or no training. There is certainly no customer-centric culture. They will stagnate, and their remaining customers will disappear. They are in a race to the bottom.

Some companies have a great deal of customer turnover, which puts pressure on sales to rapidly bring new customers. Business development and marketing for many companies represent a high investment level, with an uncertain or unquantifiable ROI. The ROI on Marketing expenses is difficult to measure. A 'push' marketing campaign may be well designed and automatically delivered to the client list, but most are ineffective at meeting the customer's need at the time and place they need it.

Wouldn't it be great if this investment was put into developing a culture of obsessing over customers? We would train employees to deliver well-defined processes that are built to delight the customer over and over again. It would distinguish the company, setting it apart as unique and different. This is an excellent business strategy every leader should adopt. Blaine's approach in this book gives this freely to everyone who dares to change their culture to be one that is truly differentiated in the eyes of your customer.

Most companies desire to please customers but cannot do so on a systematic and repeatable basis. They do not have a reliable feedback system and often experience high rates of customer turnover. It doesn't have to be this way. You have a choice. You can allow everyone in your company to continue doing what they are doing, trying hard to please, but working in an environment where many feel no connection to the customer. Or you can begin to examine your people and processes, take control, and begin to lead your company in a new direction. You can change your culture to one that is customer obsessed. With this book's approach, we can create a culture where you have raving fans excited to tell others about their experience with you and your company.

Blaine Millet has focused on teaching others about the importance of customer-centricity throughout his distinguished career as a consultant, business coach, author, and speaker. His first book *'Creating and Delivering Totally Awesome Customer Experiences'* is a step-by-step guide for companies who have a strong desire to focus on the customer experience.

Now, with *'STOP Marketing, Your Customers are DYING to DO IT FOR YOU,'* Blaine takes the concept and practice of customer obsession to a much deeper level. In the pages that follow, you will learn about 'Why' it is vital to become customer obsessed and gain insights and instruction on 'How' to do it. Blaine provides a roadmap that takes the reader sequentially through the steps needed to completely change the way business is done, creating a customer obsessed and customer-centric organization. The result is building an army of raving fans who love what you are doing for them and are willing and excited to tell others about you. These customer 'fans' actually do your marketing for you.

Frequently, the best business relationships start with a common interest, which grows into a friendship, and ultimately mutual respect for each individual's professional accomplishments over time. I've known Blaine Millet for over 20 years, and he is my good friend. I have a great deal of respect for his work and have learned much from him, utilizing his model in my practice.

An enduring characteristic I admire in Blaine is his relentless passion for helping CEOs and their leadership teams understand how to deliver their services or products to customers with excellence. In the pages that follow, you will learn a better way of operating your business, one that goes beyond the products that you make or the services that you provide.

In Blaine's model, the company becomes the product, executing flawlessly and delivering a seamless and outstanding experience that consistently exceeds customer expectations at every level. And when this happens, your customers (and others) will gladly (and excitedly) go out of their way to do your marketing for you. You have entered into a completely new culture and way of doing business. You have become, as he puts it, "*REMARK*" able™!

Mike

Michael Langhout

Founder and Managing Partner, Langhout International LLC

Contents

Introduction

> *That's been one of my mantras – focus and simplicity. Simple can be harder than complex: You have to work hard to get your thinking clean to make it simple. But it's worth it in the end because once you get there, you can move mountains.*
>
> STEVE JOBS

Here's the deal...I have one purpose and only one purpose for this book...to get you more Advocates and Marketing Agents™ who are anxious to tell others how incredibly awesome and amazing you are as an organization so they can do your marketing for you...period.

There's a better way to market. There is a better way to GROW your business. A better way to build awareness, demand, gain new customers, keep existing customers, and grow profits. There is a better way to create a culture that sets your company on fire with excitement and enthusiasm, unlike you have ever seen before. And there is a better way to truly and completely DIFFERENTIATE your company from your competitors.

All this happens when you become "*REMARK*" able™.

You see, this book isn't actually about **MARKETING**. It is a book about your **ENTIRE BUSINESS**. Since marketing is a significant pathway to building your business, it's something that needs to change...and fast. Change the way you market and change your overall focus on your audience, and you'll change your business forever!

I believe the way many companies market today is dead...it just hasn't been buried yet. We've been duped into believing that marketing is working today. I'm afraid I have to disagree completely...it is not. It is broken and not delivering anywhere near what it should. And I believe it is impeding companies from growing and scaling, it is lowering their enterprise value, and it is stifling the culture we truly want.

Marketing affects more than your advertising and communications with your audience...it affects your entire business enterprise!

I want to offer you a different solution. A solution that is so simple, so common sense, I challenge you to tell me it won't work. In a world where we overcomplicate most things, I want to go back to simple, "dirt simple," actually. You will see this permeated throughout this book...dirt simple.

I don't have all the answers...not by a long shot. What I do have are two things...experience and insights. And I know two other things for sure...

First...complex models dazzle leaders but don't work. The more complex the model, the more people think you are super smart, so they should follow a model they don't understand. They try working with the complex model for a while, wasting Time, energy, and financial resources, only to find out it doesn't make sense or work the way they thought it would. I used to be that way...not any longer...I stopped doing that many years ago. I grew up and realized it didn't work. You won't find any of that nonsense here. I focus on two factors we all know work...**simplicity and common sense**. Complex models don't pass the "**Common Sense Smell Test**."

We have "gut instincts" for a reason...it's our common sense kicking us in the gut and telling us this doesn't make sense. You know this...you operate this way. We use analytics to confirm our gut instincts...and they're more often right than wrong. When we use analytics and other fancy

tools to prove our gut wrong, we usually pay...I know I have many times. Maybe you have as well. Everything you will read here is simple...it is going to pass your "Common Sense Smell Test" in everything you read. No smoke, no mirrors, just simple, common sense put into an easy-to-understand model you can implement. Which brings me to the second thing...

Second...there is no model out there worth a grain of salt UNLESS EVERY EMPLOYEE embraces it, internalizes it, and can execute it...none. The reason models (and change) fail isn't because the model won't work...it just can't (or won't) get implemented (and supported) by the entire organization. The model is so complex that most don't understand it and just told to do it, or they just don't see how it will help...so it fails. It is not embraced, internalized, or executed.

You can't fix these two issues by throwing money at them. I created some of these complex models in my early consulting days, and they stunk. They were intellectually stimulating and correct, but they stunk up the room. They were never going to get implemented because of the two factors I just mentioned above.

One day I had an epiphany. I realized that no one wants complex models, other than the ones who build and sell them. Employees (and leaders) hate them. And if they hate them, there isn't a chance they will ever get executed. They're doomed before you even sign the consulting agreement.

Marketing is the same way. The campaigns, models, programs all stink up the room. They don't work...which is why we get excited when we get a .05% return on something...really? Common sense tells us this isn't going to work, but we do it anyway...I want to help you STOP that.

The bottom line is this...you have an INCREDIBLE OPPORTUNITY in front of you...today...to be different...to become the envy of your industry. I want you to seize this opportunity...and I'll tell you how you can do it.

Ask yourself, "*What would our company look like if our entire company culture focused on simplicity and common sense? What would our customers think?*" You would have one hell of a competitive advantage since your company would eclipse everyone in your industry. You would have a line of people waiting to work for you and buy from you, not to mention the army of people who couldn't wait to **TELL OTHERS** how incredibly awesome and amazing you are as a company. That is what I want for you and your company...and it is **the entire purpose of this book.**

Ask yourself another question, "*If we implement a solution that is easily understood by everyone in the company, and they know what their role is in making it happen, would our chances of it being executed and implemented increase or decrease?*" Probably rhetorical...you know the answer. Your chances would skyrocket!!

Marketing is often viewed as manipulative, coercing, high-pressure, misleading, inaccurate, smoke and mirrors, self-serving, bait and switch, and a host of other unpleasant terms. I want you to be in a different place where you leave all this nonsense behind. I want both marketing and your business to be incredibly successful so you can eclipse your competition and rise to the top in your market. I can help you make this happen.

This book is much **MORE THAN MARKETING**...it is about **YOUR ENTIRE BUSINESS**. This book (and model I will give you) will change your company's culture, your DNA, to one that is laser-focused on making your customers feel incredibly special. Your company or organization will be completely different and unique from your competitors.

My model is a recipe, if you will, for building massive (and lasting) differentiation in your industry...regardless of your industry.

My model will transform your employees and your leadership team into a company your customers (and others) will rave about and tell others. My goal is simple and straightforward. I will give you the formula and roadmap to be Customer Obsessed so you can become "*REMARK*"able™.

I truly want you to **STOP MARKETING** the way most companies market today. I want to guide you through a process that will create a **Customer Obsessed culture**. Your customers will welcome it and want to participate in it with you...they are **DYING TO DO YOUR MARKETING FOR YOU**.

When you are "REMARK" able™, your audience can't wait to tell others how incredibly awesome and amazing you are. I want them to go out of their way to tell others why they should be your Customer. **It doesn't get any better than this.** Since the beginning of Time, there hasn't been a more powerful way to generate business...and it's no different today.

Let's get started...turn the page to begin what could be your most extraordinary Journey.

My Passion... My Why

The presence of passion within you is the greatest gift you can receive. Treat it as a Miracle.

WAYNE DYER

What is your "Passion" for "WHY" you are in business...for what you do...for what gets you up in the morning?

My WHY...My Passion...I don't want any organization to ever have to market again...ever. I want to help them become so incredibly unique and differentiated (in the eyes of their audiences) that their audiences will happily and gladly market for them.

This is what causes me to leap out of bed every day! Often I get introduced as "This is the guy you need to talk to if you want to build your business faster and stronger. He will help you do something we all want to do but never seem to make happen...getting our customers doing our marketing for us. He'll show you how you can become truly differentiated and unique in your market. He does this by helping you transform your company culture into being Customer Obsessed so you can become "*REMARK*"able™."

While this might sound great, it isn't my "WHY." It's "WHAT" I help companies do, "HOW" I help them do it, and some of the benefits they will receive...but not "WHY" I do what I do. "WHY" I do what I do is pretty simple.

It's why I wrote this book. I want this for you and your organization. Together, we can make that happen...I have the formula. But I also have a PASSION and WHY that relates specifically to you and me as a customer.

I want every Customer on the planet to feel incredibly important and special with every interaction they have with any organization.

We deserve it. We pay our hard-earned money to organizations for their products and services (or a donation)...don't we deserve to feel special and important? I think it should happen for all customers. It should be a given.

I love seeing companies become "REMARK" able™. Helping them along "their Journey" is exhilarating and rewarding. And I absolutely despise and hate being "pimped" by companies. I'm tired of being manipulated through their marketing and other communications just for the privilege of spending my money with them. I want to feel like I matter and that they genuinely appreciate my business. Is that too much to ask? I don't think so. I think it is how a business should operate...at a minimum.

Also, I don't particularly appreciate it when I'm forced to feel like an idiot and embarrassed if I don't buy their products or services. And I hate getting low value for my investment of Time and money. But most of all, I hate being treated like I am just "another customer" and just another "transaction" to them. Are you with me? And I want the hamburger they show me in the ad, not the one they serve me.

I want to help every company I can eliminate marketing...the "pimping" marketing we all hate. I want your customers (and all of us) to love you and rave about how incredibly awesome and amazingly you treat your audience. I want your customers to be insanely loyal and passionate Advocates for you and your company that they literally act as your Marketing Agents and do your marketing for you. I want your customers to bring in boatloads of new customers. Is that too much to ask?

I don't think this is too much to ask...I believe it should be the new baseline for every organization...making us feel like we matter!

Deep down inside, don't we all want this? Wouldn't it be a much better world if all the companies we dealt with were Customer Obsessed and treated us like we were truly special and important? Why is this the exception rather than the norm? Why do we get so excited when we finally find a company that treats us this way? Shouldn't they all?

Helping organizations understand this, create it, and deliver it to their customers and others is what gets me up in the morning. I hope by writing this book and sharing it with thousands (maybe millions) of business leaders, more will make this happen. That would be awesome!

I firmly believe customers are dying to be your Advocates and Marketing Agents™.

We haven't "armed" them with anything to talk about...so they don't talk about us. I'm talking about giving your audience an incredible, over-the-top rock your world experience, specific ways to help them improve their life and/or their business, and you keep your promises, building enormous amounts of Trust. When you do this, you eclipse your competitors...catapulting your company ahead of everyone!

I want you to be the organization with an army of Advocates and Marketing Agents™ who can't wait to tell others about you. The beauty of it all...not many are doing it today. What an INCREDIBLE OPPORTUNITY! And I want you to seize this opportunity. That's my WHY... that's my PASSION.

Utopian? Possibly...but not unachievable. Why not you?

Helping you become "*REMARK*" able™ is my "beacon on top of the hill," "my guiding light," "my pinnacle." It's what I strive for every single day. If I can help move you to wanting this for your organization by the time you turn the last page, I will consider this book a success and well worth the time and effort it took to develop the model and write it.

My goal is to see your business change. I would be thrilled if you bought one book, dog eared all the pages, passed it around to all your employees to read, and implemented it in your organization. I would rather sell this one book than have you buy 100 books that sit on the shelf.

I hope you get as excited when reading this as I have been writing it over the past five years. I hope you get all "jacked up" and energized to the point of saying, "This is exactly the type of company I want to lead...we need to get started...yesterday."

Thank you for starting the Journey with me... it's going to be AWESOME! Let's get things kicked off...

The END...in the BEGINNING

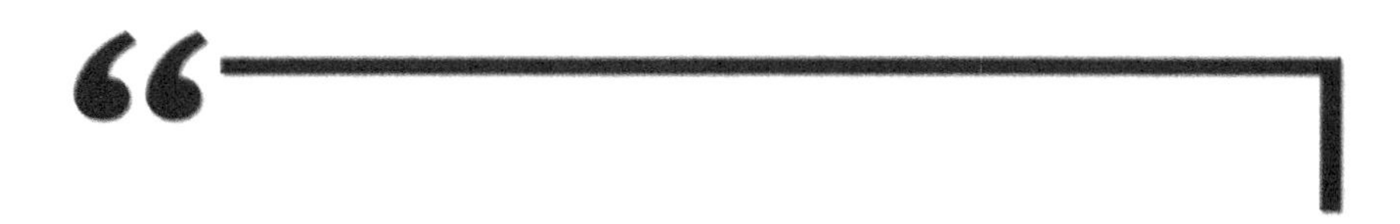

The end is in the beginning and lies far ahead.

RALPH ELLISON

What would your business look like if you had the majority of your audience (including customers) telling thousands of others you are THE ONE they should be doing business with...every single day?

I don't want to waste your TIME. After all, it is our most valuable asset today. I'll talk more about that in the upcoming chapter, "**Our Most Important Asset**." Time is something I am very conscious of in everything I do...I **Promise** not to waste yours.

I want you to know precisely what you will have when you finish reading this book. In essence, I want to tell you the ending before you begin reading, so you are excited to turn the pages. I want you to know what this book is about BEFORE you invest your valuable Time reading it.

I use the word "end" loosely since I refer to it only in the context of where you will be when you finish reading the book. The "Journey" to becoming "*REMARK*" able™ has no ending...it just gets stronger and stronger as you continue to do more of what you will learn in this book.

Being Customer Obsessed and becoming "*REMARK*" able™ isn't a "project."

Becoming "*REMARK*" able™ is a continuous process, only getting better each day you obsess over your customers. It may start out feeling like a project because there are activities, milestones, goals, and accountability, but you will soon find out it is truly a Journey. You will learn much more about this in the chapter, "**What is Customer Obsession.**"

The END I refer to is giving you a specific recipe and formula, along with a vision of what your company could look like if you are Customer Obsessed, and you become "*REMARK*"able™.

I'm sure you have noticed the word **"*REMARK*" able™** looks and feels a bit different. "*REMARK*" able™ is simply the result of what happens for Customer Obsessed organizations. When your company is so incredibly awesome and amazing that people can't wait to tell others about you, you've become **"*REMARK*" able™**...they are "**REMARKING**" about you to others. To me, that's the ultimate end game...having your audience telling everyone else they know why they should buy from you.

I want your entire audience to become your Trusted Advocates and Marketing Agents™, who do your marketing for you...period.

I wrote a specific chapter on this, "**Becoming "*REMARK*" able™**," which will help you learn more about it. The keyword is "**becoming.**" It describes the reward you get when you implement the three "cornerstones" of the model I will share with you. You will learn what it means to **BE Customer Obsessed**. And when you being Customer Obsessed, the end result, the reward, is **BECOMING "*REMARK*" able™**. Reaping the rewards of becoming "*REMARK*" able™ is the book's entire objective and goal. **I want you to become "*REMARK*" able™...period.**

Getting talked about, or I should say, "promoted," by your customers (and others), is the envy of every company on the planet!

Regardless of their industry, every organization would love to have their entire audience telling other potential customers about them...**doing their marketing for them**. The result we all want is to have our organizations "**remarked**" about to as many people as possible who are relevant to our business...period.

Today, you probably have some people in your audience "remarking" about you to others...this is common. For most, it's around 5% - 20%. If you have an audience of 1000, that's 50 – 200 people out there telling others how wonderful you are. Congratulations... that's fantastic.

But what if that number was, say, 60%? What if you had 600 people out there telling others how incredibly awesome and amazing you are to work with? How would that change your business? How would that improve your bottom line? How would that impact the culture and happiness of your employees? My bet is your company would significantly improve.

What if there were 800 - 900 people in the market telling others how they completely trust you and recommend you without question? How would that change your business? My bet is it would elevate your company to a completely different level from where you are today. This is what happens when you **become "*REMARK*" able™**. Together, we can make that happen.

How can you become "*REMARK*" able™?

I will be giving you a "Formula" and "Recipe" that is simple to understand. It is a thing of beauty if I do say so myself. It will make complete sense to you because you are also a customer, in addition to being a business leader. I know you will say, "***This is exactly how I would like to be treated and feel as a customer.***" My model is how you, a customer, would want to feel if you were going to "*REMARK*" about an organization.

The real question I hope you ask yourself continuously throughout the book is, "***How would this make me feel if I was a customer of my own organization and I was being treated this way by our employees?***"

I designed the model, **The "*REMARK*" able Triangle™,** to be simple and straightforward so everyone in your organization can understand it, internalize it, and execute it. Your audience will become your Advocates and Marketing Agents™. They are more than happy to tell others about you and create **unique and powerful differentiation for your company.**

You will have everything you need to start building your Customer Obsessed foundation. I won't hold anything back...you get it all. The magic is in the model...simple, straightforward, and common sense.

I will also give you a variety of "Tools" and "Exercises" to use with your leadership team and employees to help you implement **The "*REMARK*" able Triangle™**. You will end up with the knowledge and recipe for what is needed to become "*REMARK*" able™.

Are you in? If becoming "*REMARK*" able™ sounds like a Journey you would want your organization to be on, then let's GET STARTED!

Getting Started...

> *"We are at our very best, and we are happiest when we are fully engaged in work we enjoy on the Journey toward the goal we've established for ourselves. It gives meaning to our time off and comfort to our sleep. It makes everything else in life so wonderful, so worthwhile."*
>
> EARL NIGHTINGALE

Why should I care about being Customer Obsessed? Why do I need to become "REMARK" able™? Do my customers really care?

You have just started your Journey to getting talked about more in the market and leveraging your audience to do it for you...CONGRATULATIONS! This book will be incredibly uplifting and encouraging for you and your entire leadership team while learning how to become "*REMARK*" able™.

This book is for the top leaders in any organization who have the ability and authority to change their business. It is for those who can make it happen, build culture, and drive change when they see a significant opportunity to differentiate their business.

It is for the CEOs, Presidents, Business Owners, C-level suite leaders, Innovation Team Leads, and anyone else who can "influence" or "drive change" within an organization. It is for the individuals who have the foresight to see a vision of something incredibly powerful and different and execute on it. But most of all, this is a book for visionaries, not naysayers.

Let's start with some questions I hope you are asking yourself as you begin to read this book...

- "WHY should I care about Customer Obsession?"
- "WHY do I need (or want) to become "*REMARK*" able™?"
- "WHY would I want to transform my company into a Customer Obsessed business?"
- "WHY do my customers really care?"
- "HOW do you become a Customer Obsessed organization?"
- "HOW can I turn my customers into my Advocates and Marketing Agents™, so they are not just passively telling others about us but are proactively (and passionately) telling others about us?"
- "HOW can I leverage (and change) my marketing in today's crowded and noisy world, so my audience actually notices us and looks forward to hearing from us?"
- "HOW can we make more money being Customer Obsessed?"
- "HOW will this truly differentiate my business from my competitors and give me a significant competitive advantage?"
- "WHY is this such a "game-changer" and not just another "shiny object" or a short-term quick fix?"
- "WHAT can we specifically do to become "*REMARK*" able™?
- And many other WHY, HOW, and WHAT questions...

These (and many others) questions will all get answered as you read through the book. Once you get the answers to these questions, then YOU can decide if the benefits of becoming "*REMARK*" able™ by being Customer Obsessed are worth it to you. I think you will see pretty quickly how it will change your business forever...more than you could have imagined. I hope you will want to jump in with both feet and drive hard to reach the desirable state of becoming "*REMARK*" able™.

I also want to **Change your mindset** to one of "**investing in your customers**," not spending more money in marketing and other low return activities designed to attract and keep your customers. The concept of "**customer investment**" should be in the front of your mind throughout this book. Only then will you truly see why you need to...

Stop "SPENDING" in marketing and start "INVESTING" in your customers (and others) so you can create more ADVOCATES AND MARKETING AGENTS™ who are DYING TO DO YOUR MARKETING FOR YOU.

When you start "investing" in your customers, you are on the path to creating a powerful "leveraged" return on your investment. The more you put into it, the more you will get out of it. It isn't spending again and again and hoping to get a better result. You treat it like any other investment you make in your business (plant, equipment, or people) where you invest in getting a more massive return. Customer Obsession operates exactly the same way. Like all the other investments you make, this one can also create a significant increase in

"Enterprise Value." Your business's value will go up when you are Customer Obsessed and become "*REMARK*" able™.

Here is how I organized the book, so you know exactly what to expect as you read it...no surprises.

FIRST...I will give you some "**FOUNDATIONAL ELEMENTS.**" These are areas every organization needs to know about, regardless of whether they end up being Customer Obsessed. I believe these areas should be top of mind for every business leader as they run their business. I have zeroed in on two that are so "**mission-critical**" you can't ignore them, regardless of your particular industry. These two are incredibly powerful. If you focused on just these two elements and nothing else, your business would improve...guaranteed. These foundational areas will help set the stage for answering the question of "WHY you would want to be Customer Obsessed to become "*REMARK*" able™.

SECOND...We will look at the **PROBLEMS and ISSUES** I consistently hear from business leaders like you. Many of these have evolved because we now live in the new **Customer Economy**. I'm sure you will identify with one or more of these in your own business. If you can, you're in luck...you will be getting answers which will help you improve in every one of these areas and significantly reduce or eliminate these problems and issues.

THIRD... Once we recognize the issues and problems we all face, I want to open your eyes to see the vast **OPPORTUNITIES** waiting for you when you overcome them. Becoming "*REMARK*" able™ allows you to take full advantage of these many opportunities...quickly and well into the future. There are six primary opportunities I will share with you for **WHY** you would want to **be Customer Obsessed and become "*REMARK*" able™**. These opportunities are available to you when you have an army of **Advocates and Marketing Agents™** telling others they should be buying from you...it is a real "game-changer."

FOURTH... Since I am asking you to **STOP MARKETING**, it's only fair to talk more about why I believe **marketing is broken**. I want you to see HOW you can use "**Customer Marketing**" in a completely different way to get significantly better results. I will give you a better understanding of how marketing "should be done" in the new Customer Economy, where the Customer is in complete control.

FIFTH... This is where the fun really starts...we jump into the deep end of the pool, and I share with you my **RECIPE AND FORMULA** for how you can be Customer Obsessed and become "*REMARK*" able™. These chapters make up the bulk of the book. I will give you a very simple and straightforward model for **HOW to transform your organization to become "*REMARK*" able™.** It will help you look beyond how you are doing things today and how incredibly awesome and amazing they could be tomorrow. I don't hold anything back...you get it all. Your role is to understand it, adopt it, internalize it, and execute it.

FINALLY...We end our Journey together with some **TACTICAL ACTIONS** you can start doing tomorrow to move forward on your own Journey to becoming

"*REMARK*" able™. I will give you some very specific actions you can take almost immediately to move forward on your Journey. Regardless of whether you decide to jump "all-in" on being Customer Obsessed and becoming "*REMARK*" able™, these will help you improve your company overall...guaranteed.

I hope that you would read through the book in its entirety to fully grasp how everything fits together, like pieces of a puzzle. If you are open to exploring a new way of thinking, a new way of differentiating yourself, and a new way to be a leader in your industry, you will love this book.

I see the world a little different than most. I look at it well into the future and through the eyes of the Customer. I hear what Customers want that makes them feel special, important, and valued. I listen to what they think makes memorable and differentiated companies. And I want to help you become one of those companies. Sadly, not every leader gets it. I hope you are one that does. The ones that get it stand out and are differentiated and unique in the eyes of their customers. And since customers are the only ones who pay us, I think we need to listen.

> SPOILER ALERT: One thing this book isn't is another rah-rah book full of pithy quotes, feel-good phrases, and hollow promises. It is a book of substance...a model, to be exact. When followed, my model will help you create an army of **Advocates and Marketing Agents™** who want to do your marketing for you. This book won't leave you hanging, not knowing what to do next. It is full of actionable items and a formula, not platitudes that won't create any change. It is a book on transformation, not hype.

Telling your employees just to smile more, be happier, and be more pleasant won't change your business. Providing beer on Fridays, bring your pet to work days, free food, and other perks will build your culture...but in the wrong direction. Being a Customer Obsessed company will change your company, your culture, and your employees...period.

I don't believe in dressing up the pig, so everyone thinks things are better when they aren't. I don't believe in superficial fixes that don't stand the test of time and give you improvements today and well into the future. Customers are super smart and can see right through these hollow promises and actions...just like you can see through them when you are a customer. They don't work...and they don't last.

This is a book about change...transformation...tough stuff. It is a book for those who want to invest the time and resources to make the Journey. Those who want to reap the rewards of being at the top of the mountain. The model for becoming "*REMARK*" able™ will, without a doubt, catapult you ahead of your competitors so you can win...and win big! I'm going to give you the plan. It's up to you to execute it.

If you are the type of leader who is genuinely open to change and can support it throughout your company, you will love this book. It is for leaders who want more **innovative ways to differentiate** and rise above the competition. It's not for the mild, non-action oriented faint of heart leaders...**it's for bold leaders who want to be at the top of their industry**.

The mind shift that takes place inside your company will not be subtle...it will be loud and bold, and every Customer will feel the change...and LOVE IT! Competitors will be jealous and try to copy what you are doing. They can't...they won't have the formula you have.

Often companies operate in 'organized chaos'...like a hockey game. They react to the latest urgent matter in react mode, like chasing the puck on the ice. Customer Obsession, as opposed to a hockey game, is a well-orchestrated symphony. Everyone's part is well understood, and the end result is a thing of beauty...and your customers get an incredibly awesome and amazing experience with every interaction. You and your employees will earn buckets full of trust from your audience when they see how you help them improve their lives and/or their businesses. The "combination" of everything you will learn in this book is what creates beautiful music for your employees and your audience.

Before we dive into talking about the **PROBLEMS** almost all businesses face today in the new Customer Economy and the **OPPORTUNITIES** you have sitting in front of you, I want to share with you two critically important "**foundational elements**" to keep in mind throughout the book and beyond. These two areas exist RIGHT NOW in virtually every organization.

The **first foundational element** focuses on what our customers (and everyone) consider their "**Most Important Asset.**" If we are aware of this in everything we do, we will do better at what we do. It is an absolutely critical ingredient to get your arms around, regardless of your industry.

The **second foundational element** is what I call the "**Silent Killer.**" I can guarantee this is happening in your organization today. I'm sure you will see it clearly once you learn more about it. The "Silent Killer," as well as your "Most Important Asset," are critical ingredients to understand as you embark on your Journey of being Customer Obsessed and becoming "*REMARK*" able™.

After we discuss these two foundational elements, we'll jump in...talking about WHY this could be the most incredibly awesome and amazing game-changer you may have ever experienced as a business leader.

Are you READY?

MISSION CRITICAL

Our MOST Important Asset

My favorite things in life don't cost any money. It's really clear that the most precious resource we all have is Time.

STEVE JOBS

Are you "wasting" your customer's Time, or are you "saving" them Time when they interact with you?

Which of your assets yields a significant return? Which of your assets helps you get more customers? Which of your assets helps your company to be a leader in your industry? Our assets and investments are the foundation and catalyst to help us get more done, receive a greater return, and differentiate us from our competitors.

I want to kick things off by sharing with you something that will be pervasive throughout this book. It is an **essential element to dramatically improving your company**, whether or not you ever decide to be Customer Obsessed... it's that important.

TIME.

One of the most significant issues I hear from customers is how companies "**waste their time**" or "**do not value**" their Time. We're all guilty of doing this to one degree or another. Yet, it is paramount with customers. It is one of the first complaints I hear from customers when I ask them how they feel when working with an organization. It comes up almost every time.

I can't emphasize how important TIME is to your audience. That is why you will hear me nagging you throughout the book about TIME, to make sure we help our customers maximize it when they work with us. I want this to be burned into our minds and our thoughts. Everything I share with you throughout the book will help you improve in this area. And, at the end of the day, if your audience feels like you have honored and valued their Time, you will stand out...guaranteed.

As you think about Time, here are some questions I would encourage you to ask...

- *"If you were to prioritize your personal assets, where would "Time" rank on your list?"*
- *"If you were to rank your customer's most valuable assets, where do you think "Time" would rank on their list?"*
- *"When you think about your business processes, do you think your processes save (or cost) your customer's Time?"*
- *"If I interviewed your customers, would they tell me you save them Time or waste their Time in how you serve them?"*

If someone asks you what "assets" you own or possess, it's a pretty easy question to answer...everyone knows their "physical" assets. But what about the "intangible assets" we all own? What?!? For example, relationships are an "intangible asset" since they are essential...they just don't make it on the "balance sheet."

Our "assets" are important and add value to us, both as individuals and our businesses.

According to Forrester Research[1], there is one asset more valuable than all the others...our **NUMBER ONE ASSET**. In a study by Forrester in 2017, they found that "***66% of US online adults said that valuing their time is the most important thing a company can do to provide them a good online customer experience."*** **TIME** was their most valuable asset! Not money or other assets. **TIME** was most valuable.

Respect my Time, or I'll find someone who will.

How many times have we heard, "*Don't waste my time*"? Or, "*My time is valuable. Get to the point.*" Or, "*Why are you telling me this? It's wasting my time.*" **We value our Time**. And it is even more important today.

Customer Obsessed organizations show their audiences they value their Time...they don't waste it.

Customers often tell me they feel like they save Time when working with Customer Obsessed organizations. Customer Obsessed organizations understand how important it is and build it into their culture. It is one of the ways they differentiate themselves.

The real question is, "*How do we, as customers, get more from the time we have so we don't waste it on worthless activities*"?

Today, our customers have countless options and choices available to them. However, having more choices can also cause us to waste more time. In the past, there weren't as many choices for consumers or companies. The choice was easy...and, most importantly, took virtually no time. When there was only one color of the car, black, the decision was easy. The purchasing decision was based on when you could afford it, not what model, color, availability, price, or size you wanted. It was fast and efficient. People didn't waste their time searching through hundreds of products, reviews, prices, and other information to make their decision.

While you might argue it is much better today because we have so many choices, I would argue that it isn't all it's cracked up to be...it causes us to waste more of our most valued asset, Time. If "Time" is our most valuable asset, then why do we spend so much of it trying to shave a few dollars off the price of something when it uses up more of our most valuable asset?

All of these extra choices and options simply take up more of our TIME!

Today, we have to evaluate the quality of products, the pricing, the financial terms, the availability, ability to deliver, the technology, and other factors before making a decision. All this takes TIME.

All these components are "Commodity" elements. More choices have forced our audiences to evaluate us based on commodity factors...this is not good for any business. It tells the customer we are "all the same." This is messed up. It is NOT the way any of us want to be viewed as a business. We need to change this...and change it fast. Having all these choices is almost becoming more of a curse than a blessing.

What if you could genuinely help your audience SAVE TIME and help them get to the right answer...faster and more efficiently?

If Time is our number one asset, other factors should be of less importance...including price. Often, we think the price is the key determinant, but is it really? Maybe not. Perhaps the real reason price rises to the top is because our audience doesn't think we can help save more of their number one asset, TIME. Maybe if they felt we could actually save them Time, the price would fall further down the list in their decision-making criteria. Perhaps they would view us as different from our competitors if they genuinely believed we could save them more of their most valuable asset. How would this change the game for you?

Think about this from your own perspective as a customer. If you were the Customer of a company that said they could save you Time above all of their competitors, wouldn't you want to know more about them and how they do it? I would. They would get my attention immediately. Think of Amazon and others who have streamlined ways for you to purchase from them. They are focused on helping their Customer save Time. Amazon didn't create "Buy with 1-Click" for nothing.

We immediately associate more "value" to companies when they demonstrate they can help us save our most coveted asset...Time.

Customer Obsessed organizations know this value equation and go out of their way to help their audience save Time. They add "**more value**" to the relationship because they value their Time. As these companies become "*REMARK*" able™, we, their customers, tell others how they helped us save this valuable asset. I just told you about Amazon...that was free marketing I just gave Amazon. See how this works? Word gets around quickly when you help your customers get more of their single most valuable asset.

What if you were that business that could help their customers save Time? They would love you. Here's something to think about and how to relate this to your own business. Virtually everyone reading this book has had the experience of spending (wasting) Time on the phone with an issue. Usually, this is a very painful and unpleasant experience if the company isn't Customer Obsessed. Unfortunately, we have come to expect a "low bar" to be the "norm" for these types of calls.

We expect to be barraged with a host of automated choices to choose from. Then, after struggling to (hopefully) get to the right area, we end up getting put on the infamous "indefinite hold" with unappealing music we can't turn off. Our anxiety increases when we hear the infamous message, "*We apologize for the inconvenience, but our wait times have increased due to the increase in call volume.*" When "wait times have increased," what does it really mean in terms of Time. Or what about when they tell us we are number 9 in line...how does that translate to Time? How long does the average call take? Is this going to be 3 minutes or 30 minutes? Our anxiety continues to increase. When we finally get the answer, the person on the other end of the phone isn't usually the happiest or friendliest. Overall, we still end up with a less than pleasant experience. Sound familiar?

Does any part of the above example apply to your company? Does this experience (or something similar) apply to how you treat your customers (or prospective customers) when they call your organization? Here's a super easy test you can do yourself...right now. Put down the book and pick up the phone and call 1-800 Your Company. See what is happening when someone calls your organization. Is it what you, as a customer, want?

When you have a goal of becoming a "*REMARK*"able™ company, your culture is about having "every customer" become an Advocate and Marketing Agent™ for your company.

Companies who go out of their way (noticeably) to save their customers Time. What do YOUR customers say about how you treat their most valuable asset of TIME? Customer Obsessed companies put the Customer in the center of everything they do, including valuing their Time. They redesign their processes to give their Customers a maximum positive impact. They demonstrate how much they care and appreciate their Time with every interaction. They are essentially "giving them the gift of Time" back. When the Customer sees this behavior (consistently), they realize how incredibly important, respected, and valued they are to your company.

When you focus on helping your Customer with their number one asset...TIME...you are viewed as more valuable and differentiated from your competitors.

And here's the big bonus and the entire focus of this book. When you help your audience get back more of their Time, they will go out of their way to tell others about your company...period. It's human nature. My primary goal is to help you create your own posse of Advocates and Marketing Agents™, who can't wait to tell others about you. One thing they will tell others is how you saved them TIME!

Now that you know what is most important to your audience, let's look at the second "Mission Critical" foundational element that is consistently plaguing your customers.

I call it the "**Silent Killer.**"

The "Silent" Killer

Now is the age of Anxiety.

W. H. AUDEN

Do your customers experience anxiety and stress when they interact with your company? Are you creating "unknowns" that leave them wondering, "what's going to happen next?"

There are three things we absolutely need (and want) less of in our lives... stress, anxiety, and risk. Simply commuting to work, especially in the Seattle area where I live, gives us enough anxiety and stress. Since we experience all three of these in our life on an everyday basis, we certainly don't need (or want) to add any more of them to our lives.

Unfortunately, as you will soon discover, organizations actually create MORE stress and anxiety for their customers simply by the way they do business. What?!? Why is that? What is it we do that feeds these undesirable monsters? More importantly, what can we do to eliminate them and give our customers more peace of mind?

Stress and Anxiety are the "Silent Killers" in business today.

The critical question to ask yourself is whether or not you "add" or "subtract" stress from the lives of your customers? Let me share with you a few questions to see if this is happening in your organization...

- *"If you were to ask a random sample of your customers whether you increased or reduced their anxiety when they work with you, what would they say?"*
- *"Do your employees create or alleviate customer anxiety and stress in how you interact with them?"*
- *"Do your processes and procedures create anxiety and stress with your customers?"*
- *"Would your customers say you eliminate or create surprises?"*

According to Dictionary.com, anxiety is "***distress or uneasiness of mind caused by fear of danger or misfortune***." When I interview customers, most tell me they have some degree of anxiety when dealing with businesses...some considerably more than others. They have anxiety before, during, or after interacting with them. Given the number of "unknowns" and "surprises" they receive with each interaction, it's no wonder customers feel this way.

Anxiety happens because of the "unknown."

Think about it on a personal level. The only time you don't have anxiety is when you either "know what to expect" (and it isn't bad) or when "you don't care" about the situation. Other than these two times, we have some degree of anxiety because of the uncertainties.

Do you "create" anxiety in your audience?

Think about this question for a minute. I ask customers this same question, *"Does working with this company increase your anxiety? Do they create uncertainties or give you surprises?"* Sadly, most customers feel like this happens more times than not. Unknowingly, the company is "creating" additional stress and anxiety when they with their customers. Most of us don't think about it in the course of our day...but it should be top of mind in everything we do. We may be "creating" it for our audience or even "experiencing" it as a customer ourselves.

Put yourself in your Customer's shoes for a minute. How would you feel as a customer of your own business when you interact with various people inside your organization? Do you feel like this is one of the best parts of your day? Is it one of the easiest, least anxious things you do? Is the interaction with your company stress-free, or does it make you anxious? Do you provide enough information to eliminate the unknowns? Do you get surprised in any way throughout your experience? When leaders answer these questions honestly, they quickly realize they probably are creating stress and anxiety in their audience's lives. And, in many cases, they actually may be increasing their customers' anxiety. What?!? How can this happen? Why does it happen?

Evaluating the amount of "stress" and "anxiety" we create for our customers should be a top priority.

What causes companies to increase our anxiety and stress throughout our buying process and customer Journey? Why do companies allow stress and anxiety to be part of their processes? Why do they hire people who create more stress and anxiety with their approach and personality? Often, we don't even know it is happening. Why do we do this to our customers?

We don't "purposefully" create Stress and anxiety. It is usually gets created because we don't eliminate our audience's "perceived" anxiety.

For example, let's say you have to place an order with a company for a product you need by a specific date. Even before you make the call, you are anxious about several things. **First**, am I going to reach the person who can help me and make it happen? **Second**, do they even have the product? **Third**, will they be able to get it to us on time to meet our deadline? And **finally**, what will my experience be dealing with this organization before, during, and after the sale? These are "perceived" areas of uncertainty and the unknown, which causes our customers to be anxious.

Whether your business model is B2C (Business to Consumer) or B2B (Business to Business), your customers have some anxiety. **Anxiety happens because they don't know everything that is going to happen**. It is the "**Silent Killer**" and is "**foundational**" to every business. Every organization, Customer Obsessed or not, needs to know this is happening. It is a significant barrier to creating Advocates and Marketing Agents™.

It is impossible to become *"REMARK"*able™ if you are creating anxiety in your customers.

If we don't reduce (or eliminate) our Customers' anxiety, we can't get to our ultimate goal of becoming *"REMARK"*able™...never happen. But once you are aware this is happening inside your business, you can start to eliminate it. I will give you a very specific recipe to help you eliminate this from your company. Being Customer Obsessed will help you significantly reduce or eliminate anxiety with your customers. When you purposefully reduce or eliminate stress and anxiety from your audience, THEY NOTICE...and THEY TELL OTHERS.

We have become a bit numb to anxiety today. We expect to be a little more anxious or stressed when interacting with companies. The pace of society, business, and technology has increased our anxiety, not reduced it.

When was the last time you called up your insurance company, for example, and didn't expect it to be stressful and almost argumentative to get what you want? Or when you purchased something online and weren't quite sure about how they were handling your purchase or delivery?

When the stakes and outcomes are high, our anxiety level goes up. And the higher the level of anxiety, the less opportunity we have to enjoy the experience. We are so concerned that we don't get to enjoy the experience along the way from one moment to the next. It is NOT what we want.

However, when a business purposefully lowers or eliminates our anxiety as part of what they do, our odds of enjoying the experience increase significantly. I know I would. When this happens, we can remember the experience and even tell others about it. What a concept! Reducing our audience's anxiety allows our Advocates and Marketing Agents™ to do their job...telling others how incredibly awesome and amazing we are to work with.

Take another example, one which probably creates a bit more tension. Let's say you are interacting (in a B2B environment) with a new company, one you have never worked with before. You need to buy some essential parts or products. You have a significant (and large) order you need to get placed and delivered. It creates much higher anxiety...the "bet your job" kind of pressure. You decided to work with this new company, and if they let you down, you could get fired. A significantly higher level of anxiety has been created for a routine purchasing decision.

As a company, if you were able to alleviate this Customer's anxiety, do you think they would remember you? Do you think they might tell others (inside and outside their company) how incredibly awesome and amazing you are to work with? I believe they would...I would, and I think you would. Anxiety is in our face all the time at work and in our personal lives. There are different levels of anxiety we experience for a variety of reasons.

One of the problems we have, as business leaders, is that we often don't know what level of anxiety we are creating for our customers. We have become so anesthetized to how we do business that we don't understand how we create anxiety or its severity, at least not from our Customer's perspective. We usually don't have an accurate assessment of the level of anxiety we are creating. Knowing our customers' anxiety levels is critically important to understand before we can move forward to eliminating it.

Customer Obsessed companies understand the perceived level of anxiety their customers may be going through. They proactively handle it in such a way as to significantly reduce or eliminate it, allowing their customers to enjoy the experience...and talk about it to others.

When you are Customer Obsessed, you focus on your Customer's level of anxiety...it is part of the formula for how to be Customer Obsessed. I will share a recipe with you later in the book to build specific plans to eliminate it before it even begins. I will discuss this recipe in detail in the chapter on "**How you become a Customer Obsessed organization**."

Customers are anxious about two things...the PROCESS and the OUTCOME.

PROCESS ANXIETY is where the Customer doesn't understand what is going to happen next. They are left wondering what will happen next, who will do what, and when it will happen. Their Journey is one of ongoing anxiety as they try to understand the process. Their anxiety increases when they don't know the plan or what will happen next. By the way, this also wastes our Customer's Time...their number one asset.

OUTCOME ANXIETY is where the Customer doesn't fully understand what the outcome might be. While they hope it turns out the way they want (in their mind), there is a significant risk the outcome won't match what they perceive. When someone doesn't know the outcome, I guarantee you they will be anxious.

Regardless of whether it is **process anxiety** or **outcome anxiety** (or both), your Customer wastes a lot of energy and Time worrying about this situation. And no customer wants to waste their Time. They will stop this on their own and seek out another alternative...a competitor. For organizations that want to have their customers "**REMARK**" (talk) about them, spreading massive positive word-of-mouth, anxiety is enormous. No customer will ever say anything positive about a business that causes them to be anxious...ever.

Anxiety kills word-of-mouth and our chance to become *"REMARK"*able™.

A close relative to ANXIETY is the issue **SURPRISES**. There are good surprises and bad surprises...but all of them create anxiety. For example, when someone is expecting to get engaged, there is definitely a high degree of anticipation and anxiety. But when the big question is popped, it is a delightful and well-received surprise. On the other hand, if you were expecting to get a critical shipment of something by Friday and it doesn't arrive by Friday, your anxiety just went through the roof...a nasty surprise.

Anxiety is the "**Silent Killer**" for an organization because it happens without people thinking (or knowing) about it. Unless the Customer specifically says something about it, it doesn't get addressed...it just merely happens without most employees recognizing it. Customers typically don't mention it because they get met with excuses or the most famous phrase of all, "*I don't know, it's not my job.*" These actions create or enhance customer anxiety.

When the Customer is anxious, it is virtually impossible for them to enjoy the experience. How can you sit back and enjoy the experience when you're trying to figure out what will happen next? The company just wasted what could have been an incredible experience because the Customer was so anxious about the **process** and the **outcome**.

Why do we do this to our customers? Why do we allow this "**Silent Killer**" to penetrate our organizations? Why do we not recognize this is happening and put some changes into place to help eliminate customer anxiety? All great questions, which is why I call it the "**SILENT KILLER**." I think it would be fascinating to measure the blood pressure and heart rate of a customer before interacting with a business, during their interaction, and after their interaction. These numbers would most likely be higher than we would like to see for our customers' interactions.

However, you may not be the only one creating their anxiety. Often, someone may be anxious about an experience because of their previous experiences. They may have a **mind map** (my term) about what they "believe" is going to happen during their experience (their perceived experience). "Mind maps" are "**pictures or feelings we have in our head about what we believe will happen.**" These are formed from either our prior experience or one we have heard about. Often, they are referred to as "**preconceived notions**" of what is going to happen.

For example, going to buy a car in a traditional dealership can give you a mind map of being made to feel uncomfortable and pressured. If you are a car dealer and don't want customers coming in who have a "mind map" about having a bad experience and creating anxiety, you will have to go out of your way to change their "mind map" for YOUR dealership.

Customer Obsession helps you change the mind maps of your audience...to be viewed as completely different from your competitors.

The goal is to move your customer interactions from "anxiety" to "awesomeness." When you create Customer Experience Maps, for example, you design the experience with the sole purpose of eliminating anxiety and creating an incredibly awesome and amazing experience. I'll talk about these "Maps" in the chapter, "**The Map to the Treasure,**" or you can check them out in even greater detail in our first book, "**Creating and Delivering Totally Awesome Customer Experiences**." These "Maps" allow you to change the "mind map" from negative to positive quickly.

When a customer's mind map is changed, they are now excited to tell others because it is such a dramatic difference from what they expected and possibly experienced before. What if the dealership had Customer Experience Maps focused on delighting its customers? They would leave saying, "*WOW, that is not what I expected from a dealership at all. It was actually a positive buying experience and the best one I have ever had*." If this happened, you would most likely get customers spreading incredibly positive word-of-mouth about your dealership. You successfully changed their mind map from being distasteful to enjoyable. You eliminated their anxiety and replaced it with awesomeness and uniqueness. And they will tell others about it because it was so incredibly different and enjoyable.

And if you aren't quite convinced (yet) that people have already created mind maps about specific businesses, just ask them. For example, ask them to describe their experience (and mind map) for the following companies and listen to their anxiety and stress as they describe their experience...

- Car dealers
- Investment advisors (stockbrokers and other wealth advisors)
- Insurance companies
- Lawyers
- Other service companies
- Auto repair companies
- Possibly YOUR company???

I, and probably you, have personally lived the car dealer experience too many times in my life. It wasn't that long ago when my daughter was looking to buy a car...a used car, since she was just starting her new career. Our anxiety was spiking because of our "mind map" for what a used car salesperson and dealership was like...not pleasant, and downright distasteful. We were anxious and nervous about the experience before we even stepped onto the car lot.

Even though we knew it was coming, it still created anxiety. My daughter's anxiety level was off the charts...her mind map said this would an unpleasant, uncomfortable, and insulting experience. We were gearing up to do battle before we entered a dealership.

Unfortunately, our mind maps were correct. Everything we had anticipated happening happened. It was a shark pit...all the lowest-paid sharks waiting for the next prey to swim by. One leaped out of the pit and, in seconds, was on us before we could even reach the building...we'd been intercepted.

Then the usual question about what kind of car we wanted to buy. When we said, "*An inexpensive quality used car*," the guy seemed annoyed...not a big commission coming his way, so he was visibly disappointed. I explained the mind map I had of what was going to happen...he shows us cars, lets us test drive a few, asks us if this is a car we could see ourselves driving away today (they really need a better line than that old one), and what would it take to earn our business today.

Of course, he disagreed and told me this dealership was different, and they don't operate like all the other dealerships in the market. I said, "*That's great to hear. Exactly how does your process work, and why is it so different from all the others out there? What do you do that is going to make this a pleasant experience?*" He went on to explain how they worked and how they were so different. They weren't different...they were exactly the same as everyone else...they just changed the language to convince themselves they were different. There wasn't any part of the experience that didn't match my mind map...they failed.

Welcome, Tesla. Tesla changed the experience...completely. They saw the **opportunity** (which is in front of every car dealer and manufacturer) and said this is broken. They proceeded to blow it up and change it completely. They made it easy, comfortable, and a pleasant way to buy a car. Granted, they aren't the average priced car and are only for a select group of people, but they changed the experience. They created a pleasant car buying experience and one every other car dealer could follow if they wanted.

If we want the Customer to change their mind map, we have to have an alternative that delivers an extraordinary buying experience. It is the **OPPORTUNITY** staring everyone who sells cars (or anything else) right in the face. Some dealers (like Sewell Automotive I'll talk about later) have ventured out to be different and unique. Some have succeeded. If you buy from them, you get to have a delightful experience...a new mind map.

Does any of this translate into what might be happening inside your organization? Maybe this is a good time to pause and think about how your customers feel after each interaction. Perhaps your industry has some stories like the car dealer. Great Time for some introspection and thinking about your industry and your situation.

One question I often ask in speeches that get most CEOs and Leaders thinking...

> ***"Why is it we (as an organization) are willing to give our customers an experience we, as customers, would not find acceptable?"***

Recognizing and **eliminating the SILENT KILLER** represents an incredible **OPPORTUNITY**. Just because the "mind maps" for our industry may have created, we get the opportunity to **stand alone**, to be **truly differentiated**, to **be unique** in the eyes of our audience. It's sitting right in front of us today, in just about every industry.

Customer Obsessed companies seize this opportunity. They know if they can significantly reduce or eliminate their audience's anxiety and delight them beyond belief, they will create an army of Advocates and Marketing Agents™ who will tell others about them. They know they will be happy to do their marketing for them and eliminate the **Silent Killer** from their organization. Take a moment and reflect on your organization...ask these questions...

- Are we creating unknowns for our audience?
- Do we create surprises for our customers?
- Could we improve our communication with our customers?
- Are there things we are doing as an ordinary course of business that creates undue Anxiety with our audience?

If you answered YES to any of these questions, you're not alone. I want you to stand alone in how your customers think about you when it comes to Anxiety. I want them to feel minimal Anxiety, if any at all. And I want them to create a new mind map for how incredibly wonderful you treat them...so they won't hesitate to tell everyone they know. How much happier would your customers be if they had no Anxiety when they interacted with you? How different would you be viewed if you were able to eliminate your customers' Anxiety?

There are some things YOU CAN DO TODAY, which will help you eliminate the "Silent" Killer, even before you are Customer Obsessed. You can start to change things almost immediately to alleviate customer Anxiety.

In the chapter, "**AKA**," I will give you some concrete steps to eliminate this **Silent Killer** from your organization. I hope you'll wait for it, but if you can't, read the chapter and then come back.

Now, let's dive into some of the "**Problems**" or "**Issues**" most organizations face today. It will help you see WHY becoming "*REMARK*"able™ is so incredibly powerful when you understand these. We'll then explore many "**Opportunities**" you will have available to you as a "*REMARK*"able™ organization.

THE PROBLEMS

Blaine W. Millet

Our World Today...

We can't solve problems by using the same kind of thinking we used when we created them.

ALBERT EINSTEIN

”

What issues or problems are you facing because there are now more competitors, and it is harder to differentiate in your customers' eyes?

When the Internet happened, the world changed. And everyone loved it...or did they? We, as consumers, love having everything at our fingertips. Now we have more choices than we could have ever imagined. In just about every business on the planet, **the Customer is firmly and absolutely in control**. It is critically important to understand this as we learn **WHY** being Customer **Obsessed** is now mission-critical.

I am a "glass half full" kind of guy, so I don't want to dwell on the problems, but we need to understand what they are to eliminate them. The good news is that these problems create tremendous **opportunities** for you and your company...especially if you decide to become "*REMARK*"able™.

The section on **OPPORTUNITIES** will give you some deep and rich strategies for WHY being Customer Obsessed and becoming "*REMARK*"able™ is such a game-changer. You will see WHY being Customer Obsessed will change your organization...forever...guaranteed. But before we can appreciate the opportunities, let's identify some of the primary problems and issues almost every organization faces today.

If these problems hit a nerve and help increase your desire to become truly differentiated and unique in the eyes of your customers, you're reading the right book. You can also relax. I will give you the recipe and formula for HOW to eliminate these issues and capitalize on them. Let's take a quick look at the most significant PROBLEMS or ISSUES I see organizations facing today...and the ones that also represent the most significant "Opportunities" when you become "*REMARK*"able™.

FIRST...I firmly believe we are "Leaving Money on the Table" in the form of Revenue, Profits, and Enterprise Value.

Money is always top of mind for any organization, whether it is a "for-profit" or "not for profit." We are always striving to make more revenues, profits and increase our enterprise value. It is one of the top 5 most critical areas leaders focus on. How have the "monies" been growing in your organization? While your numbers may have been growing, leaders tell me they aren't growing at the rate or amount they believe they should be in today's competitive economy. If this describes where you are as an organization, you are not alone.

While you may feel you are doing everything you can to increase revenues, make more profit, and increase your enterprise value, I believe most organizations are leaving a pile of money on the table. I see this happening all the time. However, when companies become "*REMARK*"able™, they improve in each of these areas...scooping up some of this extra money they are leaving on the table. Being Customer Obsessed allows any organization to improve in one or all three of these areas. In the section on "**Opportunities**," I'll dive into how you can take advantage of these Opportunities by becoming "*REMARK*"able™.

SECOND...More and more competition...companies "Look the Same" to the customer...there is a growing lack of differentiation.

One big thing that happened with the birth of the Internet Revolution was increased competition. Depending on the industry you are in, two things have probably happened. **First**, more competitors have shown up that look just like you in the eyes of the customer. **Second**, the "barrier to entry" is virtually gone (or is extremely small) in just about every industry, allowing new companies to show up out of nowhere. Is your business experiencing either one of these in your industry? My bet is you are answering YES to one or both...there is definitely more competition.

To the customer, this is awesome. More choices give them more power in the market. No longer does the customer have to "settle" for what's available. Customers see your company as a **commodity...everyone looks the same**. And when your customers believe your products or services are a commodity, they choose who to buy from based on commodity criteria, such as Price, Availability, Terms, and other such items. Commoditization is a massive problem for almost every industry today. Is this an issue for your organization?

Customer Obsession lets you rise above commoditization and be seen as unique and different in the eyes of your customer. I'll show you how to "not to play" in the commodity game. You can avoid the "**race to the bottom**" Customer Obsessed companies that become *"REMARK"*able™ separate themselves from the pack of competitors.

THIRD...Customer Loyalty and Retention are at ALL TIME LOWS.

Have you experienced a decrease in Customer Loyalty and Retention? Is your "customer churn" increasing? Almost everyone tells me their customers "just aren't as loyal as they used to be." Sound familiar? If so, you're not alone. I'll give you some data in the Opportunities section that will help you understand WHY this is happening and HOW you can elevate yourself above your competitors so your Customer (and employee) Loyalty and Retention goes up...significantly.

Creating more Loyal Customers is an absolute necessity to becoming *"REMARK"*able™. You can't become *"REMARK"*able™ without focusing on Loyalty. You can only create **Advocates and Marketing Agents™** when you have Loyal Customers and an audience that trusts you. The path to Advocacy and people doing your marketing for you goes through Loyalty.

You will see why changing your strategy from "acquisition" to "loyalty and retention" will elevate you above your competitors. It is a game-changer, and one most organizations don't take advantage of to its fullest extent. I will show you how you can change your company forever.

FOURTH...Employee Happiness is extremely low...they aren't excited.

Employee turnover is a huge issue today and costs organizations considerable amounts of money...money that could be redeployed to more productive uses. Depending on the employee's level in the organization, studies have shown that turnover can cost up to 7 times their salary or more. The market for talented people has become fierce, and the employee is reaping the rewards. They, like customers, switch companies faster than any other time in history. Wouldn't it be great if the employee turnover was drastically reduced?

Employee happiness is very similar to the issue of "Customer Loyalty." Employees see a greenfield out there because there are so many more choices, more than ever before. And with the shortages of employees in almost every industry, employers are doing everything they can to attract the best talent.

This situation isn't going to change anytime soon. By all accounts, it is only going to get worse. But what you can change is how employees view your organization. **People generally leave people, not companies.** Employees have a strong desire to be valued for their contributions. Employees love to work for Customer Obsessed companies...they have happier employees. You will hear more about Zappos, a Customer Obsessed company that is one of the most coveted places to work. This area alone could change your business forever.

FIFTH...Culture has become a buzzword, not who we are. It means less to employees because it is inconsistent and confusing.

Customer Obsession is all about Culture. It's about changing the organization's DNA to be one of teamwork, helping others, putting the customer first, and creating a group of employees who are the envy of your competitors. Having a culture with a common purpose that everyone rallies around is game-changing. Your customer (and audience) is that common purpose.

You will get a formula and recipe for how to build a culture that is unlike any other. It focuses on building your culture around "helping" your audience (customers and others) in various ways. It changes the way your audience (customers and others) think about you. They feel like they are part of your team, special, and important...not just another dollar.

I'll show you how this can be transformed and improved within your company just by focusing on the elements of "The "*REMARK*"able Triangle™, which is the foundation for becoming "*REMARK*"able™. The "Triangle" will change your company...forever.

SIXTH...What customers (and others) say about us isn't consistent...it's random, inconsistent, and confusing...it's eroding our brand.

Brand erosion is cancer in the Customer Economy. No one really knows who companies are any longer. Ads and promotions don't work, nor do they have much impact on changing your audience's mind. The opinion of their buddy on Facebook carries more clout and believability than anything you have to say in your promotions or advertising. **The power of branding** has completely changed. With more choices, there is more confusion. Companies seen as a commodity have lost their unique identity in the eyes of their audience. Their audience ignores their pimping and promotions. It doesn't matter what they say, only what they think and perceive.

When this happens, your audience doesn't have a consistent (and accurate) perspective of who you are as a company. We might know what your company sells, but not who you are or what you stand for. When this is remedied, your company can tell your story and elevate yourself above your competitors. Think about Disneyland...everyone knows they are "the happiest place on earth." Not just because they use it as a tagline, but because they deliver it consistently every single day. Their "guests" feel it and experience it...and then tell others (lots of others) about it. They are a Customer Obsessed company...they have become "*REMARK*"able™. Their brand and messaging are consistent, and it spreads like wildfire through thousands (or millions) of Advocates and Marketing Agents™. And this "Marketing Wildfire" happens at little to no cost.

All six of these issues and problems represent tremendous **OPPORTUNITIES** for those who want to be Customer Obsessed and become *REMARK*"able™. You can eclipse your competition and rise to the top of your industry. This book will help you get there.

Now let's dive into the OPPORTUNITIES. I'll show you how you can squash these problems to be unique and completely differentiated...

THE OPPORTUNITIES

Let's Talk About the MONEY

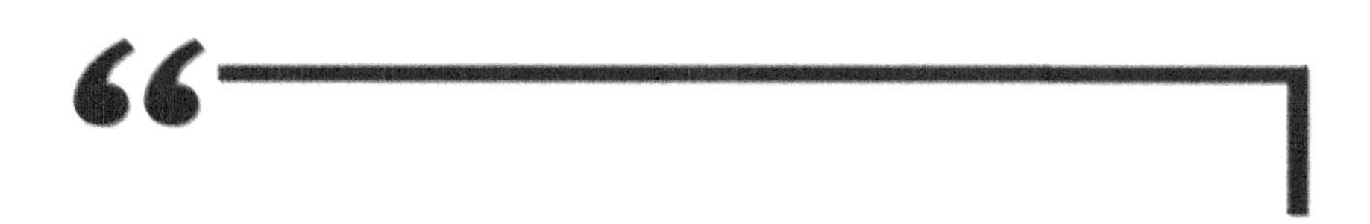

All money means to me is a pride in accomplishment.

RAY KROC

How would the revenue, profitability, and overall enterprise value increase if your customers were actively sending you lots of new customers?

There are many "OPPORTUNITIES" for Customer Obsessed organizations to become *"REMARK"*able™. The one that always catches everyone's attention is the one related to **MONEY**. Being Customer Obsessed gives you the foundation for taking advantage of this opportunity...it will definitely make you more money...period!

Becoming *"REMARK"*able™ is a direct path to more revenues, increased profitability, and growing enterprise value for virtually any organization.

Since you are either the top person running an organization or a leader who has significant influence in the organization, revenues, profitability, and enterprise value are a big deal...you are close to the MONEY. You make decisions that impact the money. Even if you are leading a non-profit organization, your decisions affect what is happening with charitable contributions and other revenue sources. Any true leader is close to the money.

Let me cut to the chase. I will talk about how much more money you can make if you are a "*REMARK*"able™ organization and how much you may be "leaving on the table" and not even realizing it is available and ready to scoop up. It can be significant.

There is plenty of research available in the market from a wide range of sources to help guide us in our discussion relating to money. While it may not be industry-specific, it is, at a minimum, an excellent guide to help us see how rewarding becoming "*REMARK*"able™ can be for any organization.

For example, based on Salesforce.com's research, they came up with robust numbers on how impactful having an excellent customer can be for revenue. Their research[2] shows that 67% of customers say **they'll pay more for a great experience.** I have seen other research reports say this increase can go as high as 89%. That's an enormous number when we're talking about money. If you did nothing more than give your customers an experience that rocked their world, you would make more money...period.

The Salesforce.com study also said that 57% of customers have **stopped buying from a company because a competitor provided a better experience.** Companies are literally handing money over to their competitors by having an above-average customer experience. I'll share with you why the experience you deliver to your customer is an absolute necessity to becoming "*REMARK*"able™.

> **SIDE NOTE:** When I speak to top leaders, most really don't understand what it means to have a **customer experience that "rocks."** Most tell me their experience is "outstanding" and "better than their competitors," so they think it rocks...it doesn't. They feel it is "under control" right now, which means they may be delivering an "above average" experience at best, but not one that rocks their customer's world. How do I know this? Their customers tell me...and rarely do they say it is "over the top" and "rocks." It is good enough, but not memorable.

If you already give an incredibly awesome and differentiating customer experience, you will probably get some of this 89% additional gain in revenue and profitability. If you aren't getting a chunk of the 89%, you have just identified a potential "**greenfield opportunity**" you can take advantage of...its **money sitting in front of you on the table** right now.

Let me share another number that might also shock you a bit. The Watermark Consulting Company has done some exceptional work in tracking the profitability of publicly traded companies who deliver (or don't deliver) amazing customer experiences. For example, in their 2019 study[3], they found that companies who are "**Customer Experience Leaders**" in their industry had a cumulative total return of 183.8% in stock performance over ten years from 2007 - 2017. For reference, the S&P 500 had a cumulative gain of only 138.7%

over the same period. Those companies who were (recognized) customer experience leaders had a cumulative **increase of 45.1% over the S&P 500.**

While these companies can't attribute all of their gains to being more Customer Obsessed and having a more robust customer experience, they couldn't have achieved these higher numbers without one. A substantial percentage of this gain was from having a differentiating and positive customer experience...above and beyond their competitors. There is no question that having a customer experience that rocks was a major contributor to them achieving a 45% increase in return over the S&P 500.

But here's something even more impressive that came out of the Watermark analysis. Watermark also identified the "**Customer Experience Laggards**" in their study...those who were not delivering a great customer experience and hadn't done anything (or very little) to focus on it. They found that the "laggards" only had a cumulative return of 63.1% compared to the 138.7% return by the S&P 500. They were **75.6% below the S&P 500** for their cumulative return and **120.7% below the Customer Experience Leaders** in cumulative return! Now we're talking massive numbers.

We're talking about real money...big money. There is no question the companies who focus on treating their customers better make more money. The difference isn't even close. This is money "sitting on the table" for those focused on their customers and who want to be Customer Obsessed.

Let me share with you another shocking number. Currently, 43% of the customers surveyed said they would "**accept an inferior product or service in exchange for a customer experience that rocked, and that made them feel special.**" What?!? That's right...almost half the people said they don't need the very best product or service if the company treated them incredibly well, showed them how much they cared about them, and made them feel awesome. More and more people care about how they are treated than having the latest and greatest product or service. I know this will be mind-blowing to some of you, but this number keeps going up!

I've also done some informal studies and found similar results...sometimes even higher in specific industries. Customers are always telling me they don't need the very best or latest and greatest product to be loyal to the company.

Companies don't need the best product to be differentiated.

Customers tell me they want the company to make them feel special, important, help them in various ways, make things happen, and continually communicate with them. These are the reasons why they love working with them. It all translates to money. While I could share many other statistics about how much more money you can make when you become "*REMARK*"able™, I want to touch on three additional areas I hope you will investigate when focusing on the money.

The first area organizations either aren't aware of or ignore...**Customer Lifetime Value or CLV**. The research tells us that 76% of companies see CLV as an important "concept" for their organization, yet only 42% can measure it. Larger companies typically measure CLV, whereas smaller ones don't. I'll talk a lot more about CLV in the section on Customer Experiences.

CLV allows you to calculate the "**lifetime value**" of any customer (or group of customers) you have. The goal is to identify which ones give you greater profitability so you can invest in them more than those who don't. They give you a long-tail of revenue (and profitability). If you have a customer who stays with you longer, you generally make more money from them since you have eliminated one of the highest costs...acquisition costs.

With the ever-increasing costs of acquisition, combined with the lower returns from traditional marketing, focusing primarily on acquisition is rapidly becoming a losing (and expensive) proposition. Even with the costs associated with retention, they are usually lower than acquisition costs.

Increasing the CLV for your customers is money in the bank...money sitting on the table. Focusing on increasing CLV directly impacts profitability and enterprise value. When I suggest you STOP MARKETING, this is one of the components included in this statement. Stop focusing on acquisition and use your money and resources to improve your retention (CLV) rates.

The second area where you can make more money is related to the core of what this book is all about...**becoming "*REMARK*"able™**. "*REMARK*"able™ companies win big money because they have created an army of **unpaid Advocates and Marketing Agents™** who are happy to help **do their marketing for them**. The keyword here is "unpaid." No one is paying these customers (and others) to go out of their way to market for you...no one. They are doing it because they trust you and appreciate the way you treat them as a customer. They love being your customer, and as such, they return the favor by being your Advocate and Marketing Agent™ in the market.

The third and final area is "**Enterprise Value**." Being Customer Obsessed can help you raise the value of your enterprise...often significantly. It makes perfect sense when you think about it. Being Customer Obsessed and creating an army of raving Advocates and Marketing Agents™ who are raving about you to others is "**money on the balance sheet**." It is an incredible asset. It carries tremendous value. It is something a buyer of your business would compensate you for. And when it comes to an ESOP (Employee Stock Ownership Program), it becomes a significant advantage.

By the time you finish this book, you will have a new appreciation for how profitable it is to be Customer Obsessed so you can become "*REMARK*"able™. You will see exactly where the money is and how you can scoop up all the money being "left on the table" in front of you...it is yours for the taking!

Now let's look at another massive opportunity in front of you when you become "*REMARK*"able™...

Loyalty and Retention...The Holy Grail

> *Exceed your customer's expectations. If you do, they'll come back over and over. Give them what they want – and a little more.*
>
> SAM WALTON

How would you rate your ability to "keep" the customers you have spent a ton of money on to acquire? How much could you reduce your customer acquisition costs if the ones you already have stuck around longer?

Another significant OPPORTUNITY you have when you become "*REMARK*"able™ is to **increase Customer Loyalty** (significantly)...the Holy Grail for any organization. No one wants a "one and done" customer who just stopped by to pick up a deal and leave. Customer acquisition costs money. Losing a customer shortly after acquisition costs is expensive.

Keeping your customers longer is money in the bank. Business leaders feel customer turnover, or churn, is one of their most important areas of concern...the more churn, the less profitable. Customer Obsessed companies create strong Customer Loyalty by how they treat their customers. Here are some reasons WHY you might want to increase your focus on Loyalty and Retention rather than acquisition.

Customer Loyalty and Customer Retention are at an all-time low.

Loyalty is at an all-time low in just about every industry. Improving it represents an **incredible opportunity**. Customer Loyalty is as much a "mentality" as it is a result. When this is the case, you often get comments from your employees such as these, "*They are so hard to deal with I'm glad they left*," or "*It doesn't seem like there is anything we can do to please them, so it's good they went somewhere else*." With this "mentality," our employees don't think it is all that critical if we lose some customers. Marketing (or sales) will just find some new (and better) ones. Nothing could be further from the truth.

When you look at the cost of losing an existing customer and the expense of acquiring a new one, it makes absolutely no sense why we wouldn't do everything we could to keep our hard-earned customers. **Having a mentality where customers can be easily replaced is a very dangerous mindset. It is a mindset of complacency, not Customer Obsession.**

When employees have this mindset, it increases customer defection, lowers loyalty, and increases turnover. It is an "**acquisition mentality**" where they emphasize acquisition, not retention. It can also create "**complacency**" in your employees. Complacency is one of the worst diseases a company can have. It means they don't care enough to fight for Customer Loyalty. Complacency is non-existent in Customer Obsessed company employees. Their Culture and DNA focuses on building Customer Loyalty because they know it leads to Advocacy...and Advocacy leads to becoming "*REMARK*"able™.

Do you know what the level of "employee complacency" is in your company? Here's a quick way to see if this is an issue or not for you...

I recommend doing a **Customer Loyalty Audit™**. Let me share an abbreviated version of how to conduct one in your organization. Start by looking at your entire customer base and ask yourself, "*What percentage of customers are "loyal" to the company.*" Use a simple definition of customer loyalty, which is, ***"You can mess things up once in a while with your customer, and they hang in there with you...they give you more than one chance."*** For most companies I talk to, customer loyalty ranges anywhere from 10% to 25%.

Once you determine your percentage, you can see what type of "**customer strategy**" you have in place today. For example, if you have a low customer loyalty percentage (higher degree of churn), you most likely have an "**acquisition strategy**" as compared to a "**retention strategy**." Performing a Customer Loyalty Audit™ will work for you regardless of your sales cycle.

Any customer worth acquiring is worth retaining.

If you spend a chunk of resources (time and money) finding and attracting a customer, they should be the "right" customer and worth keeping. According to Kissmetrics[4], **63% of marketers felt "new customer acquisition" was their most important advertising goal**. Yet, at the same time, Econsultancy[5] says that 82% of companies agree that **customer retention costs less than customer acquisition**. And Invesp[6] says that 44% of companies focus on customer acquisition **compared to only 18% that focus on retention**. They tell us that it **costs five times more to attract a new customer than to keep a customer**.

The **profitability math on retention vs. acquisition** has been around a while and tells us the same thing...if we **increase retention rates by only 5%, we can increase profits by anywhere from 25% to 95%!** To add even more fuel to the money fire, a **repeat buyer spends 33% more than a new customer**. And when it comes to selling your products or services, the probability of selling to an existing customer is 60-70%, while selling to a new prospect is only 5% - 20%...a substantial difference in cost, time, and results. The final key reason you want to adopt a solid retention and loyalty strategy is that more than 70% of the Invesp survey respondents agree it is cheaper to retain a customer than acquire a new one.

It is more expensive to acquire new customers, yet there is substantially more return in retaining those you already have.

With such overwhelming evidence supporting the case for building loyalty and focusing on retention, I don't understand why companies don't go all in and do everything they can to keep the customers they have worked so hard to acquire. I have some theories why this might be the case...

One theory (maybe more of a reality) is that **marketing is usually in charge of this area**. From my experience, marketing leaders are far more comfortable acquiring new customers than retaining those they have. I know I will probably get some hate mail from the marketers out there, but these are my observations. Marketing is very skilled at advertising, attracting visitors to the website, building SEO engines to capture unsuspecting visitors, etc. Customer acquisition is easier to define and measure against the efforts expended. Customer retention is a "companywide" effort and doesn't fall under the marketing umbrella. Creating Loyalty and Retention should be part of your culture, your DNA.

Customer Obsessed companies have a substantial focus on customer loyalty, retention, and ultimately advocacy.

Customers stay when they feel special, like they matter, and we genuinely care about them. They feel like they are the center of our universe...because they are. When they feel this way, the opportunity to retain them and turn them into a loyal customer goes up significantly.

Another benefit to focusing on loyalty and retention is that selling costs go down, marketing costs go down, revenue per customer goes up, and profitability goes up. Who doesn't want this formula working for them?

Increasing Customer Loyalty and Retention is one more reason WHY you can **STOP MARKETING. Your loyal customers become Advocates who are dying to do your marketing for you.** It's leveraging every dollar you spent on acquisition when you turn them into your **Advocates and Marketing Agents™**.

Customer Loyalty is the starting line for creating Advocates and Marketing Agents™!

And since we're on the topic of crazy numbers, here's one that will blow your mind. Research shows that **92% of people trust the recommendations from someone they know**. That's right...92%. Who in their right mind would ignore the ability to leverage such an enormous number? As a business leader, I would be everything I could to figure out how to get this number working in my business. This is precisely why I wrote this book...I want you to reap the reward of this incredible number. I want you to turn your organization into a marketing machine...**where your customers and others do the marketing**.

I eat my own dog food, as the saying goes. I don't market at all...no ads, no promotions, no obnoxious buy now or the deal will be gone type stuff. The majority of my speaking engagements, for example, come from people who have heard me speak somewhere and then told others they should have me speak at their company or convention. It also happens exactly the same way for my Advisory and Consulting engagements. It works.

I will give you the exact model, blueprint, recipe, and formula for how you drive significantly more Customer Loyalty, increase Retention, and build an army of Advocates and Marketing Agents™. Now let's talk about the incredible benefits you get when your company is truly unique and differentiated from your competitors...

Why Does Everyone Look the Same?

In a crowded marketplace, fitting in is a failure. In a busy marketplace, not standing out is the same as being invisible.

SETH GODIN

”

Do you look the same as all your competitors in the eye of your customers? Do you feel like your business has become a commodity where Price, Terms, and Availability have become the dominant decision-making criteria for your customer's buying decisions?

The third massive **OPPORTUNITY** and the reason WHY you would want to become "*REMARK*"able™ is so your company **doesn't look like everyone else.** Nothing can be gained when your customer sees you as the same as your competitors...nothing. Customer Obsessed companies are truly different and unique...and this pays big dividends.

Being viewed as "truly different" by your customers is a goal every organization should do whatever they can to achieve.

How would you answer the following questions about your organization?

- *"Could our company grow faster if our customers honestly viewed us as being completely different from our competitors?"*
- *"Do we feel customer loyalty would go up if they viewed us as being uniquely differentiated from our competitors?"*
- *"Would we have happier (and longer-term) employees if our customers stuck around longer and loved interacting with us?"*
- *"If we called our customers today, would they emphatically tell us were truly different and unique from our competitors?"*

Today, being viewed as UNIQUE and DIFFERENT is like handing you the treasure map and telling you where the treasure is buried!

With the massive increase in competition and competitive offerings, most organizations look the same to their customers. This opens the doors for incredible opportunities for those who are different. With our transition from the "third" Industrial Revolution (starting in the 1980s) to the "fourth" Industrial Revolution (starting in 2015), we have ushered in many changes for how we interact with our customers (and audience,) according to Klaus Schwab[7]).

According to **Forrester**[8], there are four distinct **Sources of Dominance**[8], defining who "dominated" over the past century. The four stages are...

- Age of Manufacturing - 1900 - 1960 (the longest of all the periods) (Ford, Boeing, P&G and others)
- Age of Distribution - 1960 - 1990 (Walmart, UPS, and others)
- Age of Information - 1990 - 2010 (Amazon, Google, Intuit, etc.)
- Age of the Customer - 2010 - present (Facebook, Apple, Tesla, etc.)

We are firmly in the **Age of the Customer**, where **the customer is completely in control**. Customers can dictate what happens because they have access to massive amounts of options and information. And there is one thing that hasn't (and won't) change anytime soon...

How did we get here? What caused COMMODITIZATION?

Let's step back for a minute and look at what got us to where we are today with Commoditization. Then we can look at what Customer Obsessed organizations do to **avoid looking the same** to their audiences. Whatever we, as customers, can easily find, so can our customers. Our customers have the power to find new companies, products/services, better pricing, better availability, different terms, and a host of other information using the wonderful invention of the internet and search engines. Everything has changed...it will never be the same again.

A little bit of history. Many of you probably remember the "good old days" where businesses could charge what they wanted and deliver what they wanted when they wanted because the customer had limited options. And even if there were other options, the buyers' cost to pursue them, find them, and purchase from them was much more difficult and expensive. Customers were literally "handcuffed" by businesses...leaving them will little choice but to buy a particular product at a specific price. Henry Ford said it best, "*You can have any color you want, as long as it's black*." This was the era when companies were in complete control.

Suddenly, **the Internet changed EVERYTHING** when it came to our role as a customer. Almost overnight, businesses were turned into **COMMODITIES**. They were experiencing the dreaded "C" word...**COMMODITIZATION**. The balance of power shifted from business to customer. Companies slow to adapt are at high risk of extinction. Several of the most respected consulting and research firms have been saying (almost shouting) this for the past few years. They believe, "***If you don't change your business model to become Customer-Centric, you have little to no chance of survival as a business***." Strong words backed up by lots of data and trends showing this is our new world.

The process of serving the customer has changed forever.

I was fortunate enough to be on the cutting edge of this revolution, more by accident than on purpose. My brother and I released our first book, ***"Creating and Delivering Totally Awesome Customer Experiences,"*** at the beginning of this storm. It came out when Amazon was newer in the market and started to disrupt the way people shopped.

When we first introduced our book to the public, we printed it and listed it on Amazon. We wrote an excellent summary of the book and why everyone should buy it. Then I came to the "shocking realization" that the customers' opinions carried more power in the market than the author's views! What?!? What was happening? It was my accidental introduction to the. I saw the NEW **CUSTOMER ECONOMY** first hand while most businesses were still clueless.

Some companies flamed the fire and capitalized on commoditization. Companies such as Groupon, Retail Me Not, Honey, and hundreds of others help us navigate to find the lowest prices. They are "**commodity aggregators.**" We love them as consumers...we hate them as a business.

Commoditized businesses almost instantly started losing margin on their products and services. With a few clicks or swipes, the customer could find a lower price on just about anything. Suppose you believe a product or service is indistinguishable from other products and services. In that case, the commodity elements of price, terms, location, and availability become the determining factors for your purchasing decision. If the customer can't see a substantial difference, they will buy based on commodity criteria.

In the Customer Economy, being a commodity is death. Customers always vote with their wallets.

When you compete in a commodity marketplace, you have to reduce prices and give up some profitability to remain competitive. And the application of technology is deflationary. Suppose a company in the commodity sector cannot determine how to reduce cost commensurate with price reductions. In that case, that company will not withstand the decline in margin and soon go out of business. **This is the "Race to the Bottom."**

Customer Obsessed companies focus on differentiation and being unique in the eyes of their customers. They choose not to participate in the game of commoditization and the race to the bottom.

The "barrier to entry" is virtually gone in our world economy. There are more "**disruptors**" to contend with. How can you act like these disruptors and take advantage of what they are offering to their audience? How can you be the disruptor in your industry? Ask yourself these questions...

- How did Uber or Lyft change the transportation market?
- How did LegalZoom become a dominant force in legal documents?
- How did Quicken, Quickbooks, and TurboTax sweep into a very stable and controlled accounting market?
- How did SouthwestAir dominate a niche in the airline industry?
- How did Tesla turn the auto industry upside down?
- How did Zappos show up out of nowhere in the highly commoditized area of shoes and become an incredibly successful company...then purchased by Amazon for a premium?

They came into well-established markets almost overnight and now either dominate or take billions of dollars away from the established companies. Most never saw it happening. Blockbuster had an opportunity to acquire the startup Netflix in the early days but turned down the opportunity because they were heavily invested in their storefront business model. And this isn't over yet...disruptions happen every year. I would be very uneasy if I were in the banking, real estate, and auto industries...I believe they are ripe for disruption. Companies like Mastercard, Zillow, and Tesla created new **customer-centric models** using technology, having a disruptive effect.

Companies forget the CUSTOMER is in control in the Customer Economy!

The disruptors (and others) figured out that treating their customers special, unique, and of high value endeared them to these companies. They figured out how to create happiness within their customer base...and their customers loved it. You can turn this doom and gloom commoditization situation into something advantageous. If you follow and execute The "*REMARK*"able Triangle™ model, it will change your business forever...guaranteed!

The focus of Customer Obsession is to eliminate commoditization.

The entire foundation of Customer Obsession is to build uniqueness and differentiation into your organization. At its very core, Customer Obsession demonstrates to your audience how unique and different you truly are in everything you do. **Differentiation** is what allows you to elevate yourself above your competitors in the eyes of your customers. Later in the book, I will give you some tools and methodology to create a culture, your DNA, to be one that demonstrates this to your customer with every interaction.

Customer Obsession is the roadmap that gets you to differentiation. And differentiation is what keeps you from becoming commoditized.

When your customers see you as different, they not only love it, they want more of it. Customers want you to be different...they want you to stand out and not look like everyone else. They want you to make their buying decision more comfortable, so they don't have to waste their time (their most valuable asset) shopping around to find the best deal. Customers want you to obsess over them. They will reward you with their dollars and their loyalty...becoming **Advocates and Marketing Agents™** for YOU!

Customers, you and me, want this. But most importantly, we want to feel so incredibly special that we can't wait to tell others about you. This is what it means to become "*REMARK*"able™...to be seen as completely different.

By the end of this book, you will know exactly how to kill commoditization. You will have a model to ensure it doesn't raise its ugly head. You will learn how to become differentiated in the eyes of your audience. You will be participating in the "**race to the top**" and leave your competitors behind. And your employees will love it! Speaking of employees...

Employee Happiness

If your employees are disengaged, and they don't take care of your customers, it doesn't matter how good your strategy is – your customers will still go somewhere else.

KEN BLANCHARD

How happy are your employees...really? Is your turnover higher than you want? Do you have trouble finding great employees? Are your employees marketing your company to potential employees?

One significant advantage of being Customer Obsessed is that you have happier employees. What?!? Yes, employees are happier in Customer Obsessed organizations because of how their audience treats them.

Customer Obsession is all about "Culture," your DNA. It is WHO YOU ARE!

Being Customer Obsessed is not for the "Customer Department" or the "Marketing Department" or even "Sales Department"...it is for EVERY DEPARTMENT. It is the Culture of your entire company, your DNA. It is who you are and what you stand for as an organization. And it is demonstrated in everyone's actions, internally and externally.

A Customer Obsessed Culture puts your customer (and your entire audience) in the center of everything you do. Employees are continually thinking about how to make their customers' life/business better. Customers love it, and your employees enjoy serving them. When the company's culture focuses on delivering ***WOW*** and delighting your audience in everything they do, you have HAPPIER EMPLOYEES!

No employee will ever complain when your audience is always raving about how awesome they feel and how well they are treated.

Employees are much happier when their customers, partners, vendors, prospects, and others are also happy. When your employees treat your audience incredibly well, your customers treat your employees exceptionally well. There is one critical factor that drives "Employee Happiness"...**CONSISTENCY**. Employees, like customers, love consistency. Employees love to know what they should be doing so they can do it over and over again. It doesn’t mean they can’t be creative. It just means they want to know their role to do it better and better each day...not having it changing all the time.

The "unknown" creates tremendous anxiety, stress, and discontentment in employees (and customers).

When employees are left to "figure it out" and do what they think is best, it puts stress on them. Employees naturally want to please leadership, and one way to do this is to perform better today than they did yesterday. But they can’t do this if they don't know exactly what to improve upon or what leadership expects from them.

Inconsistency drives employees nuts! They hate surprises.

When your employees are inconsistent in delivering an experience to the customer, the customer doesn’t know what to expect...they will be surprised. It’s really tough (if not impossible) to delight our customers when they are always left guessing about what will happen next. Both your employees and customers are much happier when they know what will happen next...no surprises. We'll talk a lot more about the customer side of this in the section on **Customer Experience**. For now, it is important to know there is a massive opportunity available when your processes and customer experience are consistent...this combination will deliver happiness to both your employees and your audience.

When I talk about “consistency,” I'm talking about how your employees deliver this process, with their own personality and style that capitalizes on their creativity and innovative nature. When this happens, your customers get a consistent experience with your employees' individual flair and personality. The combination creates a fantastic interaction...a WOW experience for your audience and your employees. Let me give you an example of a distribution and fabrication company I worked with several years ago before they were Customer Obsessed.

Jim was an older gentleman responsible for sweeping the floors in their warehouse...that was his full-time job. Jim's role was keeping the floors clean, walkways cleared from debris, tearing down boxes, and making sure the warehouse looked great. He helped them reduce accidents and keep things looking nice for their customers.

I watched Jim work and noticed a few things that were quite telling...and what turned out to be what was happening throughout the organization. Every day Jim did his job differently. Some days he would start by sweeping out the office for the warehouse employees. Other days he would begin by cutting up boxes before he swept the floors. Still other days, he would clean the back of the warehouse where the employees hung out and put a lot of the extra materials.

And each day, the warehouse employees would ask Jim what he was doing and why he was doing things a particular way. They didn't know what to expect from him daily...there was no consistency. The employees were confused, often frustrated because they didn't know what to expect. Jim was also frustrated because the warehouse personnel didn't seem happy with what he was doing, even though he felt like he was doing an outstanding job. The result was unhappy warehouse workers and an unhappy floor sweeper. Joe used his own "creativity" in how he did things and thought he was doing a great job and being responsive to what the warehouse employees wanted.

We talked about how the customers felt with all this going on behind the scenes and realized they were probably not happy. It was a lose, lose, lose situation. Since Jim focused on making the warehouse employees happy, the customers' entrance where they pick up their orders was usually the last area to be cleaned. It led the customers to think the entire warehouse was probably a mess as well...giving them a less than desirable customer experience.

Everything changed when the CEO committed to being a Customer Obsessed organization. As soon as they started their Journey, Jim became a "true" member of the warehouse team. The team's responsibility was to make the warehouse "something special" in their customers' eyes. We created a plan with some Customer Experience Maps (you'll learn about these later), so everyone knew exactly their role in delivering an incredibly awesome and amazing customer experience.

Once they had a plan, everyone knew their role (including Jim) in dazzling the customer every time. The warehouse employees knew how to greet them, how to handle their orders, how to process their requests, and how to get them on their way quickly (I just summarized in one sentence their 18-page Customer Experience Map).

Jim's role also changed. As a very respected and necessary part of the warehouse team's success at delighting the customer, he knew that the number one goal was to take care of the customer and make them feel special. Now, for the first time, Jim had something he could focus on...consistently. Every morning, before any customers came to the warehouse, he spent an hour cleaning and organizing the entryway and waiting area...it sparkled and was very inviting.

Then Jim moved on to the warehouse and made sure everything was out of the way for the employees to do their job. Jim only focused on other areas when he was all done with the customer-focused areas. Several times during the day, he would go back "up front" (while the customers were coming and going) and made sure it stayed looking great.

What happened next was nothing short of pure magic. Jim had a spring in his step, a smile on his face, and a song he would whistle while working because he was so happy. He used his creativity to put on a little show for all the customers when they were coming and going...and they loved it. They talked about it, told him how amazing he was, and often commented on how he had the cleanest warehouse they had ever seen. Jim was on cloud nine, and, of course, this encouraged him more every day. He got more and more creative in "how" he delivered the "consistent" experience their customers loved (their Customer Experience Map).

The result was amazing. The warehouse employees completely embraced Jim and treated him as a "highly valued" member of their team. They included him in everything they did, even social events. They could see how he was helping them all achieve what they wanted from their customers...happiness. It fed each of them, and they were all happier.

They started hearing the magic phrases from the customer, such as, "*This is the absolute best warehouse I get to visit...I really enjoy (and look forward to) coming here. You guys treat me better than anyone else, and you're always happy and ready to make my day better. Whatever you are doing, keep doing it...I love it!*"

Imagine what your warehouse (or any part of your business) would be like if your employees experienced (and heard) this type of feedback from your customers? They might just feel happier than they are feeling today. And when they are getting this kind of feedback, they want to do more...continually raise the bar. They want to do even better tomorrow than they did today. They have a purpose and a consistent "Map" to follow...yet their personality shines through to their customers.

When your employees are happier, there are a ton of benefits you get as a company.

They aren't line items on the P&L statement, but they can impact your bottom line dramatically. You get benefits such as lower turnover, more productivity per employee, happier customers, more creativity, and more innovation, to name a few. If your company could benefit from any of these, they are within your grasp when you become "*REMARK*"able™ because of being Customer Obsessed...as the warehouse found out.

The company was realizing their ultimate goal...their customers were telling others they knew how awesome they were to work with...they were becoming "*REMARK*"able™...**their customers were doing their marketing for them.** It didn't take very long before they were the place every driver wanted to have on their list of places to stop. This company was definitely doing something different than anyone else.

Word got out how happy their employees were. Employees from other companies wanted to work for them. They became the "top dog," all starting with how the warehouse was being cleaned and operated.

Customer Obsession helps you create Employee Happiness.

And Employee Happiness enables you to reap these kinds of benefits for your organization. Happy Customers feed Happy Employees. And Happier Employees encourage and energize your Customers. It's a definite Win-Win for you and your Customers.

And when it becomes "who you are" as an organization, it becomes your Culture, your DNA...

Blaine W. Millet

It's in Your DNA

Businesses often forget about the culture, and ultimately, they suffer for it because you can't deliver good service from unhappy employees.

TONY HSIEH

Is your culture, your DNA, "internally-centered," or "customer-centered?" Your culture defines WHO you are...and your customers (and others) see it every day. How would your customers describe your culture?

Make no mistake about it. CUSTOMER OBSESSION is all about CULTURE. When you create a Culture where the Customer is at the center of everything you do, magic happens every day.

A company's Culture, or DNA as I call it, is who we are, how we act, and how we treat each other...inside and outside the organization. You can't fake culture...at least not for very long. When you have a culture committed to your customer, your organization comes alive.

Your "old" DNA (or culture) got you where you are today...an established and successful business. You built it for a specific purpose, or it happened by accident (which many cultures are). Regardless of how it happened, it is what it is today. If you want more growth, eclipse the competition, and lead your industry, your culture may need to change.

Your culture has probably evolved over the past few years (or more). Cultures evolve as people and leaders evolve. But, in some cases, it might still have the same foundation and tenants it did initially. Regardless of where your culture is today, it will most likely change if you decide to be Customer Obsessed and become "*REMARK*"able™...it is just different than most cultures. It's different because the focus changes from "**product-centric" to "customer-centric.**" When the customer is in the center of your business, your culture needs to support the shift.

As the experts in culture tell us, when the company's focus changes, so does the culture. For example, I worked with a company in the services industry that wanted to measure their employees differently. They felt their employees were "slacking" a bit and wanted a high utilization and efficiency model. They hired an efficiency-oriented manager to make changes to measure every aspect of an employee's production.

I came in to help develop a business strategy...a new Vision, Mission, and Values for the organization...one that centered on their customers. We spent quite a bit of time identifying and capturing the Values the owner of the business wanted. We identified and defined them in a way every employee could understand and relate to...they were simple and impactful. We then created a long-term Vision and Mission. As you would suspect, they put the customer at the center of the business since they wanted to embark on a Journey to being Customer Obsessed and "*REMARK*"able™.

All this sounds great, right? And it was, right up to the point where the new "efficiency manager" kicked into gear. While their values would have supported an awesome Customer Obsessed Culture, the management of their day to day activities was fighting against these values...creating the wrong Culture. They went in a different direction because of a conflict between their Values and the new efficiency standards. He demanded efficiency and utilization above and beyond providing what was most important to their customers. The organization was adopting a Customer Obsessed culture while the CEO was insistent upon improving efficiency and labor utilization first and foremost...instant conflict.

The employees were confused. While they wanted a Customer Obsessed Culture, they were motivated to deliver on their utilization numbers. There was pressure to get utilization up while they were supposed to serve their customer's extraordinarily. They were being compensated based on utilization. They were in direct conflict, and their culture was suffering.

I share this particular story because it didn't have a happy ending. I like to be transparent about everything, including things that don't work out as planned. Not everything is rosy and works out the way you want. The efficiency manager won. He won the CEO over with promises of higher profitability. The Culture of the company started to tank. The Values were not adhered to since they conflicted with their unreasonable goals of efficiency and utilization. Over time, the company eroded, and employee turnover skyrocketed. They got their efficiency up, but their customers became more and more unhappy and progressively left. Efficiency went up, customer (and employee) happiness went down, only now with fewer employees and fewer (unhappy) customers.

I share this story with you to illustrate how these kinds of factors can have a significant impact on your culture. Household name companies like Zappos, Southwest Airlines, Starbucks, Disney, Nordstrom, Ritz Carlton, and many others have the customer firmly in the center of their business. And their successes over the years have shown this to be a worthwhile (and profitable) decision. It works...and it changes the culture.

Creating a Customer Obsessed Culture is a game-changer.

Regardless of where you may be today, you can create a Customer Obsessed culture with consistent effort, strong Values (customer and employee-based), and a Vision and Mission focused on obsessing over your customers. You will be amazed at how fast culture can change when leadership is committed to this, supports it, and puts it in the center of everything every employee does in the company.

Consistency is the secret ingredient to creating a Customer Obsessed Culture. When leadership is unwavering, Culture will follow.

Here's the great thing about Culture...it follows consistency. If leadership is consistently demonstrating the Values and always supporting having the customer at the center of their business, the Culture changes.

Let me share another story about a company whose owner successfully changed their culture because of the Values he created. Once we established the owners' values, we put them all over their walls...where both employees and customers could see them. It allowed them to be "self-managed" by each other. Now, when someone wanted to do something for a customer, all the other team members had to say was, "*Is this living and demonstrating our Values and helping us achieve our Vision and Mission?*" If it wasn't, they came up with a different answer. If it did, they could defend it, support it, execute it, and move forward.

This repetitive checking, always asking this question on everything, cemented it in everyone's brain. Everyone started thinking differently. Everyone acted differently. And a new culture was created based on company Values and focusing on their Mission and Vision of being Customer Obsessed. It was the check and balance of continually asking and checking up on each other (in a friendly way) that moved the needle. Their Culture changed because they were consistent.

They moved from being "mediocre" to being "outstanding and unique" in their customers' eyes. They became differentiated and stood out among the pack of "me-too's" in their industry. They looked different, acted differently, and supported their customers differently. It didn't mean they did everything the customers wanted or always the way they wanted, but their customers knew they had their backs and did their best to help them along in their Journey. They were now starting to realize all the benefits and opportunities I described in the previous chapters. They are a Customer Obsessed company becoming

"*REMARK*"able™. Their Culture transformed from "company-centric" to "Customer Obsessed."

I often describe the process of becoming "*REMARK*"able™ as similar to climbing a mountain and having the goal of enjoying what's on the other side...a lush green valley with the bluest water lake you have ever seen nestled under snowcapped mountains. Sounds great, right? But the climb up the mountain isn't easy...it's fraught with peril all the way along. Only those well-prepared for the Journey, have commitment and fortitude, have the right culture in place, and who are relentless about reaching their Vision and Mission will succeed. But the reward is unbelievable!

The number one reason companies don't make it over the top is commitment.

Their commitment isn't strong enough to see them through difficult times. Translated, they have a hard time enforcing their values and living them every day, without wavering. Everyone has good intentions and a desire to succeed. But without **commitment**, **consistency**, and the right **culture** in place, the Journey ends before it can be realized.

The Journey is enjoyable (and rewarding). There are so many triumphs and highs along the way up the mountain. It can be this way for your employees and business. They will be right alongside you, cheering each other on like a strong, committed team does. You will be working together to support each other, improve as you go along, develop new ways of making the Journey easier and more fun, and get over the mountain...together. The Journey will transform your new DNA and build a Customer Obsessed CULTURE. And the best part is that **your CUSTOMERS (and audience) LOVE IT!!** They will notice the changes and applaud your efforts and focus on them. Maybe for the first time, they will see how special you make them feel and how important they are to your company. They will feel a part of what you are doing. They will embrace your creativity, your commitment, and your consistency in helping them improve their own life and/or their business.

This is what a Customer Obsessed Culture looks like...and it is what allows you to become "*REMARK*"able™.

When you have a culture that thrives on making your audience feel special, important, and that you are doing everything possible to "help" them improve their life and/or their business, you have a Customer Obsessed culture...period.

There are two key components to changing your company's culture to becoming "*REMARK*"able™...

First...create a customer experience that blows your customers away. Help them "**feel**" so incredible they can't believe how well you treat them. When this happens, they want to be your **Advocates and Marketing Agents™** and are **happy to tell others about you**. You build deep and lasting Trust that will elevate you above your competitors.

Second...treat your employees like family and build a Culture where they support each other and focus on delivering the first component. Establish the Values which support a Customer Obsessed mindset and make sure everyone "lives" these values in everything they do. Check out Zappos Values, some of the easiest to understand and live.

Investing in your customers and your employees change the game...changes the culture...changes your DNA. It takes work, being consistent, and a strategy to becoming "*REMARK*"able™. Peter Drucker coined the phrase, "***Culture eats Strategy for breakfast.***" I disagree...**Culture eats everything at every meal.**

Now let's talk about one final benefit and opportunity...your BRAND. It may not be what you were thinking...

What Will YOUR Customers Say?

Brand is just a perception, and perception will match reality over time. Sometimes it will be ahead, other times it will be behind. But brand is simply a collective impression some have about a product.

ELON MUSK ”

How do your customers FEEL when they interact with your company, and what do they say about us? What is your "brand message," and what are your customers telling others about you?

I hope you have these same questions...they are the right ones to be asking. We use all sorts of methods to find the answer to these questions... surveys, questionnaires, NPS (Net Promotor Score), focus groups, and various other techniques. The sole purpose is to determine if they will continue to be our customers and continue spending their money with us.

Let me offer you a much simpler (and more accurate) way to get better information you can act on...TALK TO THEM.

Investing the time (and resources) to talk to your audience (including customers) will give you mountains of information. Or get an outside specialist to speak with them for you if you want to get even richer and more in-depth information. A quality outsider can help you get to the core of what they like and don't like...it's worth the investment.

There is one question I would strongly suggest you always ask if you some golden nuggets of information. I can guarantee it will get your customers talking...and it has nothing to do with your products or services. Here's the one question I would encourage you to ask...

> *"So, (Customer name), I would like to ask you one question. How do we make you FEEL when you work with our company? In other words, how do you FEEL when you interact with our employees?"*

Now sit back, LISTEN, and take notes...it will be a gold mine of information. Every leader should be doing this with every customer they meet. Leaders need to demonstrate how valuable this feedback is from their customers (and audience). Don't lead or steer them in any way. Just listen and ask more refinement questions such as, "*That's interesting. Can you tell me more about that?*" Then simply LISTEN some more. You will learn more than you ever thought possible. I guarantee it will be valuable time spent.

In my earlier days in the Big 5, I would coach my partners to follow my "**20-minute rule**." Here's how it works. You simply ask the open-ended question above and then let your customer talk for 20 minutes before you talk about anything else. You get to the "gold" (or their big issues) after 20 minutes. They usually run out of "surface issues" after 20 minutes and start giving you what is really important to their organization." It always works.

> CAUTION: Whatever happens and whatever is said, DO NOT TRY TO FIX IT. Don't try to offer some quick solutions or ideas or anything else that smells like a solution. You are there to listen and learn. When you hear about an issue, our first instinct is to fix it...don't. You can do that later, just listen and take notes.

When they are done, dried up and drained from talking, now you get to say something. This is what I recommend you say...

> *"WOW, that was amazing, thank you! This time with you was incredibly valuable to me as a leader in our company. Thank you for spending the time to share all this with me. I sincerely appreciate your honesty and the information you shared. As you can see, I've taken a lot of notes. I will take these back and discuss this with my leadership team. As you know, our mission going forward is to be a Customer Obsessed organization. Your feedback will be incredibly helpful to us in that Journey. After we have had time to discuss this and process it, I would love to schedule another time to review how we will be changing concerning these items. Does that sound OK to you? Would you be willing to meet with me again?"*

CONGRATULATIONS...you are now on your Journey to being Customer Obsessed! Your customers will, possibly for the first time, feel like they were truly heard. It means the world to any customer. This process allows you to tap into the "emotions" of your customer (or buyer). It is an excellent kickoff to establishing an emotional connection and moving this customer from feeling like they are a "transaction" to developing a deeper "relationship." And as you will learn in the chapter on "**Promises, Promises, Promises**," building a "relationship" is one step closer to turning your customers (and your audience) into Advocates and Marketing Agents™ for your business. It's one step closer to helping you understand how to become "*REMARK*"able™!

From my experience, I find it virtually impossible for a customer to have an INCREDIBLY AWESOME AND AMAZING EXPERIENCE if we haven't tapped into understanding their emotions during their experiences with our company. I know you will find this true for your company as well.

Let me give you a short yet potent **5-minute exercise** you can do with your leadership team and employees. I think you'll find it to be quite fun yet very insightful.

First, write down 3 of the experiences you have had that blew you away and rocked your world. The ones that were so over the top incredible you felt ecstatic about being their customer (business or personal). These are the experiences you would go out of your way to tell someone about because they were so memorable and incredible. The ones that made you feel special, important, and made you just smile thinking about them. Name each one of them.

Second, take one of the three experiences you just wrote down and answer these questions. "***WHY was this experience so incredibly awesome and amazing?" WHY was it so memorable? WHY was it so unique that it made your top 3 list of unbelievable customer experiences?"*** Start writing...just throw down some words, short sentences, draw pictures, or whatever you want that will help describe WHY it blew you away, dazzled you, and caused you to think it was something special. There is no limit on this exercise...write (or draw) as much as you want here and take as long as you want.

Third, look at the words (or pictures) you just wrote down. Circle the ones that have to do with how the organization or experience made you "**feel**." Not about the product or service they provided you, but the way they made you feel when you interacted with them, no matter what form of interaction it was (in-person, over the phone, online, email, etc.) Now sit back and look at the words you circled.

Like most people who do this exercise, most of the words you circled are the "**emotional**" aspects of the experience. They are what caused you to feel special, cared about, and important. These emotional elements created something memorable and unforgettable. And, most importantly, these are the elements **YOU WILL TELL OTHERS ABOUT** when describing your experience. These are the elements you will "*REMARK*" about to others. These are the elements that make the organization "*REMARK*" able.

What you won't find on this list are "commodity" elements...they aren't nearly as memorable as how you felt. You won't see price as one of the topmost memorable items. Price is rarely remembered when it comes to describing an unforgettable experience. Think of the last time you went to Disneyland (or Disneyworld) and tell me the price you paid for your tickets and how much you saved off the regular priced ticket...you probably can't. Commodity elements aren't the reasons we remember something we experienced 20 years ago. Emotions create this type of memory. Just like when your family went to Disneyland and Cinderella talked to your daughter. It made your daughter feel like the most important person in all of Disneyland. It was memorable. Even when your daughter grew up, she remembered how Cinderella made her feel ten years ago.

Ask yourself these questions about your business...

- How many of your customers would have listed YOU on their list of "Top 3" most extraordinary and memorable experiences?
- How many of your customers would give me, if I was to interview them tomorrow, a similar list of "emotional" words to describe their experiences with your organization?
- How many of your customers, after several years, could tell me some of the most memorable things you did for them that caused them to remember you and set you apart from your competitors?
- How many of your customers would tell me the one thing they remember is how you made them "feel" so special and important?

If the answers to these questions aren't what you would want today, don't worry, I'm going to give you a formula and recipe for how you can start getting the right answers from your customers tomorrow. I'm going to help you transform your experiences into "memorable" and "unforgettable" so your customers can rave about you to others. Because, at the end of the day, **this is your BRAND**. It is “who you are” to your customers. And, most importantly, this is what they tell others is your BRAND. Most people misunderstand Brand. It won't happen when you build a **Customer Obsessed Brand** that everyone knows and can communicate with others.

Your Brand is simple. Branding takes work.

I want you to see your company's brand through the eyes of your customers. It is different from what many of the "branding experts" might say. Often, customers view your brand differently from what you think about your brand. Let me give you another way to think about your Brand and how you can ensure it is in alignment with your customers.

Your BRAND is simply "*what your audience (customers and others) say about you to others when you aren't around*." That's it.

Your Brand is definitely in your hands to build. But it is in the hands of your customers to "communicate" to others. You cannot control what your audience says, but you can control the inputs they receive from you to formulate what they will tell others. It is a critically important point to grasp and understand...it is the **heart of Branding.**

Test this out for yourself in your next leadership meeting. Ask your team to answer these two questions, "***What do you believe is our "brand message?" What would you want our customers to say about us in the market?***" I will bet you the price of this book that the "brand message" your leadership team came up with isn't the same message you would hear from your employees or your customers. Don't feel bad...this misalignment happens in most companies. And when there isn't an alignment of your brand message between your employees and your leaders, there is zero chance it will be in alignment with your customers. In marketing terms, this is called "**Brand Confusion.**"

Customer Obsessed companies eliminate Brand Confusion and create Brand Synergy. Brand Confusion leads to defection...customers leaving because they don't understand the brand or are getting mixed messages in the market. Customers don't like to be confused.

In today's Customer Economy, **your customer (and audience) control your brand message.** If you tell the customer you are red, and they believe you are blue, you are blue. Your audience will tell everyone you are blue, despite your desire to have everyone know you are red.

Before the Internet, companies were in control of their brand...completely. They could blast you with ads on TV, radio, newspapers, magazines, billboards, direct mail, flyers, and through a variety of other distribution methods. They told you what they were about, and they owned the brand message.

This form of Branding ended with the Internet Revolution, and Branding got turned entirely upside down.

The customer's voice is now more powerful than the company voice because it was authentic and real. After all, the voice of the person having the experience of using the product or service, not propaganda from the company, is what we want to hear. It is from someone, just like you, who tells thousands, or millions, of people what they honestly think.

The customer is firmly in control. They have a microphone.

I was an early entrant into the world of social media and gave thousands of speeches to leaders showing this had happened and suggested they change the way they brand and market. Those who saw this opportunity and took advantage of it were able to take advantage of their brand's misalignment and changed how they communicated with their customers. They were the winners.

Unfortunately, Marketing firms, Agencies, Brand Experts, and many others still use the old model in the new Customer Economy...it doesn't work any longer. Customers aren't listening, regardless of how much gets "pushed" at them through traditional messaging. Customers simply tell others what they have personally experienced and believe. The customer shares what they believe is true...because it is their own truth.

Marketing groups created "Influencers" to get around this misalignment of Brand Message to combat this issue. Influencers are individuals with large groups of "followers" who try to influence your opinion. We, the audience, see through this more and more, so they are losing their influence in the market...we want to hear from actual customers instead. Influencers, and other shenanigans, were simply created because customers don't trust the companies. If we did, we would be getting input from the most credible group on the planet...their trusted customers and audience. Influencers aren't a new phenomenon. Influencers have become nothing more than the "online spokesperson" in today's Internet Revolution. Anytime something appears to be "tainted" or "manipulated" by an organization, the organization loses trust. And when a company loses trust, they lose all credibility for their message with the customer.

TRUST is the CURRENCY of the CUSTOMER ECONOMY.

When you have Trust, you reap the rewards of becoming *"REMARK"*able™. When you have the trust of your audience, you win...and win big. We'll talk about Trust a lot more later on in the book. And because it is such a critically important topic, I am currently writing a book dedicated to Trust.

What is the **Brand Message YOUR audience** is spreading in the market? Many companies don't know their "**audience Brand Message.**" Don't worry. Your Brand Message will become crystal clear when you are Customer Obsessed. Your audience will become your new spokespeople in the market...your **Advocates and Marketing Agents™.** They will passionately and proactively communicate your Brand Message to your audience...**they are doing your marketing for you.**

It's a different way to think about your Brand and your Brand message. **It's what your audience wants**...because we want it as customers. Nothing I have shared with you isn't what you, the customer, desire. Having your audience in charge of your Brand Message is a MASSIVE OPPORTUNITY!

Another reason why you can STOP MARKETING...because your customers are dying to do it for you! You just have to help them...arm them...support them...and nurture them with the right experience and content to share as part of your Brand Message. When this happens, you've changed the game. And your competitors are now firmly in your rearview mirror.

You've now seen some of the significant opportunities sitting in front of you today when you become a *"REMARK"*able™ organization by being Customer Obsessed. Now let's dive into **WHAT** being Customer Obsessed is all about and **WHAT** it means to become *"REMARK"*able™...

WHAT IS IT?

What is Customer Obsession?

We've had three big ideas at Amazon that we've stuck with for 18 years, and they're the reason we're successful: Put the Customer first, Invent, and be Patient.

JEFF BEZOS

Before I dive into helping you understand what Customer Obsession is, let me first share with you what it ISN'T. Sometimes it's easier to eliminate what it isn't to help us get a clearer definition of what it actually is.

Customer Obsession isn't about "liking" your customers more than you do today. Everyone likes their customers...they write us checks.

While liking your customers more isn't bad, it isn't the same as "Obsessing" over them. Customer Obsession isn't about trying to make them happy by giving our audience everything they want. It also isn't about telling your employees just to be nicer to your customers. These aren't bad things. They just aren't "obsessing" over them. None of these have any staying power. They won't last since there isn't a framework for employees to build upon with each interaction. They won't have many tangible results.

When you are a **Customer Obsessed Company**, you are literally saying...

> ***"We, as a company, have a Customer Obsessed culture. It's who we are, our DNA. Because it is our culture, we "Obsess" over helping our***

> *audience (customers and others) improve their lives and/or their businesses. Our processes, operations, interactions, and decisions have our customer at the center of our universe and at the center of everything we do.*"

Customer Obsession is a state of "BEING," not a result.

Customer Obsessed companies ask different questions and simply act differently. Customer Obsession is **how you behave**. It is also a continual "Journey," without an end destination. It is an exciting Journey your customers can see and feel as you continually focus on their happiness. The more they interact with you, the more evident it becomes you are Obsessed over their success and well-being.

Since "being" Customer Obsessed is an ongoing, never-ending "Journey," it can't ever be a "result." The result is "becoming" "*REMARK*"able™.

I use the term "**Customer Obsession,**" as opposed to "**Customer Centric**" or "**Customer Focused,**" because it is simple, emotional, and immediately captures your attention when you hear it. Everyone understands the word "Obsession." It carries much stronger emotions than any other word you can use to describe your commitment to something. It jumps off your tongue and says you aren't passive...you are over the top committed to your audience. You are all in...your OBSESSED with making their life and/or business better. It is the feeling you want your audience to have when they think about your entire organization...over the top committed to their happiness and success!

I don't believe a customer (or member of your audience) doesn't want you to be obsessed over their happiness and success.

Customers want your very best...your complete focus. And they want to feel they are significant and special to you. What customer doesn't want to feel this way? Customers don't want to feel like they are just one of many customers or a transaction. They want to feel like they genuinely matter to you. Don't you, as a customer, want to feel this way? Don't you want (and expect) to feel special and important to the company you are giving your hard-earned dollars to? So do your customers.

I can guarantee you one thing. When you tell your customers you are "obsessed" about their happiness and success, you will not only gain their immediate attention, but you will earn their trust and respect. You can quickly put their mind at ease when you explain what it means and how it will help them improve their life and/or their business.

Most customers will think this is interesting and want to know more. What an excellent opportunity for you to share your passion for making their life and/or business better. Who doesn't want to hear you are 110% focused on making them feel special and important!! When they hear this, they immediately start seeing you as **DIFFERENT** from your competitors.

For example, when you give them an unbelievably awesome customer experience and show them how you are helping improve their life and/or their business, their natural inclination is to be much more positive and collaborative. This alone can be a massive change for a business. To have customers calling you with the intent to "work through" a problem rather than "complaining" about an issue is a game-changer for most companies.

And as we discussed in an earlier chapter, this has a significant benefit to your culture and employees. You have happier employees when customers call with the intent of "working through" an issue instead of "ripping them a new one" because something went wrong? You get my point...happier customers = happier employees. And happier employees help change your culture, your DNA, and ultimately your entire business.

In Customer Obsessed organizations, **employees are empowered to work through issues with customers on the spot** instead of referring their issue "topside." It's how the employees speak, act, and treat their audience. Your employees now operate based on what is best for your customers in every situation, ahead of their own interests.

Here's an example of how this actually works. Let's say you are in one of your leadership meetings, and someone brings up an idea that would improve your organization's productivity and revenue. Non-Customer Obsessed companies would dive into this like a dog on a bone and start asking questions about how it would fit into the product line, how long would it take to create, how much are the development costs, and how much money would they make from selling it. These are pretty basic (and normal) business questions.

A Customer Obsessed company handles this differently. The conversation (and questions) would have a different focus. Leaders would now ask...

> ***"Tell me how this would impact our customers if we were to launch this product? How would it impact (or improve) their life and/or their business? Would this help them more than something we are already doing? Would this help save them time or money? Would they see this as something that would benefit them, or us, or both? Is this so awesome they would want to tell others about it?"***

There is different questioning in a Customer Obsessed leadership meeting (and all team meetings). All changes start with how it will affect our customer's life and experience. If it isn't an improvement, we need to determine if this is a viable product/service or solution. If we aren't sure how it will impact them, more analysis is necessary before discussing the idea. Customer Obsessed organizations start every discussion with how this will affect their customer. Then they work back to the appropriate answer. We still analyze how the change impacts our company and our profitability, but we always start with how it affects our customers.

"*You've got to start with the customer experience and work back toward the technology, not the other way around.* The customer, not technology, must be the core of your strategy." – Steve Jobs

A natural (and expected) outcome Customer Obsessed organizations enjoy is a significant increase in **TRUST** by their audience. You will learn much more about how this works by reading the chapters in the Section on Trust.

Customer Obsession is...OBSESSION! It's essentially saying...

> ***"We are always cheering for (and helping) our customers to be as successful as possible in whatever they do...we are their biggest fan. We go out of our way to help them be successful. We get incredibly creative and look for ways to help them grow. We find ways they could improve their business. We save them time when dealing with our company. We help their people be more productive and share content we believe could help them do better. We go out of our way to give them the absolute best and most positive experience possible. We are "proactively" thinking about them all the time. And in the end, we earn their respect, their loyalty, and above all, their Trust."***

Think about when you were dating and found the person you truly loved. You wanted them to be a part of your life. You couldn't get them off your mind...you thought about them 24/7 and thought of ways you could have fun with them and make them happy. You wanted to do whatever you could to make them feel good and enjoy your time together. You were Obsessed over wanting them in your life and couldn't get them off your mind. You were creative and innovative in ways to make them feel special. This is the same feeling Customer Obsessed companies have for their customers and everyone in their audience.

Customer Obsessed companies are continually looking for ways to make their audience happier and improve their lives. You can't get them off your mind, and you care about them so deeply that you want to find ways to make them smile. When you are Customer Obsessed, your audience says, ***"WOW, I can't believe how great you treat me and how special you make me feel every time I interact with you...and how much you care about me and my life."***

The result of being Customer Obsessed is becoming "*REMARK*"able™ and building an army of Customer Advocates and Marketing Agents™ who literally do your marketing for you.

Customer Obsession goes way beyond customer satisfaction. Today, customer satisfaction benchmarks and measurements are mediocre and for amateurs. Customer Obsessed companies want their customers to feel ecstatic...exhilarated...and incredibly special, not merely satisfied.

A critically important word to keep in front of your mind as we talk about Customer Obsession is **PROACTIVE**. Most companies operate in a "reactive" mode, merely responding to their customers' requests and demands. Customer Obsession is about being "**PROACTIVE,**" thinking ahead of your customers. They

"**ANTICIPATE**" what will happen along the Customer Journey and are more "Proactive" in responding to situations. This is an **incredible differentiator** for Customer Obsessed companies...it becomes the way they operate. I'll give you a very specific formula for how you can capitalize on this concept of being "Proactive" and "Anticipating" your audience's needs in the chapter, "**AKA**."

Customer Obsessed organizations end up **ELIMINATING SURPRISES** and **LOWERING THEIR CUSTOMERS ANXIETY.** You are giving them more **PEACE OF MIND** when they interact with your company. You do this because it's "who you are" and "how you do business." It is in your DNA, your culture.

I hope your mind is racing, and you are already asking, "**what would it be like if we were a Customer Obsessed organization? *What would it look like if we were to become "REMARK"*able™*?***" Now let's see what becoming "*REMARK*"able™ is all about...

Becoming "*REMARK*"able™

Word-of-mouth now has an unprecedented influence because it spreads so far and so fast.

ALEXIS OHANIAN

Is your audience (customers included) anxious and enthusiastic about telling others about how incredibly awesome and amazing you are? How much stronger would your organization be if you had an army of people singing your praises and encouraging everyone to work with you?

Becoming "*REMARK*"able™ is not just a play on words...it is an actual result. I want you to be in the enviable position of having an army of Advocates and Marketing Agents™ who can't wait to tell others how incredibly awesome and amazing you are to work with. When this happens, you can reap the many benefits I discussed at the beginning of the book.

Shortly, I will give you the recipe and formula to being Customer Obsessed so you can become "*REMARK*"able™. Just so we are all on the same page, let me spend a few minutes on what becoming "*REMARK*"able™ is all about.

Without question, any organization's ideal goal should be to BECOME "*REMARK*"able™...getting others to "remark" about them.

I break the word into two components..."**REMARK**" (getting **talked about**) and "**able**" (**making it happen**). My one overarching goal and passion for decades has been to help organizations get talked about, "remarked about" by their audience of customers, prospects, partners, vendors, friends, and colleagues. You get talked about, "promoted," and "sold" to your prospective audience **BY** the most credible people on the planet, the ones who TRUST you. To achieve what every organization dreams will happen...their audience **does their marketing for them!** Now it can become a reality for your organization.

Any size organization in any industry in any country can become "*REMARK*"able™.

All organizations want the benefit of becoming "*REMARK*"able™. They just don't know how to create it, lead it, implement it, and do it consistently every day. The model I will share with you shortly will get you over that hump so you can make this happen in your organization.

Becoming "*REMARK*"able™ can be a significant catalyst for any organization. The beauty of becoming "*REMARK*"able™ is that everyone in the company can understand it...which means it gets implemented. It becomes the driving force for employees to focus on. You consistently ask, "***Is this going to help us dazzle or WOW our customers to a point where they would be happy (and go out of their way) to tell others about us?***" If what they are doing does, you do more of that. If it doesn't, you stop doing that. It's easy to grasp, understand, get passionate about, and adopt, so it becomes part of our culture and DNA. It is always easier and more powerful to focus on "**the one thing**" we are striving for in whatever we do...the beacon on the hill. If you are sailing a boat, you have a specific destination you want to reach. You understand it and focus on it. It is precisely the same in your Journey to be Customer Obsessed and become "*REMARK*"able™.

You're probably asking yourself, "***If this is so simple, why doesn't every company in the world do it***?" Great question. Let's explore why only about 20% of companies are reaping the rewards of becoming "*REMARK*"able™.

Unfortunately, while the concept and recipe are simple, the execution of being Customer Obsessed isn't as simple or as easy as it might appear. If it were, everyone would be doing it without much effort. The keywords here are "**consistent execution**." If you are relentless about it...making it part of your culture and DNA...making it purposeful...executing it consistently from the top down through every employee...you will get there.

I will hand you the recipe, the formula, the roadmap for how to be Customer Obsessed so you can become "*REMARK*"able™...the rest of this book. But like with any good recipe, the proof is in the execution. This isn't any different. I can't think of a single reason why any organization wouldn't want to be Customer

Obsessed with so many rewards waiting for them when they become *"REMARK"*able™.

Becoming "*REMARK*"able™ is PURPOSEFUL. It only happens when you are "all in" and commit to following the formula every day, making it part of your Culture and DNA.

The two keywords, "**consistent**" and "**purposeful,**" describe the Journey. To become *"REMARK"*able™, you have to stay consistent in your Journey and stay focused on your purpose. Someone, hopefully you, who has a deep desire to become *"REMARK"*able™ will reap the rewards because they are committed, focused, and consistently execute the recipe. And you definitely measure your success. I dedicated an entire chapter to help you see how to measure your success, "**Measure What You Don't Measure.**"

Here's something to think about and wrap your head around that hopefully will help you understand why Customer Obsessed companies are so purposeful and focused on becoming *"REMARK"*able™...

> **"One of Google's biggest fears, when it comes to someone searching for a business, isn't other search engines...it's Word-of-Mouth. If someone you "trust" has already "experienced" what it is you are looking for, why would you need to waste a bunch of time searching the internet...you wouldn't. You would buy from a place you can trust and will treat you incredibly well and make you feel special. We all would. You don't want to be found via search. You want others to find you because someone who trusts you told them about you. Google (and others) hate that"**

Suppose you can go to a "trusted" source (via your communication channels of social media, email, or in-person) for answers, recommendations, or information. Why would you waste my time doing an organic search to get a solution you don't trust? You wouldn't.

For example, let's say you want to find a great Italian restaurant in Seattle. You want one that is extraordinary, and you don't want to spend a ton of your valuable time trying to find it. At this point, you have three choices.

Your first choice...jump onto Google (or another search engine) and search for "great Italian restaurants in the Seattle area." It actually returned 143,000,000 results. Now I have to spend my most valuable resource (**time**) to narrow down the searches to get the result I want. However, even when I narrow down my search results, I have to find out how well it was rated and review the comments...what a time suck. Even then, I can't really **TRUST** them...they just had higher ratings and some positive comments.

Your second choice...go to the review sites such as Yelp, Trip Advisor, or another similar review site. They return fewer results but still consumes a tremendous amount of my most valuable asset (**time**) to go through all the reviews. And in the end, I am still relying on the opinion of people I don't know (or trust) and hope the reviews I read weren't "paid reviews" to boost the restaurant's rating on the review sites. Whew...this is beginning to be a lot of work and takes a lot of time. And you still aren't entirely sure this will be a great Italian restaurant because you still can't **TRUST** the reviews.

Your third choice...this is the easiest solution, takes **less time**, and virtually guarantees me a great result. And it is easier than either of the previous choices. I simply **Ask those I TRUST**. I send out a message to my friends and ask them if they have been to any incredible Italian restaurants that serve fantastic food and have an incredible (and memorable) experience at a reasonable price? I start getting responses from my "trusted network" of friends and colleagues who are more than happy to give me the places they have experienced that were really spectacular. The probability I will go to one of these is incredibly high...they are "trusted" results.

Keep in mind that this process **only works** if the restaurant is **"*REMARK*"able™**. If the restaurant treated my friends incredibly well and made them feel special, they get to be in this unique and differentiated class of restaurants...they have become "*REMARK*"able™. If they just gave them an ordinary product and a mediocre experience, my friends won't recommend them. They won't put their credibility and reputation on the line for mediocre or even great...they put it on the line for someone who delivers an incredibly awesome and amazing experience. This is the restaurant they will rave about and happily "**do their marketing for them**."

And how much did the restaurant pay my friend to tell me about their restaurant? That's right, ZERO. They didn't have to buy an ad or spend a lot of money on the review sites to rank higher or a variety of other low return activities. Following the Customer Obsessed model, the restaurant could literally **STOP MARKETING**. Option three just saved me a boatload of time, energy, anxiety, and stress I would have otherwise spent researching and reviewing other opinions. Why would I want to do that? Why would your customers (and audience) want to do that? They don't. They won't.

Becoming "*REMARK*"able™ is about allowing others to **do your marketing for you**. Isn't this a better way to market? Isn't this a better way to run your business? Isn't this a better culture to have in your company? I think so...I hope you do as well.

I am an "unpaid" Advocate and Marketing Agent™ for my financial advisor Roger Reynolds at Coldstream. He is incredible at what he does and how he manages my money. More importantly, I trust him completely. He has earned my trust and loyalty (remember the Advocacy Architecture™), which is why I am a strong advocate for him and his firm. I am also a huge advocate for Detlef Schrempf, Coldstream's Director of Business Development. You may remember him best as a former NBA star with the Seattle Supersonics. The relationship I built with him over the years was because he always kept his promises and played it straight with me in everything. He also earned my trust and loyalty. Because they followed the Advocacy Architecture™, I enthusiastically became their Advocate and Marketing Agent™. I help do their marketing for them because they make me feel special, important, and give me an incredibly awesome and amazing experience. I "proactively" tell others about them and recommend they meet with them. They don't pay me a dime to do it.

> **SideBar:** Being an **Advocate** is different than being a **reference**...it's important to understand this distinction. A **reference** is someone you "ask" to tell someone else you're great...**it is solicited**. An **Advocate**, on the other hand, is someone who **proactively** tells others about you...**it is unsolicited**. They offer your name up whenever they are in a conversation where this topic comes up.

Who are your **Advocates**...the ones who go out of their way to do your marketing for you? Do you need more of these working on your behalf? The recipe and formula I will share with you shortly will help you get more of them working on your behalf...for free. Having a business where your audience proactively tells others about you is what becoming *"REMARK"*able™ is all about...and what this entire book is about. I want your organization to be *"REMARK"*able™.

Allow me to share a very simple story with you, one about cows...they're pretty simple. But I think it will really help you get your head around what it's like to be Customer Obsessed and become *"REMARK"*able™...

How Grandpa Bought Cows

Word-of-mouth will trump media attention every time.

CAMILLE PERRI

My grandfather, William, grew up like most of our grandparents. They worked the land or had jobs that produced things. They had very few services and lots of product because they needed something to eat, wear, and simply survive. He was living in the middle of the Great Depression.

My grandfather was a farmer and a rancher, so they were pretty self-sufficient in what they produced. And when they had some extra, they gave it away to others who didn't have enough or sold it at the markets. They were very typical for the early 1900s through the depression, post-depression, and early war years.

My grandparents knew the value of hard work and could easily distinguish between what was right and what was fake or superficial. They could read people like nobody's business. It was a vital skill for buying things that would help them grow and raise their products. In his case, it was farm products and cattle. If they ended up getting bad advice or something wasn't as it was supposed to be, they got hurt...badly. It could mean the difference between eating and surviving one month to the next. So, it was necessary for them and was literally their ability to survive! To say it was critical would be an understatement.

The same held true when my grandfather bought his cows. He didn't go down to the local feed store and look on the bulletin board for who was selling cattle (we would call that the Internet today). These were the advertisements in his day for the cattle dealers marketing their cows. They were people he didn't know. How could he trust his family's success (and survival) to a listing on the bulletin board? There were lots of people selling cows...some at a pretty good (cheap) price where he could get more cattle for his money. But there was one big thing missing...he didn't know them, and he didn't trust them.

So how did my William buy his cows? He would walk down to the end of his fence and talk to Bob. Bob was his next-door neighbor. They would shoot the breeze and swap stories. They talked about the weather and whether they thought it would be a dry or wet year, and how it would affect their cattle and crops. They would talk about the latest issues and how they handled them...sharing their knowledge about anything and everything relating to ranching and farming. It was like getting the latest news from others in the biz...what could be better or more accurate?

One day my grandfather told Bob he was in the market to buy some more heads of cattle and mentioned that he admired some of the cattle Bob had bought over the past few years. So, my grandfather asked Bob, "*Where did you get those great head of cattle? They look really healthy and strong. Do you know someone that sells high-quality cattle, will treat you fairly, and offer them at a reasonable price?*" Bob replied, "*Yes, I do...do you want to talk to the guy?*" Of course, my grandfather said yes, and would love to get some cattle without all the hassle and risk.

Then Bob leaned over the fence and said...

> "*I'll let you in on a little secret...Joe is the guy. He is the one you want to buy your cattle from. He is a great guy that treats you right and fairly. He sells great cattle but does way more than just selling you his cows. He helps you pick out the ones that work best for your ranch and then makes sure they are healthy before he ever sells them to you. And he does all this for a reasonable price. Not the cheapest, but fair and reasonable. And if anything goes wrong with the cows, he stands behind them and will make it right...it's almost no risk buying from Joe. He's the only guy I go to for my cattle.*"

My grandfather thanked him for telling him about Joe and went directly to Joe to buy his next head of cattle. From that day forward, grandfather bought all his cattle from Joe. But there's more to this story. When some of my grandfather's friends saw his great cattle, they asked him the same question he asked Bob several years earlier, "*Where's the best and most trusted place to buy your cattle?*" Of course, my dad gave them Joe's name, and they bought their cattle from Joe as well.

Let's look at some questions you should be asking yourself from this story. They are just as relevant today as when my Grandfather bought his cattle 100 years ago...

- Do you think Joe ever put up a notice on the bulletin board in the general store or the feed store to advertise his cattle?
- Do you think Joe ever had to go out marketing his cattle and offer special incentives and deals for people to buy his cattle?
- Do you think Joe ever had to worry about the competition and what kind of cattle they were selling?
- Do you think Joe was ever hurting for buyers of his cattle?

The answer to all of these questions is NO...Joe didn't have to do any of this. And neither do you. You see, Joe was "*REMARK*"able™. Joe **STOPPED MARKETING...his customers were dying to do it for him**. Joe built an incredibly successful cattle business by being Customer Obsessed. Joe had more positive word-of-mouth from his Advocates and Marketing Agents™ than all of his "bulletin board" competitors combined.

While this might be a simple story, it is not that dissimilar to our world today concerning what works and what doesn't. I love to tell this story...not only because it's part of my history but because it shows us that some things never change...nor should they. It's a story everyone can relate to at some level in their life. It is a story about how business is done today, has always been done, and will continue to be done in the future.

There are five great takeaways from this story. I want to point these out and explore them a little further.

First, you have to start with a **quality product**...not always the best product, but a quality product. The old adage that you can only dress up the pig long enough until they find out it's a pig still applies. Joe had quality cows that didn't have a lot of problems. They were above average but weren't the best cow's money could buy...that wasn't his secret sauce.

There are some crazy numbers that illustrate how people don't always choose the highest quality products...and not because of price. One number I have seen says that almost half (43%) of the people will knowingly select a lesser product in exchange for an incredible customer experience. This number is growing and clearly demonstrates that having the absolute best product isn't the deciding factor.

Second, Joe provided an incredibly awesome and amazing experience. He ensured that the buying process was simple, friendly, personable, and made his customers feel special and important. Joe went above and beyond in his service to these customers. He offered a guarantee that he stood behind his cows and would make it right if something went wrong. Above and beyond his competitors, he also did other unexpected things, such as delivering the cows to the people who couldn't pick them up. He also made sure they were inspected and healthy before selling them. He enhanced the customer experience above and beyond what others were doing. Others just sold cows...Joe sold the experience that could be trusted.

Joe was the guy selling quality cattle and giving his customers an incredibly awesome and amazing experience that helped them reduce their risk and anxiety. He was selling "peace of mind." It is what everyone was buying from Joe. He didn't sell a commodity at the lowest price they had to worry about throughout the year. He sold happiness for his customers.

Third, he **didn't advertise**. Joe didn't hand out bulletins and flyers or mail things to people (that would be like using traditional media such as direct mail, brochures, radio, TV, etc.). Nor did he post flyers at the local feed store (the internet today and social media). He didn't have to "convince" anyone to buy his cows through a bunch of sales literature and information...he **had his customers doing the marketing for him**.

When someone came to him looking for a cow, they were sold before they got there. He just closed the deal by telling them what a great experience they would have when they bought from him. Customers were coming to him via **"trusted recommendations," not marketing materials**. He had the best marketing force working for him...his trusted and ecstatic customers.

Today, the numbers still support Joe's approach. Less than 10% believe an advertisement, while 90% believe the recommendation from someone they know. They couldn't afford to take the risk just because it was a bit cheaper because it could cost them their livelihood.

Fourth, Joe sold ALL his cows via **word-of-mouth**. He sold every cow because his **Advocates and Marketing Agents™** were telling their friends to buy their cows from Joe. He worked hard to earn everyone's trust. And if something went wrong, he made it right. But it was more than just standing by his product and giving them a refund or a new cow...he was selling an experience, happiness, and peace of mind.

Joe "**invested**" in his customers. He knew that building **TRUST**, creating an incredibly awesome and amazing **CUSTOMER EXPERIENCE**, and **HELPING** his audience throughout the relationship built massive **DIFFERENTIATION** from his competitors. Joe knew what people wanted, and he gave it to them...consistently and honorably. His investment in his customers was worth far more than any investment he could have made in anything else.

Finally, because Joe knew what he could deliver, he could **choose which customers** he wanted to work with. He knew if someone were referred to him by one of his "ideal" customers, they would most likely also be an "ideal" customer. I'm pretty sure Joe didn't know about the concept of identifying his "**personas**" back then, but that's precisely what he was doing. He didn't sell to those that wanted the cheapest cows or the best bargain...he sent them to others selling cheaper cows. He didn't want those customers who wanted the absolute highest-grade cow that money could buy...he sent those to the few that dealt with this elite level of cattle. He knew his niche of customers and sold to those that fit into his niche.

A significant benefit of leveraging your Advocates and Marketing Agents™ is to know who you want as customers and who you don't. **Not all money is good money.** Just because someone wants to pay you for your product doesn't make that "good money,"...nor does it make them the "right customer." Joe knew his lane on the freeway, and he stayed in it. He didn't drift into other lanes and get in trouble by selling to the wrong customers.

If you want to be the "Joe of your industry," the recipe and formula you will be learning will help you get there. It will help you change how your customers see you and show you why your customers are dying to do your marketing for you, just like they did for Joe. It will transform your culture into being Customer Obsessed so you can become "*REMARK*"able.

With my grandfather's story about Joe as a backdrop, let's look at some specific ways you can STOP MARKETING and start to get your customers to do it for you...

STOP MARKETING

Marketing is Broken

The aim of marketing is to know and understand the customer so well the product or service fits him and sells itself.

PETER DRUCKER

Are you happy with the ROI of the marketing dollars you are spending? Do your customers welcome your marketing? Would you embrace the marketing you are sending to your customers?

Put yourself in the shoes of your customer. After all, you are a customer as well. Think like a customer while you read this chapter, not just as a leader in your organization. Ask yourself some simple questions, "*Do I really want to be marketed to? Do I really want to figure out what the truth is and what is a lie? Do I really want to waste my time trying to figure out what this product (or service) is all about?*" We all know the answer to these questions when WE ARE THE CUSTOMER...it is a resounding NO.

We don't have time. And since time is our most valuable asset, we don't want to waste it on nonproductive activities such as marketing. Why would we (or our customers) want to waste it playing detective and trying to figure out what the real story is behind a particular product or service? We don't.

Marketing is BROKEN.

Marketing forces us to determine what is fact and what is fiction. And it has operated in this mode for decades. If we aren't willing to invest the time to investigate what we are buying, we could get burned, costing us even more time and money. Figuring out fact from fiction is the last thing we want to spend our most valuable asset on...we have better things to do with our time.

Today, unfortunately, marketing forces us to spend even more time than we did before. This is messed up. **Marketing needs change...it is broken**. Let's avoid making these mistakes and let our competitors make them instead of us. You can be different. Your audience wants you to be different. You can be the one everyone loves to work with because you aren't playing these marketing games with them. You can stand alone.

When you STOP MARKETING, you can stand alone as the one who is different and unique.

This book is not just about marketing...it is about your entire business. It is all about **culture**, **leadership**, and a **commitment** to the one thing that is absolutely, positively vital to any organization...**CUSTOMERS**. Without them, we don't exist. Without them, we don't have a business. They are the linchpin for every business.

Marketing usually focuses on getting more customers, the lifeline for business. The more you market, the more thriving the company should be. Everyone wants this to happen. I just believe the ways we go about getting these new customers (and keeping the ones we have) is broken.

When you actually STOP MARKETING, your business can genuinely shine...because your audience will be doing it for you. Your audience of customers and others will see a completely different approach and will reward you by helping you get more customers, just like them.

That's right, when you STOP MARKETING, you will get more customers.

STOP MARKETING...really? That's blasphemy! I really do mean it, and I'll show you why. By the end of the book, I hope you, too, will want your organization to STOP MARKETING!

When the numbers tell us that people only trust 8% - 12% of "company advertising" (regardless of the communication channel used), it says this method of communicating just isn't working...at least not to the degree most people think it should. If marketers aren't liars (as was the title of a great book by Seth Godin, "**All Marketers are Liars**"), then they are at least masters of "truth twisting" to one degree or another.

If you're in marketing, your hair is probably on fire right now, and there is smoke coming out of your ears. If you are the CEO or President (or other C-Suite executive), you're probably shaking your head in agreement right now. You get it. Marketing has lost its effectiveness (and trust) over the last several decades. Yet, we keep spending more and more money on it, and we keep getting lower and lower results. Why do we keep doing this? Isn't there any other alternative? I believe there is a (much) better answer.

One reason marketing isn't working so well today is because of Social Media. What?!? Isn't Social Media supposed to be the new and improved channel for marketing? It's a channel, but it doesn't mean that it has any more trust than the newspaper we used to read. **It's the "content" of marketing that is broken, not the tools or the channels.**

Social Media is high-speed and easy to use. So, we pump out a lot of content on its channels, regardless of whether it is helpful or not. More is better when it comes to Social Media...or so we think. If I inundate you with enough material about how great I am, maybe I will stand out more. Perhaps you will notice me more, and maybe you will want to buy from me. After all, the "squeaky wheel gets the grease," as they say. It seems logical until you realize millions of others are doing the same thing...then we get lost. Everyone gets lost...including your customers.

To make matters worse, what happens when others are pumping out inaccurate or inflated information? When this type of information floods the social media airwaves, the audience assumes your content is the same...unless it comes from a "**trusted source.**" **TRUST is the game-changer when it comes to marketing.** We'll dive into this in later chapters.

On the positive side, Social Media allows us to share what we see, hear, and feel with hundreds, thousands, or millions of people...instantly. **They can say anything they want about you**, your products, your services, your people, and of course, the way you make them feel when interacting with your organization. And they are prolific and loud...and getting louder.

If a company (pre-internet and social media) mistreated a customer or lied to them through their marketing, their "circle of influence" was tiny...maybe 5 to 50 people. Not enough to do any serious damage to most companies. The "company was in control" and could say whatever they wanted in their advertising, and it really wouldn't hurt the company, even if they were called out on it.

Then the internet showed up and connected us to others. Companies like MySpace (very early entrant) showed up...followed by Facebook, Twitter, Instagram, and hundreds of others. They immediately gave us a platform where we, the customer, could talk to others with a few clicks. The game suddenly changed...forever.

The customer had the microphone and could say whatever they wanted when they wanted. The business was no longer in control of its message.

Marketing didn't seem to care or didn't understand the microphone was in the customer's hands. Marketing departments were set in their ways and didn't think they needed to change. They were not paying attention and soon discovered the customer could tell more people than ever before

Today, virtually everyone is using social media to one degree or another. But, instead of only a handful of people hearing about you, now there are thousands or potentially millions. If a customer is being misled, manipulated, or doesn't feel like they are important, they tell lots of people about it...instantly. Now the game has really changed, again...forever

STOP MARKETING...the customer isn't going to stand for it any longer. They no longer want to be tricked or manipulated, and they can easily find out when they are...and they will leave.

Think of the last time you ate a hamburger or something from a fast-food restaurant. Did it look anything like what it did in the picture? Why is that? Why do we create something we know we can't deliver and then tell everyone we can? Why do we believe manipulation of the facts is going to win over our audiences? Lots of "why" questions. There is a simple answer that has been around since the beginning of time. It hasn't changed over the centuries, and it won't change anytime soon. It is a surefire way to differentiate you help you stand out from the noise and the pack. It is what we, as a customer, want as well. It doesn't involve any "smoke and mirrors" or manipulation, and it's actually much easier than you think.

Turn the page, and let's start talking about what it is and how you can use it to transform your company today and well into the future, if not forever!

Your Customers are Waiting...

If you're in business, and you don't understand how word-of-mouth works, you won't be able to take full advantage of it, how to get full adoption by getting that network to talk about you.

ROBERT SCOBLE

What percentage of your revenues come from someone else singing your praises...word-of-mouth? Why isn't word-of-mouth your primary driver of revenue?

Customers, like you, are amazing people. They are eager to share their wealth with you and support your business (or your cause). If, and only if, you give them what they want. They are waiting...

Customers want you to be obsessed over them...obsessed over how you treat them and how you make them feel. They want to trust you in everything you do and say. When you obsess over them and build their trust and loyalty, you earn their Advocacy. When your audience and customers become your Advocates and Marketing Agents™, they are literally "**DYING TO DO YOUR MARKETING FOR YOU**."

Your customers are waiting...are you ready?

When your customers are thrilled with you because of how you make them feel (special and important), how they trust you completely, and how you consistently help them improve their personal life and/or their business, you don't have to ask them to market for you, they will be "**dying to do it for you**." They are more than anxious to help you out. And the absolute best way a customer can help any business isn't to just buy more. It is to tell others about you. And telling others, just like them, how incredibly awesome and amazing you are is the Holy Grail for any business. The audience of Customer Obsessed companies do this for them...are you ready to have your audience do it for YOU?

The audience(s) of Customer Obsessed companies can't wait to tell others how special they make them feel, how incredible they treat them, and to show them how important they are to them. Audiences are waiting to be dazzled and delighted, and not just because they pay us money. They can't wait to spread the word. They can't wait to be your **Advocate and Marketing Agent™**.

This book is all about helping you, and your organization, eliminate the barriers and execute the model so your entire audience can STOP WAITING and START TALKING.

And by the way, none of what I just described has anything to do with traditional marketing...nothing. My model of how to be Customer Obsessed so you can become "*REMARK*"able™ will give you everything you need to arm your audience so they can tell others how incredibly awesome and amazing you are and why they should work with YOU.

Customer Obsession is the pathway and catalyst to becoming "*REMARK*"able™ in the eyes of your audience.

When you are Customer Obsessed and ready to become "*REMARK*"able™, it will feel like you are at the Boston Marathon's starting line. There will be thousands of people anxiously waiting for the sound of the starting gun to start telling thousands of people (just like them) you are the most incredibly awesome and amazing company to work with. You can finally STOP MARKETING so you can use these funds to support your customers in a completely different way. Customer Obsessed companies don't need to market the old way. They market in a way their customers appreciate, look forward to, and find incredibly helpful.

When you change the way you market (communicate), you get talked about...you become "*REMARK*"able™.

Over the next several chapters, I'll give you a completely different way to "market" to your audience...one they are excited about, can't wait to receive, and will share with others. Your new form of "marketing" will be "**Customer Focused Marketing**" your audience will welcome, believe, follow, and share. That's how marketing should work. The world is different, your audience is different, and now you can be different as well.

Time to step up to the starting line, the starters' pistol is ready to go off...

The NEW Gold

Word-of-mouth is way more important than millions of dollars spent on advertising.

ISAAC HANSON

How many people (customers and others) do you have telling others they should buy from you? How many are doing this on their own, proactively?

Here's the deal...I have one purpose and only one purpose for this book...to get you more Advocates and Marketing Agents™ who are anxious to tell others how incredibly awesome and amazing you are as an organization...period.

I want you to be "Top of Mind" to lots of people who can create buzz and enthusiasm in your audience and "proactively" tell others about you. It doesn't get any better than this when it comes to business. I want that to be you...the envy in your industry.

To get there, you have to move from the "old school" way of thinking to a completely "new way" of visualizing how you treat your customers. No longer is having "satisfied customers" going to cut it. To be honest, I hate the term "satisfied." To me, it merely means being mediocre. I ate this meal, and it was OK, I'm satisfied...WOW. That doesn't get me excited in the least. Certainly not to the point of wanting to go out of my way to tell anyone else about this restaurant.

Satisfaction is mediocrity. We have to do better than this if we want to dominate our market. NO ONE talks about mediocrity...no one.

The "New Gold" is CREATING Advocates and Marketing Agents™.

Today, we have the infrastructure and tools to leverage our audience(s) aggressively. **They have always existed...but now we can leverage them**. And if we can leverage our audiences to help us expand our audiences with more credibility and impact, why are we not focusing a maximum amount of effort on doing that? Why aren't we doing everything possible to tap into this new vein of gold in business? Why aren't we allowing our audiences to help us by telling thousands of other people about us?

ADVOCATES are people (customers and others) who "**proactively go out of their way to sing your praises and tell others how awesome you are.**" These are your biggest fans in the market, and enjoy, no, **love** to tell others about you. They are the ones that are dedicated to you because they know you are obsessed with their happiness.

Advocates are the "New Gold," and you can't have enough of them.

What exactly does it mean to "be" an "Advocate for someone?" There have always been Advocates...this is nothing new. There have always been people who go out of their way to tell others. There has (and always will be) word-of-mouth happening. But not just any word-of-mouth. I'm talking about those who are "passionate" about your organization and who go out of their way to tell others. The difference is being **proactive**, not reactive.

When someone is proactive about telling others about you, they are genuinely acting as your Advocate and Marketing Agent™. They are the ones who are so passionate about how you treated them, how you made them feel, and how important they are to you, they "**want to go out of their way**" to tell others. They don't just offer your name when someone asks (that's merely a reference). They go out of their way to proactively tell others about you.

Proactive trusted Advocates who act as your Marketing Agents are the "NEW Gold" today...and everyone can use more of these.

Having Advocates in the market connected to many others (thousands) via their social networks opens the door to a significantly large number of people. And the people we know...the ones in our network, are people just like us. We all know people just like ourselves. So, if you want more people like me, then you should turn me into your Advocate so that I can communicate with others just like me. That's leverage.

Oh, and so we don't lose sight of it, **how much did you pay them** to be out there telling others about you...**ZERO**. They aren't asking to be reimbursed or charging you a fee. They do it because they believe in you, what you do, how you make them feel, and because they trust you.

That's the beauty of an Advocate. They do it because they want to, not because there is some reward out there for them. Advocates are pure...they are people who tell others because they want to be helpful, not rewarded. They simply fit into a different category.

Here's the "hidden gem"...Advocates don't have to be a customer!

Another significant advantage of becoming *"REMARK"*able™ is that others can promote you even if they aren't customers! Everyone misses this point. It is a big opportunity available to Customer Obsessed companies.

For someone to be a **loyal customer,** they need to be a customer. By treating them incredibly well, we can turn them into an Advocate. We want to do this with all of our loyal customers. No one disagrees with this logic. But what if they aren't a customer? Can they still be an Advocate? ABSOLUTELY! They can definitely be a **Trusted Advocate**.

I have a friend, Dave Carroll, who is in the banking industry, at least that's his day job. He is a great connector of people. He also shares new ideas with them through his organization, Cantillon. I trust him. He has earned my trust by going out of his way to help me and others I know. This is huge. Yet, I haven't ever been a customer of what he does in his career to date.

I'm his Advocate, not his customer. I go out of my way to tell others to meet him because of how he has treated me and how I know he cares. And in the banking industry, this is gold! I go out of my way and tell others they should meet him and see if he can help. And if they like what he says, they also know they are dealing with someone I trust in the banking industry.

Even though I can't speak to what it's like to "work with him," I can talk about his character...which carries more credibility than being his customer. He's someone who can be trusted to give you the right information and do what is right for you, even if it means referring you to a different bank. When I tell others about him, they don't go to Google and search for banks and bankers (that would return millions of results). They simply meet with him because they know I trust him (more on trust when I talk about The *"REMARK"*able Triangle™). They thank me for "saving them time" (our most valuable asset) and for telling them about someone I trust. Since they trust me, they feel comfortable talking to Dave.

How much does Dave pay me to do this for him? ZERO. As his Advocate, I am "**doing his marketing for him**" with my network. When I post something about him on my social channels (over 10,000 people), the ones who trust me will have an immediate and initial trust for Dave. They will be far more inclined to contact him because I am someone they trust. He gets all this for free. He invests in our relationship by helping me with questions or steering me in the right direction. I reward him because I trust him. He gets the **leverage** because of this relationship...for free.

Or take my friend and colleague, Michael Langhout (Mike). He is the best overall business advisor and growth coach I know, hands down. I have known him for over a decade and know what he does to help companies grow and scale their business from a strategic perspective. I know about his process and the results he can get for companies. I know how he operates and how he works.

But most importantly, I know his character. It is above reproach and something clearly aspirational. I trust him without hesitation. But I'm not, nor have I ever been, a client of his. I have never personally paid him a dime for his expertise or services. Yet I know he is fantastic at what he does.

I recommend Mike all the time without question. I go out of my way to suggest leaders talk to Mike about their business to see if he can help them somehow. I offer his name up in person, in speeches, and on my social channels (and even in my book). I'm his Advocate. And I'm honored to help market for him whenever I can. He is "top of mind" for me.

I am happy to go out of my way to be an Advocate and Marketing Agent™ for those I trust and who I know are Customer Obsessed. They put their customers at the center of what they do and become "*REMARK*"able™.

How many Advocates do you have (or could you have) who are not customers?

Do you have people who go out of their way to tell others how incredibly awesome and amazing you are, and who aren't your customers? Everyone has these people...sometimes lots of them. They can be friends, colleagues, partners, other professionals they work with, or a host of other people. How many can you count? Are you feeding them with great things to talk about (I'll talk a lot more about this in the Chapter on **"Truly" Helping Changes the Game**)?

There is a tremendous amount of power and opportunity in your network for creating an army of Advocates and Marketing Agents™. Regardless of whether they happen to be customers or not, they are out doing the same thing for you...telling others how incredibly awesome and amazing you are to work with. Whether you have an army of Advocates today or very few, I will help you build this army. That's my passion and my objective.

This is the "New Gold." Let's keep going and help you tap into that vein of gold for yourself and your organization. But first, there is something we need to STOP and something we need to do more of...

Stop "Pimping"... Start "Helping"

Permission marketing turns strangers into friends and friends into loyal customers. It's not just about entertainment – it's about education. Permission marketing is curriculum marketing. Permission marketing is marketing without interruptions.

SETH GODIN

Are you still "pushing" marketing out to your audience? Is what you "push" out about YOU or your AUDIENCE? How valuable is what you "push" out to your audience?

The days of "pimping" your company are gone...dead. Nobody wants to hear about how great you think you are. They want to see it for themselves or hear about it from a highly credible (and trusted) source. They can find out about your products and services and your company by simply searching Google or your website. They don't need it shoved in their face.

Today's audience has become very proficient at using the internet...we all know how to find things. We don't need to be "told" and "sold" on your company's quality and your products/services. We want those using the products or services to "help" us make the right decision!

Customers (and others in your audience) are the new "marketing force" in your company...whether you like it or not.

As you have already heard, customers are in complete control of your marketing and brand today. The pendulum has swung to customers to either sing our praises or trash us. Companies have lost the power they used to have in marketing, and it belongs to our audience. If you have some warts, received kudos, have raving or unhappy customers, or even have disgruntled employees, we see (and hear) about all of these today.

Customers (and our audience) have a microphone, and they aren't afraid to use it...a lot! And they have higher credibility than anyone else.

Before the internet, companies could promote themselves as often as they wanted because they had a captive audience. You HAD to listen, read, or watch what they were telling you...there was no other option. They put ads in newspapers, filled your mailbox with direct mail, occupied the airwaves, and interrupted your favorite show just when it was getting good. And we hated it...but we didn't have any other option.

In 1999, we saw some of the first signs of relief...TIVO was born. Remember how excited you were when you could watch your favorite show or movie from start to end and skip all the advertising...nirvana! A new day was born.

Innovations starting in the '90s were sending a thunderous message...we don't want to hear your hyped-up advertising!

The message hasn't changed...we still don't want to spend our valuable time (remember it is our most important asset) reading, seeing, or hearing about all this advertising and promotion. With all these innovations designed to help you skip the annoying ads, wouldn't you think companies would have gotten the message by now? We don't want it...and we want you to just stop it. STOP MARKETING this way, or we will ignore you.

Sadly, many organizations haven't gotten the message. We are continually being bombarded with messages we don't want. Somehow there is a disconnect between what we, the audience, want and what we get.

However, because companies still believe this type of marketing still works, your company has an incredible **OPPORTUNITY** staring you in the face. Those who realize this is not working can change the game and elevate themselves above their competitors. This is your time to shine and take the lead...and all the tools to help you get there are available TODAY! I want to liberate you from this old world of "**Pimping**" and help you create marketing that your audience actually looks forward to hearing, reading, and seeing from you.

What would your business look like if you had customers asking for more "marketing" because they genuinely wanted it and found it incredibly helpful and valuable to them?

Marketing that "PUSHES" information we don't want (or need) is nothing more than **Pimping**. Let's stop Pimping. Let's start creating such fantastic and incredible "content" that our audience can't wait to hear from us and wants to get to know us better. Let's stop focusing on "interruption marketing" and focus on "permission" marketing, as Seth Godin told us to do years ago in his book, "**Permission Marketing.**" Let's do what they are begging us to do...**help them improve their lives and/or their business**.

But let's go beyond permission marketing and move into DESIRED MARKETING...my term for marketing in a Customer Obsessed world.

It goes beyond just getting permission. It takes you to a place where your audience actually "**DESIRES**" to have your "content" and looks forward to hearing from you. Why? Because it is so helpful and individualized that your audience can't wait to see how it can help them in whatever they do.

It could be as simple as the latest trend report information with your insightful narrative that helps me in my next meeting or with my team to expand in a specific area. It could be your insights on a new law or regulation that will help me understand it better and apply it to my business. It could be a series of leadership tips to help me as I'm trying to build my leadership skills. It could be some business insights from what I have learned over the past few decades. And the list goes on and on.

When you **help** your audience by providing them with the **desired** content, they want to "**PULL**" this content into their life. Your marketing "feeds" them with helpful content, elevating yourself above your "Pimping" competitors. Your audience sees you as helping them improve their life and/or their business...not as "pimping" them for another dollar.

Customer Obsessed companies do this for their Advocates and Marketing Agents™. This is "**Customer Marketing.**" This is a different mindset. This is a different culture. This is your new DNA.

When you operate with the Customer at the center of your organization, your marketing will change 180 degrees. It is an opportunity in front of you today. The question is, "***Will you change your direction and seize the opportunity?***" I hope so. Let's look at a much better way to do marketing...

There's a Better Way to Market

Word-of-mouth works now, much more than ever. @-reply every single person.

GARY VAYNERCHUK

Would you change the way you market if you could significantly increase the ROI of your marketing efforts?

Marketing is most powerful when you can get others doing it for you. The purpose of marketing is to create a "**catalyst**" that starts the process moving forward. Once underway, we should let our audience do it for us...**this is the way marketing "should" work**.

Marketing is also about creating and supporting the identity of your organization...**your Brand**. An easily recognizable brand gets talked about and is consistent. As Seth Godin would say, *"It's about gaining "permission" from your audience to communicate with them."*

As I talked about in the last chapter, marketing isn't about "pimping" your audience with products/services in hopes of catching someone on a good day so they will buy something from you. It isn't about creating fear, uncertainty, and doubt (FUD). Marketing stoops to its lowest levels with such approaches as, ***"If you don't do something by such and such a time, you will lose out and miss your*** *opportunity*." Really? This isn't marketing in the Customer Economy and why I believe every company should...

STOP MARKETING...there's a better way to market.

Let's start with one simple fact...**customers are much more credible than we are when they tell our story.** Customers are believable because they tell others about their experience when buying your product/service. They have high authenticity, transparency, and credibility in the eyes of prospective customers. Here are a few questions you might ask...

- Why are we keeping our customers from telling others?
- Why aren't we doing everything possible to "arm" our customers (and our entire audience) with credible and trustworthy information so potential customers can't wait to check us out?
- Why aren't we focusing more on the most trusted audience we could empower to market for us...our customers (and others) who have become our Advocates?
- Why are we not investing every marketing dollar we have into someone who has a 92% credibility rating instead of our marketing, which only has an 8% average credibility rating?

It isn't that most companies don't want to get this powerful source of marketing...they just don't know how to do it. They don't know there is a better alternative. By the time you finish this book, you will realize there is a better (much better) alternative to the way you may be marketing today.

Marketing has changed in the Customer Economy. We have to start thinking of marketing differently than in the past. The new way of marketing is what I refer to as "Desired Marketing," where the customer craves your content and can't wait to share it with others.

When you provide your audience with information and "content" that is specifically valuable and relevant to them, they want more of it. When they see how it will improve their life and/or their business, they value it. When they see we aren't wasting their time, we help them grow. And we are helping them do better at what they do best. We are of value to them. Our audience "pulls" it to themselves. They request it, ask for it, and, most importantly, they share it.

I believe marketing should be about leveraging all the knowledge we have inside our organization to help our audience (customers and others) improve their life and/or their business. When we do that, our marketing is welcomed and valued.

When your audience can't wait to hear from you because you are "Consistently Helping" them improve their life and/or their business, you get talked about...you become "*REMARK*"able™. People share what they find of value and what they trust. And when your audience shares and "promotes" the information and insights you give them, there is a high probability your audience will act on it. You will read much more about how all this works in the chapter on "**The "*REMARK*"able Triangle™**."

NO ONE shares an advertisement or promotional material unless it is because of price...NO ONE.

People share advertisements when they believe your products or services are a commodity. **They share a "good deal" or "low price" or some other commodity component. We don't ever want this to happen.** Why would we want something to be shared that is costing us margin and profitability? This makes no sense. Do we really want more customers who only want lower prices on a particular product or service? Do we really want this to be our Brand?

I don't think so unless you can be the continuous leader in low prices and remain profitable. However, there will always be some company out there that will offer a similar product or service at a lower price, guaranteed. It happens all the time. This book isn't for the few who use the commodity model. It is for those who want to raise profitability by being differentiated.

Let me give you a quick example of how this works. I worked with some attorneys who wanted to change how they marketed...stop the pimping, and change how their audience viewed them. They tried to stop selling fear and uncertainty and started providing helpful content (articles, seminars, podcasts, etc.). The goal was to help their audience, so their audience would want to help them out and tell others about them. They wanted to become "*REMARK*"able™, allowing them to differentiate themselves from the countless other attorneys.

We started to give their audience valuable insights and stories they could easily relate to in their own life. We moved from fear and uncertainty to providing a ton of helpful content their audience would find very important in their lives. They were building a platform of differentiation. This was the right approach, and it worked. People started "consuming" their content regularly and wanting more of it. They elevated themselves above the pimping, and their audience saw them as incredibly relevant and helpful.

Unfortunately, their internal systems (processes) and the people who handled their "transactions" didn't exude being Client Obsessed and helpful. They fought themselves because their culture (others in the firm) was out of alignment with their Customer Obsessed approach.

Here's what happened. While these attorneys didn't get as many customers doing their marketing for them as they had hoped, they still got a significant amount...well over what they were getting before. It demonstrated that even when they weren't doing everything they should have to reap all the rewards of Customer Obsession, they were getting significantly more word-of-mouth and referrals than ever before! There were many positives for them overall.

While it was less than what it could have been, their clients were actively "**doing their marketing for them**." They were getting more referrals, and people were telling others to meet with them. They were also able to build more trust along the way, which was critically important to them.

> **SIDE NOTE:** The example I just gave is one of the primary reasons why "**the Customer Experience always leads the way to process changes.**" If they could have reengineered their processes to support their client experience, they would have pushed over the top to being completely Customer Obsessed.

There was an intriguing concept discussed several years ago that was in alignment with my beliefs about marketing. It was a concept created (I believe) by Andrew Ford from the UK. He coined the term "Customering" to put the focus of marketing squarely on helping the customer. The concept seemed to be in alignment with what you would use if you were Customer Obsessed. You can read more about his concept of "Customering" and visit his site at www.andrewforduk.wordpress.com for more on this topic. It will be well worth your time to read some of his posts.

Unlike sales, marketing tries to paint a picture of how extraordinary your life and/or business will be when you use a particular product or service. Do you believe it? Unfortunately, the majority of us don't. We all understand the message is coming from someone who is trying to separate you from your money. And, sadly, the image of what you will receive doesn't match the vision of what you actually get...which is why only 8% - 12% of people "believe company advertising" today.

Has the hamburger you bought from a fast-food company ever, ever, ever looked like the one from the advertisement? Never!! Has the car you purchased ever brought you the benefits of looking better, made you stronger, or wealthier? Never! Has the beverage ad ever turned you into a social magnet because you ordered it? Never. Lies, all lies. And because we know none of this happens, we have been conditioned not to believe advertising and marketing claims. We might enjoy them (like the Super Bowl ads), but we don't believe them.

I don't believe there is any need for the way most companies market today! It is a waste of time and money.

However, I believe there is a considerable need for a different way to market...one which actually supports **who** you really are, what **problems** you can genuinely **solve**, and how **trustworthy** you are as an organization. Marketing that leverages all the fantastic and incredible things you do to truly help your audience improve their lives and/or their business is how to market in the Customer Economy successfully. This is the marketing I am suggesting every company on the planet starts doing.

This is marketing you to do FOR your customers, not TO your customers.

Customer Obsessed Marketing puts your customer in the center of everything you do, but with a different objective in mind. No more "**pushing**" and "**pimping**" your audience to buy or take some action. You move to a "desired marketing" model where your audience "**wants your information**" because it's incredibly personalized and helpful. They can't wait and to "**pull**" it to them. It is what we, as customers, want it to be.

SIDE NOTE: This doesn't mean you should take funding away from marketing. The goal is to change the way funding is used. You will now use it as an "**investment**" rather than an "**expense.**"

Marketing, by definition, is about the value and "***helping people who need your product or service find you so they can discover how you can help them improve their life and/or business***."

Customer Obsessed Marketing focuses on "***Helping your audience (because of your knowledge and experience) to be happier in their lives (or their business) and solve their problems...without telling them how great you are. Your customers and others do that for you***."

When you look beneath the covers, Customer Obsessed Marketing is more aligned with the "intent" of what marketing is supposed to be than you might think. It merely helps improve the lives of your audience, **whether they buy from you or not.** If you consistently (and frequently) do some incredibly unique things to help improve your audience's life and/or business, your desired audience will want to tell others about you. We can stop the tricks and manipulation.

Customers WILL FIND YOU...and your audience will help them. They will lead them to you because they value and trust you...something traditional marketing has never done.

The primary goal of Customer Obsessed organizations is to create more **Advocates and Marketing Agents™.** People who will gladly go out of their way to tell others about you...whether they buy from you or not. When you have Advocates and Marketing Agents™ spreading the word about you (in-person and through various other channels) to their audience, YOU WIN. **You have changed the game of marketing.**

You have STOPPED MARKETING and started LEVERAGING your audience to be on your marketing team...and they will help you be more successful.

Does your marketing effort need to change? Are you still operating with the mindset of traditional marketing?

My challenge to you and your company is to deeply examine these questions and take a step with me to venture into the world of "Desired Marketing," where you and your company are Obsessed with Customers in every aspect...resulting in a growing army of Customer Advocates.

With this as a backdrop, let's dive into **HOW** you can make this happen...the recipe, formula, and roadmap you can follow are all outlined in detail in the next chapters. This is where the rubber meets the road. I will show you the "**cornerstones**" of being Customer Obsessed so you can become "*REMARK*"able™! Your business will start to change...forever!

HOW

Journey's Need a Road Map

> *What I found over the years is the most important thing is for a team to come together over a compelling vision, a comprehensive strategy for achieving that vision, and then a relentless implementation plan.*
>
> ALAN MULALLY

"What would your business look like if you doubled (or tripled) the number of Advocates you currently have? How would your business improve if you had twice as many people proactively telling others to buy from you?"

EVERYTHING starts with STRATEGY...everything. Actions without a strategy are nothing more than getting in your car and driving...no plan, just driving. You get somewhere, but it most likely won't be where you wanted to go.

Strategy, to me, is simple. It's a plan for **HOW** to reach the "beacon on the hill" or the "pinnacle on the mountain." It's not a Vision or Mission. It is the plan for how you want to achieve your Vision and/or Mission.

If you want to get to the top of an intense mountain, like Mt. Rainier in my neck of the woods, you need a well thought out strategy for how you are going to reach the summit. There is a strategy for climbing a mountain like Rainier.

The plan would involve how to pack, train, get to different checkpoints along the way, and successfully execute the climb.

It is the same process for how you can become "*REMARK*"able™. It doesn't just happen. And if you begin the Journey to get there without a specific plan, you won't get to the top of the mountain...you won't become "*REMARK*"able™. But with a solid strategy in place, you will get you there.

I hope you have decided you want to be Customer Obsessed by now so you can become "*REMARK*"able™. Your new Vision and Mission...your quest to reach the "summit of Mt. Rainier." If you have made this decision, it's time to develop our Strategy for your Journey. The fun is about to begin...

The rest of the book will give you a specific road map, a recipe, a formula, and some tools for your ascent to the summit. I will provide you with the critical elements needed for "leading" such an expedition. I will share the specifics of what you need if you truly desire to be Customer Obsessed and become "*REMARK*"able™. I won't leave anything out.

The key to a successful Strategy is to invest the time to build a solid plan for how the Journey will progress. As with a climb, there are unforeseen circumstances that always occur along the Journey. The more prepared you are when you start, the easier it will be for you to blast through these temporary barriers and stay the course. Many organizations want to be Customer Obsessed, but they don't have a Strategic Plan for getting there. They bail on the strategy and return to their old way of doing business when things get difficult or hit an obstacle. They are ill-equipped to push through, so they give up and retreat. Since we know these "bumps" will happen, the ones who can push through will be the ones who ultimately own the brass ring of becoming "*REMARK*"able™.

Your odds of success increase significantly with a Strategic Plan.

I highly recommend finding a "process" and "tools" to help you execute your Strategy. The essential ingredient to your plan is "consistent execution." I spent many years in a "Big 5" world assisting companies in developing Strategic Plans. I would venture to say only about 25% of these plans were ever executed and implemented. The others sat on the shelf...only to collect dust until it was time to revise it the following year. This isn't planning...this is window dressing. If you genuinely want to become "*REMARK*"able™, you must be willing to commit to the execution of your Strategy and plan. If you do, amazing things will happen.

Having a "process" for executing your strategic plan would include managing the various activities, responsibilities, and timelines for getting things done. I have used several tools and processes over the years...some work better for others. You just need one...one you and your employees will actually use. After years of working with different tools, I have gravitated to the Trello project management app (trello.com). It works on both your computer and mobile devices (I use it extensively on my phone). It is straightforward, easy to learn, and easy to use. Regardless of what you use, it needs to be easy for everyone, or it won't get used...period. Fancy programs and tools play to egos. Simple ones play to getting things done.

Once you have your Strategy and Plan in place, you can move on to execution. You will soon learn about **The "*REMARK*"able Triangle™**, the foundation for how to be Customer Obsessed and become "*REMARK*"able™. It is powerful yet simple and straightforward. If you like models that you can execute, you will really enjoy this one.

Every employee, and I mean every employee, can quickly grasp, internalize, and execute **The "*REMARK*"able Triangle™** model. To become "*REMARK*"able™, it is absolutely critical to have all your employees signing from the same sheet of music...they need to all be working together to make this work. If the model is too complicated to grasp and execute, it won't work. I can't emphasize this point enough...simple gets implemented.

As we begin this Journey together, it is crucial to always keep in mind that this is all about CULTURE, your DNA. It has to permeate the organization to become part of your culture. I can't emphasize this point enough.

Customer Obsession has to be a part of your culture for you to become "*REMARK*"able™...period. If it becomes your culture, it will happen.

To set the proper foundation for getting started on your Customer Obsessed Journey, I want to make sure we are all on the same page with what exactly Customer Obsession is all about...

HOW You Become "*REMARK*"able™

Exceed your customer's expectations. If you do, they'll come back over and over. Give them what they want – and a little more.

SAM WALTON

Does the majority of your audience proactively and enthusiastically tell others they should buy from you? Why not? How would your business change if they did?

This is where the "rubber meets the road." It is time for the **instruction manual** for **HOW** to become "*REMARK*"able™! It is exhilarating...it's the beginning of making this happen and become your new Culture!

I hope by now, you have a clear understanding of WHY being Customer Obsessed and becoming "*REMARK*"able™ is so incredibly awesome and unique...along with many other benefits and rewards. There are just so many advantages to becoming "*REMARK*"able™. I hope you are ready to dive into the process I am about to share.

You are about to embark on an exciting, transforming Journey. While the Journey never ends, it may very well be the most thrilling ride you and your organization have ever taken.

It starts with **discovery.** Discover what your customers honestly think and genuinely want, so they become your Advocates and Marketing Agents™...telling others about how incredibly awesome and amazing you are as a company. It is a time to understand how "dirt simple" this can be if you aggressively execute it according to the prescription, recipe, formula, and instruction manual you are about to receive. It was purposefully designed not to be "rocket science." It is something EVERYONE in your organization can embrace and execute. It is what you need if you want to change your culture and your DNA to be Customer Obsessed and become "*REMARK*"able™.

While I can't create a specific recipe for every industry and every size company...I can help you create your own unique formula. I give you one simple, straightforward way so you can understand and grasp how to tailor it for your organization. Customer Obsession isn't a "one-size fits all" formula. While the core "cornerstones" and components apply to everyone, they can be tailored to your company's nuances.

There is a process for helping you learn HOW to become "*REMARK*"able™...it never just happens.

Please read the next several chapters in order...there is a reason for this, and they will make more sense if you follow this sequence. Each chapter is a foundation for the next, and they continually build on the concepts.

You become "*REMARK*"able™ when you can execute the cornerstones of **The "*REMARK*"able Triangle™** I will share with you in the next chapter. You will see precisely HOW you should be using these in your organization. These "cornerstones" will give you information about how to build your plan.

Please keep in mind that becoming "*REMARK*"able™ involves using the "Triangle" and executing each cornerstones. Continually ask yourself, "*HOW are we doing today in this area, and HOW can we move from where we are to this new state?*" If you are continually focusing on "eliminating the gap" between where you are today and where you would be if you implemented these three cornerstones, you will be on your way to being Customer Obsessed. Becoming "*REMARK*"able™ happens when you are fully engaged in executing the three cornerstones.

The model I will share with you takes effort and focus. I won't lie to you about that...it won't just happen because you do a few things differently. You can't change your culture and DNA by just "dabbling" in it...you have to be "consumed" by it. Thinking about it, executing it, modifying the plan, and continuing to implement...it is a Journey, not a sprint.

I can guarantee you one thing...your business will definitely change if you are diligent and consistently improving in each of the three cornerstones...every day.

Reading the next three sections on TRUST, CUSTOMER EXPERIENCE, and CONSISTENTLY HELPING in order is critically important before creating your strategic plan. Once you have a foundation for how everything works individually and collectively, you will be able to see exactly HOW you could start to make (significant) changes in your business. I guarantee your mind will be racing at the end of these three chapters, and you will be anxious to get started. While this is awesome (and expected), give yourself the time to focus on building a solid plan before jumping in and getting started.

After you learn about the three cornerstones, I will share some things you can do...starting with Leadership. These are very tactical and will help you as you develop your strategic execution plan. These will be of tremendous help in getting you headed in the right direction.

The final section is about "what to do next." It will give you some concrete steps for how to get started on your Journey. I call it "**Lift Off.**" These chapters will get you started on your Journey where you "leave" your current place and "take off" on a new adventure to your new place. It will be where you start taking advantage of this incredible "Opportunity."

However, even with all the information you will have at your disposal, the one word that will make it all happen is **EXECUTION**. Without execution, this will just be another book of new and exciting ideas to stimulate your brain. But, when you choose to act on this new way of thinking and invest in being Customer Obsessed, you will become "*REMARK*"able™. Even if you can't execute today, having this knowledge swirling around in your brain will eventually move you forward. And when you do, you won't look back...you will sprint to make it happen. It's all a matter of "when" not "if."

> **CAUTION:** While each "cornerstone" can be executed separately and independently from the others, you won't become "*REMARK*"able™ unless you use all three of them together. You might jump all over one of the cornerstones, fall in love with it, dive deeply into it, and forget about the other ones. Each cornerstone will dramatically improve and change your business...that's the good news. But if you truly want to push through to the coveted state of becoming "*REMARK*"able™, you will need to build all three into your Strategy and Plan.

Now let's dive headfirst into the process for **HOW** you can make Customer Obsession a reality in your organization. All you need to do is turn the page...

The "*REMARK*"able Triangle™

The only difference between a problem and a solution is that people understand the solution.

CHARLES KETTERING

If someone handed you a treasure map with a very distinct path to discovering gold, would you follow it?

The "*REMARK*"able Triangle™ is a roadmap. If you follow it, you will find the buried treasure. It is a formula for how to become "*REMARK*"able™.

As you have hopefully seen (and felt) throughout the book, my goal is to keep things simple...dirt simple. Simple gets implemented...complex sits on the shelf. The "*REMARK*"able Triangle™ isn't any different. It is a very straightforward and easy way to organize and communicate the "**three cornerstone elements**" needed to build a Customer Obsessed organization so you can become "*REMARK*"able™.

In the upcoming chapters, we will explore each of these three elements in greater detail. Before I dive into these three cornerstone elements, let me give you a bit of background and perspective on how they came together to form "The "*REMARK*"able Triangle™.

While each cornerstone element will do amazing things for your organization individually, it is like supercharging each cornerstone when they are combined and working together.

As you will see, each cornerstone is something you can undertake individually. I designed the model to tackle the ones they feel will have the most significant impact on your organization. Each one can be worked on individually or in parallel with each other. However, there is an order I would highly recommend you follow to get the maximum benefit from The "*REMARK*"able Triangle™.

When all three are working together, it is much more than triple the benefit...it is like ten times the benefit (or more). It's exponential. Each cornerstone leverages the others, so you get much more impact from each cornerstone. As the saying goes, "*the whole is worth much more than the individual pieces.*" The same holds true for **The "*REMARK*"able Triangle™**.

Let's start by breaking them down individually and giving you deeper and richer insight into each one. I would encourage you to read, understand, and visualize what your company would look like if you adopted each cornerstone. As you read about each one, I would also encourage you to think about how they would work "together" and support each other. That is their real strength and power. You will start to see WHY your audience would be more than happy to "do your marketing for you."

When all three work together, it's like pouring gasoline on your campfire...it erupts with massive heat and flames. Or like pushing down the gas on your turbocharged car and feeling it kick in and thrust you back into the seat. It is an exhilarating feeling...one you will never forget. Visualize this happening in your organization...that should put you in the right mood to dive in and visualize what can happen for your organization!

TRUST - The first Cornerstone...

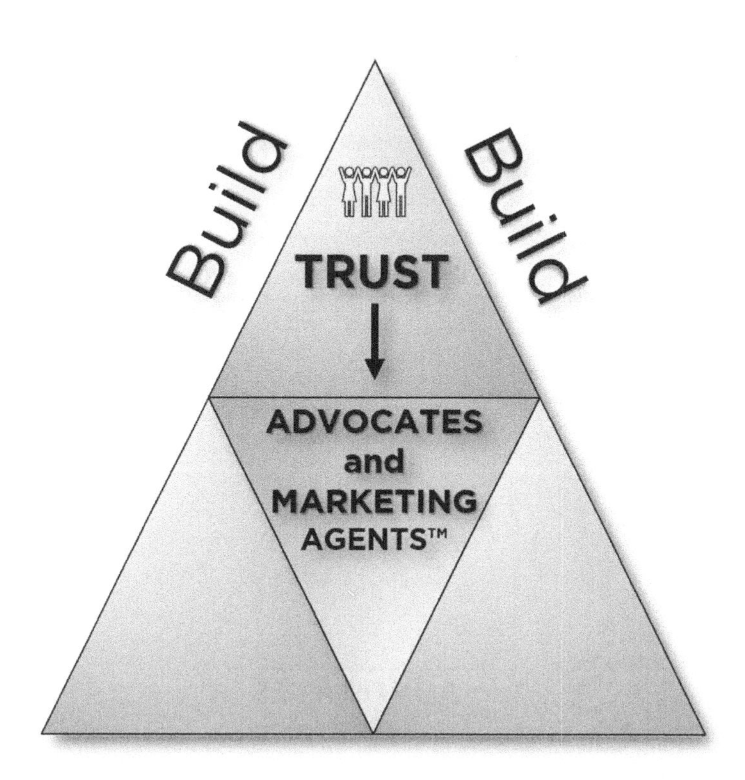

TRUST is the most powerful "five-letter word" you can incorporate into your organization. The TRUST cornerstone is an absolute necessity and critical to your success. When you have built Trust with your audience, you are in an enviable position. It will be the heartbeat of your organization, your culture, your DNA. It is the one thing you want to build as much as possible every day.

I don't believe any organization can thrive without **TRUST**. Nor can you be genuinely differentiated and unique without it. Keep in mind our single and overarching goal...getting your audience to be a proactive Advocate and

Marketing Agent™ for your company, so they do your marketing for you. You can only get there when you have Trust with your audience...period.

NO ONE on the planet will ever be your Advocate or Marketing Agent™ and tell others about you if they don't TRUST YOU...no one.

Trust is absolutely, positively critical to your success at becoming "*REMARK*"able™. I will spend a couple of chapters helping you understand how you can get more of it (a lot more) with your audience...and fast. I will give you some simple and straightforward ways to build Trust. It's a model you can use in all aspects of your life, not just your business. It will help you in all your relationships. And since you need to build relationships with your audience, it is an absolute necessity.

I will also share with you the "stages" you and your audience will progress through, which will help you build more profound and deeper trust, relationships, loyalty, and ultimately Advocacy with your audience. I call it Advocacy Architecture™. I think you'll agree, once you see it, that it should be a foundational part of how every employee acts when interacting with their customers. It's that powerful.

CUSTOMER EXPERIENCE - The second cornerstone...

The Customer Experience is the one everyone gravitates to when we talk about Customer Obsession. And it is one that area we (as business leaders AND customers ourselves) tend to focus on the most. There are thousands of books on this particular cornerstone...we even wrote one ourselves several years ago.

When my brother and I wrote our first book, "***Creating and Delivering Totally Awesome Customer Experiences***," it was a landmark book (and still is) because it was the first of its kind. We chose not to focus on the "soft" side of the customer experience, such as telling everyone to be happier and smile more with their customers, and instead, focused on the "**process**" side of how to deliver a "**consistent and repeatable**" customer experience with every employee, with every interaction.

The process we created is even more relevant today than when we first wrote it. While I have continually refined it in various areas, the concept of creating a process for the Customer Experience is vitally important for every organization to have in place today.

> **Side Note:** I am in the process of rewriting (condensing and updating) the content from this first book and hope to have the Second Edition released in 2021. Stay tuned...

Great is the new average.

The Customer Experience is an incredibly valuable cornerstone since it focuses on how we treat our customers with every interaction, so they **"feel" special and amazing.** Not good, not great, but **incredibly special and amazing.** With the rapid spread of commoditization happening in every industry, "**great is the new average.**" Every business is great today. Great merely is "being in the game" of business today. Everyone has great products and services, great technology, great employees, and great processes. We need to be "great" just to stay in business. It hasn't always been that way, but it is the new norm. We need something much better than great...we need something that is incredibly awesome and amazing!!

This Customer Experience cornerstone focuses on helping you create and deliver an incredibly awesome and amazing customer experience. I have dedicated two chapters to this topic to give you a much deeper and better understanding, foundation, and recipe for creating one in your organization. It is one of the most exciting cornerstones in the book. This one is very exciting because it is a topic that has been near and dear to me for over two decades. As I'm sure you'll realize very quickly, it is a topic I am incredibly passionate about and believe will change every organization.

CONSISTENTLY HELPING - The third cornerstone...

We all have one aspect of human nature, regardless of age, ethnicity, heritage, or anything else. It is "**helping others**." We are wired, by human nature, to help others. We all don't do it in precisely the same way or the exact amounts. And while we want to help others, we, ourselves, definitely look forward to when others can help us. It works both ways. While we might be trying to help others, others are trying to help us.

This cornerstone is one I often find absent from most organizations. Not because they don't want to, most just don't know how and haven't formally built it into their strategic plan. **Consistently Helping** doesn't focus on helping our customers buy (more) products easier or to help them decide what to purchase. We get paid to do this type of helping. This is called "sales."

Consistently Helping refers to "*helping others, REGARDLESS of whether it translates directly to revenue for our company*." It means going out of our way to help others "**improve their life and/or their business.**" It is imperative to get your head around this type of helping because it is as close to altruistic as you can get. And it will pay big dividends in terms of revenue and more customers.

Here's an easy example to give you more insight into what it means to Consistently Help others improve their life and/or their business. Let's say you deal with someone in purchasing at one of your customers. If you were Customer Obsessed, you would be asking, "*How could we help that individual "improve their life or their business?*" You might be thinking, that's hard because all they only care about availability and price. While that is their "job," it doesn't mean you can't help them.

What if you decided to help them move their career forward and become the head of all purchasing agents? How could you help them get that job? How could you help them advance their career? What kind of information and resources could you share with them to help them be better at purchasing and become the best purchasing manager possible? What type of leadership content could you share to help them grow in this area? What information could you share that talks about the "purchasing manager of the future?"

You can do a variety of things for the purchasing agent to "**improve their life and/or their business.**" And it wouldn't have anything to do with your products, or how you work with them. Do you think this would come back and pay dividends to you down the road if they became head of purchasing? Customer Obsessed companies believe (and act) this way as part of who they are and their culture. While you might receive some benefit for your business down the road, it's also just the right thing to do to help someone. And if you help them in their career, do you think they would tell other purchasing managers who helped them? Do you think they would go out of their way to tell others about your company? You have moved closer to becoming "*REMARK*"able™!

Putting all THREE CORNERSTONES together makes up The "*REMARK*"able Triangle™, and executing each Cornerstone is what allows organizations to become "*REMARK*"able™.

Customer Obsessed organizations make these three cornerstones the heart and soul of their organization.

They focus on them...daily. They strive to improve on them...daily. They deliver them...daily. And when this happens, they become "*REMARK*"able™. Are YOU ready to become "*REMARK*"able™?

Let's make it happen. It's time to do a deep dive into the "recipe," "formula," and "roadmap" to get you there. This is where the rubber meets the road. It is HOW you get it done.

Let's start with the first component of The "*REMARK*"able Triangle™, the big kahuna...

TRUST

The "Secret Ingredient" to becoming "*REMARK*"able™

If people like you they will listen to you, but if they TRUST you they'll do business with you.

ZIG ZIGLAR

How many customers (and others in your audience) TRUST you enough to stake their credibility on recommending you...without question? Do you "build" trust...or do you erode it?

No one on the planet will ever be your Advocate (someone who goes out of their way to tell others about you) and put their credibility on the line unless they TRUST you...NO ONE.

It is only possible to get recommendations, referrals, or (positive) word-of-mouth when someone trusts you. Trust is an absolute necessity if you want someone to Advocate or talk about you with a high degree of credibility. Trust is the essential ingredient and most critical cornerstone if you want your customers to **do your marketing for you**. When your audience trusts you, they will happily go out of their way to act as your Advocate and Marketing Agent™, telling others just how awesome you.

TRUST is the essential ingredient to becoming "*REMARK*"able™.

Do this simple test to see how powerful Trust is when creating Advocates and Marketing Agents™ for your organization. Let's say you are talking to a friend or a colleague about a particular service you are interested in using. Financial services, for example. The conversation would probably go something like this...

"Hey Bob, I've been thinking about switching financial advisors. The one I use is just not doing it for me. They are always charging me crazy fees, moving my money around, and I don't really know what they are doing. I don't feel like I have a solid plan. I don't want to waste any more time trying to figure this guy out, so I'm looking to switch advisors. I thought from some of our earlier conversations that you really liked them. Is that still true?"

Bob has one that is Customer Obsessed and that he loves. Here's what Bob, his buddy, would say to him, *"Absolutely, mine is incredible, and I don't have any of the issues you are having with yours. I'm happy to introduce you to him if you want."* You reply with, *"That sounds great, Bob. I just have one more question for you.* ***DO YOU TRUST THEM****?"* Bob immediately says, *"Absolutely, I wouldn't be recommending him to you if I didn't. He is not only great at what he does, but I trust him completely. I'll give him a call for you, and I'm sure he would be excited to see if he can help you out as well."*

This conversation happens all the time. I guarantee it is happening in your business today. The question is, what is "Bob" saying about you to others in your audience? Is Bob a raving fan that goes out of his way to tell his friends and colleagues about you and your business? Is Bob confidently talking to others about you and how incredibly awesome (and TRUSTED) you are? Is Bob acting as your Advocate and Marketing Agent™ in the market? If you have a Bob (or a bunch of Bobs) out there spreading the word about how awesome you are to others, you have become "*REMARK*"able™. CONGRATULATIONS!! We want more "Bobs"!

This conversation may not be what your customers (and others) are having on your behalf...yet. If this is the conversation you would like to happen in your organization, you're about to get the recipe in the next several chapters. Buckle up. I will share with you exactly how to capture this **massive opportunity** sitting in front of you right now, today!

The 2018 Edelman Trust Barometer discovered that TRUST (in the U.S.) suffered the largest ever recorded drop in the survey's history[9].

According to Richard Edelman...

> *The 2018 Edelman Trust Barometer reveals that trust in the U.S. has suffered the largest-ever-recorded drop in the survey's history among the general population. Trust among the general population fell nine points to 43, placing it in the lower quarter of the 28-market Trust Index. Trust among the U.S. informed public imploded, plunging 23 points to 45, making it the lowest of the 28 markets surveyed, below Russia and South Africa.*

While Trust is in a deficient state today and seems headed in the wrong direction, it's also one of the best times for companies to take advantage of this crisis and build more of it. One of my assertions is that the Internet has NOT helped us create more trust. It has eroded it more and faster than at any time in history. Today, the customer can easily find any product and service WITHOUT even asking the company that makes or sells it. Information and data are available anytime and everywhere.

Anyone can find out what is happening with a particular product or service independently, without ever talking to the company selling it. And to make matters even worse, we often hear customers disproving what the company is telling their audiences. Their customers are saying something different. **Contradictory information between the company and its customers creates a high degree of distrust**.

Companies tell their customers only partial truths, if the truth at all. More than ever, companies are being called out by their customers, competitors, and others in the market. **The customer has all the power today in the Customer Economy**. Companies now need to make purposeful and proactive changes in how they treat and interact with their customers. It has become imperative to turn this situation around and start building more Trust instead of eroding it.

And if your industry happens to be one of those that are known to be "untrustworthy," then the situation may be even worse...but the opportunity will also be even more significant. Think about your industry for a minute. Overall, do you feel like your industry is highly Trusted or not trusted? Do an honest assessment of your industry and your company...it will tell you just how enormous the opportunity is for your own company.

For example, if we look at one of the most distrusted industries in the country, the car dealer, you will understand how this works. If we polled 100 people and asked them if they Trust car dealers, I would bet the royalties from this book there are fewer than ten people who would tell us they Trusted car dealers. They have proven to be untrustworthy.

Some dealers work incredibly hard to change this image. But overall, the industry has a long way to go. There is an incredible opportunity for companies to enter the industry and offer alternative ways where the consumer can avoid having this experience. These companies will provide more detailed information about the automobiles, pricing, terms, warranties, and anything else the car dealer typically provides. They offer accurate information to the consumer because they know the car dealer data cannot be Trusted. **They are merely taking advantage of the lack of Trust in this industry.**

Are there any of these types of companies in your industry? Are there companies out there who are providing information to your customers? If so, it might be time to step back and see what they are providing and find a way to do it better and build Trust with your audience. In the next chapter, "**Promises, Promises, Promises,**" I'll show you a simple way to capitalize on this opportunity for our own company.

What if the car dealer (or your industry) decided to change the game and turn this equation around? What if they had a strategy to be Customer Obsessed and literally focused on building Trust with their audience? What if they took an entire customer-focused perspective, different from their competitors? An approach that would earn Trust with their audience, instead of eroding it? What if they could provide more accurate and Trusted information to their audience than others were providing? And what if they treated their customers in a way that showed them respect so they could build more Trust? They would change the game and dominate. This opportunity is available in just about every industry today.

One car dealer who does this as part of their DNA is Sewell Automotive in Texas. They are well known for their exceptional (and very different) way of treating their customers...and building Trust. Carl Sewell talks about how this has been a family tradition and what it means to their company in his book, **Customers for Life**. Worth the read. He espouses, "***Turning that one-time customer into a lifetime customer.***" You get there by creating an incredibly awesome and amazing customer experience and building Trust with every interaction. He and his family are famous for this, dating back to 1911. If a car dealer can do it, anyone can do it.

Do you think if a car dealer dramatically changed, they would stand out among all the other un-trusted car dealers in their area? Do you think they would build a reputation as the one you could go to and trust what they told you? What if you started hearing this from your friends (and others), who you trusted, that they had a completely different experience, and they were someone you could trust? Do you think this car dealer would be differentiated and have a significant advantage in their market?

I think we would all unanimously vote that they would stand out as completely differentiated from their competitors. When you read through these questions, why would a car dealer (or any other company, maybe even yours) not want to be in this position with their customers and future customers? I personally can't understand why car dealers (and others) wouldn't be leaping at this type of opportunity...an incredible opportunity to be viewed as uniquely differentiated and trusted in a crowded, distrusted market. There are car dealers doing things differently (like Sewell Automotive and Tesla), but not many. If you ever get a chance to talk to them (and their customers), you will certainly understand just how much this has helped their business rise above all the others in their area.

The opportunity to build TRUST can be one of the most valuable (and profitable) opportunities in the market today!

Yes, this is a Customer Obsessed Strategy...putting the customer in the center of everything you do so the customer puts you in the front of your competitors. As with all strategies, there have to be critical goals you need to achieve if you are to succeed at executing the plan.

TRUST is the FIRST CORNERSTONE, the critical ingredient to becoming "*REMARK*"able™. You have to earn your customers (and audience) Trust if you want to become "*REMARK*"able™...period. It is foundational. It is the linchpin ingredient.

Trust is a tricky word. Most people think they have more of it than they actually do. I can say this after talking to thousands of people (customers and others) and hearing firsthand how they don't Trust a company...even though the person (or company) thinks they do. There is a great deal of misalignment when it comes to Trust. I'm not a psychologist, but I have a theory about why this might be the case.

I believe it is due to the power of the word TRUST. It is one of the most powerful words in our vocabulary, and one most people don't throw around lightly. When someone says they Trust you, it should mean they really believe in you and support you, no matter what. Even by definition (dictionary.com), it speaks powerfully about the word...

> "***reliance on the integrity, strength, ability, surety, etc., of a person or thing; confidence***"

Those are powerful words...words everyone wants to be associated with themselves. Who doesn't want to have these words used when describing how people think about them? No one.

Since this is such a powerful word, I believe people want it associated with them in everything they do, even if it isn't true. For example, if someone asks if you think that person Trusts you, your natural (and protective) response would be, "*Yes, I believe they do Trust me*." When in reality, you aren't quite sure if they do or not. And besides, the corollary answer isn't all that great, "*Well, I'm not sure they actually Trust me*." They would rather assume they are Trusted until proven otherwise. It's a tricky word.

Before I dive into "HOW" you can build Trust, I would like to help you manage some of your expectations. By far, the number one question I get asked is, ***"How soon can we build Trust so we can move forward on creating more Advocates and get all the benefits of becoming "REMARK"able™?"*** Wrong question. Trust is not a "timing" issue. It is an "action" issue. It takes time to build. It takes **several interactions** with your customer and **the power of those interactions** to build Trust. These are different for every organization...there is no standard.

For example, if you interact with a customer once a year, it will might take you longer to build Trust with them than it does for a company that interacts with their customer several times a month. The more "actions" you can demonstrate, the shorter the time frame for building Trust. However, if you have many interactions with one customer who purchases from you annually, you could create a significant amount of trust.

The other variable is the **power of the interaction**. When your customer's interaction is infrequent but incredibly significant, you make more strides toward building Trust than if the interactions are less meaningful. Let me break this down a bit further. If you sell a product once a year, say a large piece of machinery, you have one "transaction" for that sale. But this is a big sale to the customer. It is a "**power transaction**." The "power" isn't the "transaction" itself that helps you build Trust. It is the hundreds of other "interactions" you have building up to the transaction and following the "power transaction," which will allow you to build Trust.

Whereas, if you are selling office supplies, where there are more transactions of smaller dollar volume, you won't earn much trust with each transaction. You will earn Trust by doing certain things many times throughout the year when interacting with the customer. You have many opportunities to deliver less "powerful transactions" but are focused on "**frequency of actions**" instead.

It is essential to know which one you provide as an organization and then build your "**Trust Strategy**" to deliver this to your customers. And when your organization has both aspects to it, your strategy has to be very specific for each area of your business. For example, you might sell a large piece of machinery once a year, but you sell parts and service throughout the year. This allows you to build Trust in both areas of your business. A good example is the "razor and the blade" or the "printer and the ink" type of company. Your Trust Strategy has to accommodate both types of interaction with your customers.

You only build a loyal and deep Trust with "**time**" and "**consistency**." While I will give you the recipe for HOW to build Trust, I just can't tell you the time it will take to get there with your audience. It is different for every organization. But, regardless of how long it takes for your organization, **the ingredient of being "consistent" is the secret sauce**.

There is one more aspect of Trust I want to share with you before we dive into HOW you can build trust in your organization. Let's say you have a customer who you have supported above and beyond their expectations, and they love how you have treated them. They rave about how unique and different you are from your competitors. You think you have just created a great Advocate and Marketing Agent™ for your company. And you have...you've done what you should be doing.

However, what if their network of friends and colleagues doesn't trust this new Advocate. Sadly, their audience won't put a ton of credibility into their raving comments about you...their lack of Trust in their audience won't give you the leverage you were hoping to get. But there is a silver lining to this situation. Even though they may not be the most trusted people in your audience, people will still listen to them...just not with as high of credibility as you would like.

When they rave about you and tell others how incredible you are, it still carries some weight, just not as much as you might like. However, it is usually enough curiosity where others will want to check you out, even though they don't completely trust them. That's enough...enough curiosity for them to check out how you treat your customers.

Once they come over and give you a chance to prove yourself (which is all any of us can ask), then you can work your magic and show them what it means to them that you are Customer Obsessed. You still win...you got their audience just to check you out and give you a chance. **The only difference is the depth to which they are already sold on you and believing in you "before" they get to experience it for themselves.** I'll take this any day over having to hunt down a potential customer with lame and ineffective traditional marketing and try to convince them they should trust me. That method takes significantly more of my time and resources.

You still "acquired" a new customer "without" traditional marketing...you attracted them via "**customer marketing,**" so it still costs you next to nothing since someone in your audience referred them. You can always convert them into a raving customer Advocate and Marketing Agent™ for you...it will just take a little more effort and time.

ANY customer you can get from another customer (i.e., referral and word-of-mouth) is fantastic! Just because they don't come in completely Trusting you from the start just means you will have to invest a little more time and attention (and your magic sauce) to turn into one of your Advocates and Marketing Agents™.

The key is that "**they came to you**" from someone who is already one of your Advocates and Marketing Agents™...**they did your marketing for you**. Another reason why you can STOP MARKETING and START investing in Customer Marketing! A different mindset, but an essential one to grasp.

Everything starts with your actions, which are focused on building TRUST with your customers and audience.

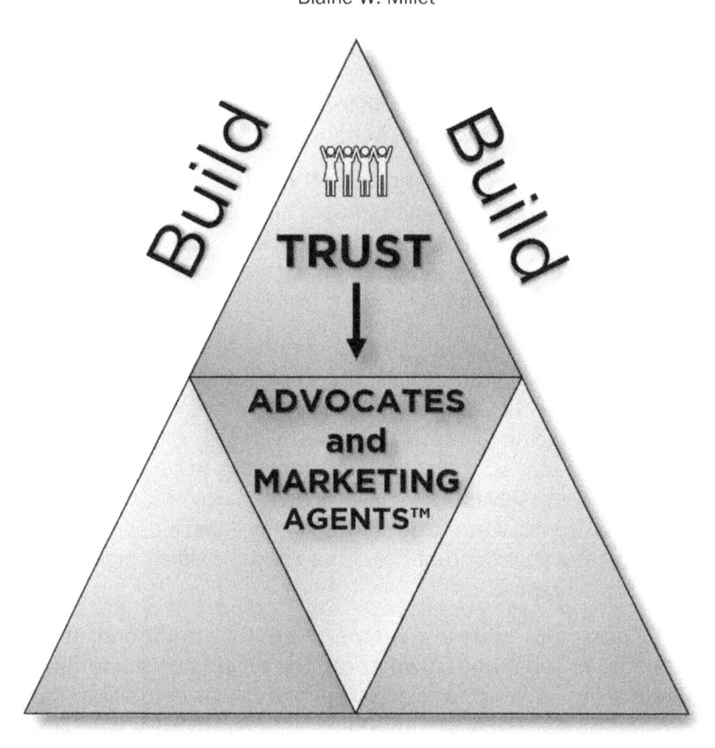

Trust is at the top of the pyramid because it is an essential ingredient for being emotionally connected and telling others how awesome you are.

As you read earlier, the ONE QUESTION you always want to be answered in the affirmative is, "*But do you trust them?*" If the person can immediately, without hesitation, and with passion, respond YES, they are going to be a highly credible Advocate and Marketing Agent™ for you and your organization. After all, isn't this the one question we all have in the back of our minds when we want to validate whether or not we should do business with someone?

While all three cornerstones of the Triangle are crucial to building an Advocate and Marketing Agent™, Trust carries the most profound emotional commitment. Without Trust, you can't leverage the other two elements of Customer Experience and Consistently Helping...these elements will lose some of their potential impacts if the customer doesn't Trust you. While you can still elevate yourself above your competitors with the other two cornerstones, the home run happens when Trust is firmly in place. It is the Big One, the granddaddy, the big Kahuna.

When you think about it, an organization can offer an outstanding Customer Experience to someone, and they will talk about it. They may even rave about it because it was so much better than your competitors. But even with all this positive feeling coming out of the experience, it won't carry nearly the same power if they don't say they Trust you or your company. This emotional connection of Trust is absolutely critical to creating a passionate and highly credible Advocate and Marketing Agent™.

The same goes for the other cornerstone of The "*REMARK*"able Triangle™, Consistently Helping someone improve their life or business. Without the Trust cornerstone, these actions just don't carry the same impact and power. Just think how much more impactful your content would be to someone who Trusted you! If they Trust you, they will go out of their way to tell their friends and colleagues to check out your content (or other ways you help). Not only is it helpful, but they Trust you...significantly increasing your differentiation and credibility.

Keep in mind that the more you deliver an incredible experience and provide ways to help your audience, the more Trust you will build.

All three cornerstones of the pyramid work together to strengthen each other when you focus on all three. It is the primary reason for being purposeful about building all three cornerstones in your organization so you can create Advocates and Marketing Agents™ in the market. They continuously feed each other when all three are working together.

When our audience Trusts us more, they look forward to us Consistently Helping them and giving them a genuinely incredible Customer Experience. Now they Trust we will do what we say. All three cornerstones are working together...continually...to accelerate and leverage The "*REMARK*"able Triangle™. They are supporting each other and building upon each other.

With this as a solid "foundation" and "mindset," let's dive into the next step...**HOW you can build Trust** with your audience. I am going to give you a straightforward, common-sense method to not only creating more Trust, but how to develop deeper Relationships, Loyalty, and of course, the Holy Grail, Advocacy. This model will definitely change your organization forever...

Promises Promises Promises

It is easy to make Promises – it is hard work to keep them.

BORIS JOHNSON

”

What percentage of the Promises you make to your Customers (and audience) do you keep? Do you even know the Promises your employees are making?

Building trust is similar to a Lego project. You start building one block at a time and do it consistently and repetitively. It's a Journey, not a sprint. But when you stay the course, the finished product is something spectacular. The same is true for when you have earned someone's Trust...it is stunning because it is the most valuable thing you can earn from your audience.

This entire book's premise is getting more of your audience Trusting you and working on your behalf as your Advocate and Marketing Agent™ in the market. If you genuinely want to become "*REMARK*"able™, it is a requirement, an absolute necessity, to build Trust with your audience.

Rather than spending tons of money on marketing programs and campaigns that yield a .001% return, I would strongly encourage you to "invest" this money back into your customers and get a significantly higher return...which includes building more Trust. It is "**customer money**" because you invest it in your customers, not flyers, ads, and online keyword advertising. The gold is sitting in your customers and your audience. It is just waiting for you when you start investing the time and money in your customers to build their TRUST.

But let's be honest with each other. Customers are confusing to a business. They come to us demanding lower prices, better availability, better terms, more selection, and a host of other things. They want more and more for less and less. Am I right, or am I right? You can change this game...today.

Trust changes the game. You can change how your customer views you and treats you when they Trust you above your competitors.

Consider these questions as you think about building more Trust...

- **HOW** can you build trust with your audience in a world where everything merely a click away?
- **HOW** can you differentiate in such an incredibly noisy world?
- **HOW** can you gain and keep your audience's attention so they will remember you and buy from you?
- **HOW** can you create loyal customers who Advocate for you in our New Customer Economy and the super-connected world?
- **HOW** can you be viewed as the one that stands out and is unique in the eyes of your audience?
- **HOW** can you earn greater profits and have happier customers?

These can all be solved or changed when our customers (and audience) Trust us. When there aren't any clear points of differentiation, our audience has no choice but to separate us based on the commodity elements such as price and availability. But when our customers Trust us, they have a powerful reason to work with us.

When our audience Trusts us, they elevate us above the competition, so we are viewed as unique and different. Trust is a great place to start when you want to build massive differentiation from your competitors.

Several years ago, I created a model which, as it turns out, is much more powerful today than it was when I created it. And while I have updated and improved it over time, the model's core remains the same. I built it for the sole purpose of **creating Advocates and Marketing Agents™**. It is simple, straightforward, and easy to understand and execute. It's a model anyone in any organization can understand and use almost immediately. It isn't complicated. Everyone in the organization will get it. The key to its success is the ease of execution. And at its core, as you might suspect, is building Trust.

The Advocacy Architecture™ model will improve your business almost immediately and help you become truly differentiated.

The model, appropriately named the **Advocacy Architecture™,** was initially created to help organizations develop **Loyalty** and improve **Retention** with their customers...what everyone needed (and still needs). Over the years, the model evolved into helping companies create Advocates and Marketing Agents™ so they could become "*REMARK*"able™. It is now the foundation for helping any organization reap the rewards of what this entire book is about...**getting others to do your marketing for you.**

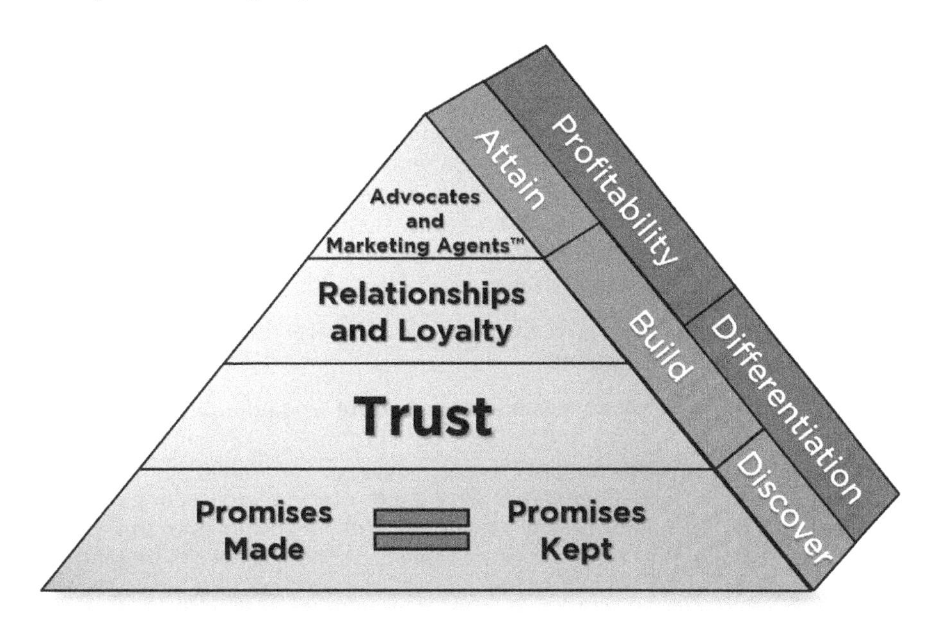

Advocacy Architecture™

The first and possibly the most critical aspect of the Advocacy Architecture™ model is that it is simple and straightforward...nothing overly complicated about the structure. No big words...only words everyone understands...straightforward and dirt simple. Let's walk through the critical components since they are essential for building the core of the foundation...Trust.

As with any structure, it is essential to have a solid foundation to support it. Without this foundation, it will collapse. The foundation of the Advocacy Architecture™ isn't any different...it is rock-solid and a primary tenant to creating Advocates and Marketing Agents™ for your organization.

The foundation is all about keeping the PROMISES you make.

Keeping the Promises you make is a requirement for building Advocacy. You can never build Trust if you don't keep your Promises...period. When you keep your Promises, amazing things will happen. The foundation is a simple formula every employee can quickly grasp and execute daily. It should be "top of mind" with every customer interaction, whether in person or via other means of communication. The formula is...

Promises Made = Promises Kept

Simple...it should be on every wall in your company to continually remind everyone what they need to do if you are going to become "*REMARK*"able™. When you **increase the percentage of PROMISES KEPT,** you will see tremendous and incredibly positive changes in how your customers treat you, interact with you, and Trust you. It is absolutely the most powerful thing you can do...immediately...to create more Trust...guaranteed!

When your audience knows they can rely on you when you tell them you will do something, without question or doubt, you will immediately lower their stress, anxiety, and give them much greater peace of mind. Your audience will notice...they always do. And when your audience sees YOU keeping your promises and your competitors NOT keeping their promises, guess which one they want to work with? YOU! You have changed the game with your audience and elevated yourself to a higher, more enviable position than your competitors.

Keeping our PROMISES is one of the most powerful actions we can take to build Trust with our Audience...period.

What makes this word so mysteriously powerful (and potentially dangerous) is that you don't even have to use the word "Promise" and someone can still assume you are making one. What?!? Have you ever said something to someone as a passing comment, and they interpreted it as something you were promising to do for them? I know I have...probably more times than I care to count. We all have. How many times has this happened to you? More than you probably care to count.

It is one of the most powerful words we have in our arsenal, yet few of us use it to its full potential. Don't believe me? Ask yourself, "*How many times a day do you use the word "Promise" in your conversations?*" I'm sure the vast majority of you will answer, "*Not very often*." Most of us don't use the word for several reasons. Either we aren't thinking what we are saying is a real Promise, or we are afraid to use the word promise because we aren't sure if we can deliver on it. Either way, we don't use it very often.

Ask yourself this question, "***What if I used the word Promise whenever I committed to doing something for someone?***" How would that change your focus on delivering what you said you would provide? How would that change what you were telling people you would do for them? How would that strengthen your commitment to whatever it is you promised them? Would it eliminate the things you weren't sure you could deliver? There is no question it would change the game.

For example, let's say you made 10 Promises during the day and actually used the word Promise. And let's say you were also able to keep those 10 Promises. What if you did this every day? Do you think you would be building more Trust with your audience? I know this is a rhetorical question, but it's the right question to be asking yourself. How would your relationships change if you started keeping every Promise you made? How much more loyalty would you earn from your customers if they knew you always kept your Promises? And how much more would they **talk about you and tell others** that you are the one that could be Trusted?

You just walked through the Advocacy Architecture™ pyramid. You went from a foundation of **Keeping your Promises** to building deeper **Relationships** and creating more **Loyalty**. But, as you will learn as you continue reading, you are now finally able to reach the pinnacle of the Advocacy Architecture™. You are now getting your audience of **Advocates and Marketing Agents™** to do your marketing for you.

Now, in a nutshell, you can see how you use the Advocacy Architecture™. I just summarized in one short paragraph. It is so incredibly powerful. I would encourage you to write the paragraph above down. Then share it with your leadership team and every employee. Then, and most importantly, commit to making it a part of your DNA, your culture, and who you are as a company. It is how you become "*REMARK*"able™.

When you execute on the Advocacy Architecture™, you will be well on your way to being **truly differentiated and eclipsing your competitors**. Your competitors won't understand what you are doing. They will just see you rising ahead of them...fast. But your audience will know...they will feel it. They will become emotionally connected to you in a way your competitors can't easily copy. Promises are powerful...are you up for the challenge?

What makes the Advocacy Architecture™ so incredibly powerful is that every employee can understand it...internalize it...and execute it. And when every employee can easily implement something, it wins the day. I hope you can now see why **keeping Promises** and **building Trust** are the core drivers behind becoming "*REMARK*"able™.

> **CAUTION:** A critically vital point to keep in mind and remember is that you cannot skip this process. There are no "workarounds" to the path to Advocacy...none. The road leading to Advocacy starts with building Trust by keeping the Promises you make every day.

Always keep in mind this simple and straightforward rule...

> **NO ONE on the planet will ever become your Advocate and Marketing Agent™, give you their Loyalty, allow you to develop a deep Relationship with them, or ever Trust you if you don't KEEP THE PROMISES YOU MAKE...no one.**

STOP here for the next 5 minutes...think about this regarding your organization. Think about where you are today. What would your business look like if all your employees were keeping the Promises they made and were able to build more (and deeper) Trust with your audience. Think about what your customers (and audience) would be saying about you if you kept the Promises you made in every area of your business. Pretty impressive, isn't it?

There is one hidden "land mine" (or **OPPORTUNITY**) that is also available to you when it comes to Promises...the every so sneaky **IMPLIED PROMISE**. An implied promise refers to something someone "thinks was said" when it wasn't actually said. We've all been there. Someone we are talking to hears something they believe is entirely different from what we think we said, and now they are holding us accountable for saying it. It happens all the time...much more often than we realize in business. And here's the real kicker. To your audience, **an "Implied Promise" is just as powerful as a "Stated Promise."** No difference. It doesn't matter whether you said the words, "I Promise" or not. That's what they heard in the conversation.

If you don't know this is happening, it can put you in a real bind with your audience. Your audience believes you made a Promise to them...and they expect you to keep it. And if you don't, they think you don't keep your Promises. It erodes Trust and makes it that much harder to establish a relationship, build loyalty, and create an Advocate and Marketing Agent™. Now you can hopefully see why every business (and its employees) must understand the Promises they are making, which are both "implied" as well as those they have "stated."

Every business makes promises all day long...lots of them. Everyone in the company is making promises to someone, internally and/or externally. While they may not use the actual word "promise," they are most likely making a commitment statement without even knowing it.

For example, if someone tells you they should have a report to you today (an implied Promise) and then call and tell you it will be tomorrow, they have broken their Promise. Even though they didn't say the word "Promise" to you, that's how we interpret it. To them, they "heard" the word Promise.

Now you can see why we can get ourselves in trouble and may not even know why. We're thinking this is something we are going to "try" to do, and it would be great if we can make it happen, but we are not committing to it...at least not to the level of being a Promise. But to the person we are talking to, they "hear" words like "commitment" or "Promise" in the conversation. Who's right? You're both right...but it doesn't really matter. What matters is what they perceive. We have lessened our chances to build Trust in this situation because we didn't keep our Promise to them.

Regardless of whether we use the actual word, "Promise," we've made a Promise in our audience's minds. If this happens once or just occasionally, the other person will most likely give you some grace, and it won't do much to erode their trust since they believe you usually keep your Promises. But if this happens more frequently, they quickly start to change their thinking. If it becomes more consistent, it will erode the Trust they have in you and the organization. Their chance of being an Advocate and Marketing Agent just disappeared...until you can demonstrate you can keep your promises. Then, and only then, will you be back on the path to building Trust, a Relationship, Loyalty, and ultimately Advocacy.

Eroding Trust with anyone in your audience can be fatal.

Erode Trust, and you will find it almost impossible to build a meaningful relationship, customer Loyalty, or Advocacy. Hopefully, you can see why keeping the Promises you make is so critical to the coveted position of building Trust. Keeping your Promises reverses trust "erosion."

I hope you have a better understanding of why Promises are so absolutely critical to becoming "*REMARK*"able™. They are the pathway...the "road less traveled," as some might say. And if you want further justification that this is the right path, just ask your customers. I always ask this simple question when I talk to customers, "*Do you Trust XYZ company and their employees...completely*?" If there is any hesitation in answering or they have to think about it, they don't Trust you. Or if they hesitate and then say they Trust you "sometimes," they don't Trust you.

Trust is black and white, not grey...you either have it, or you don't, no middle ground when it comes to Trust and keeping your Promises.

The only answer that says someone Trusts you completely is if they say, "*Absolutely*!" And they say it immediately. When you hear those beautiful words, "***I absolutely trust them***," you've earned a very coveted position with your audience. You have earned the right to continue up the Advocacy Architecture™ pyramid on your quest to turn them into an Advocate and Marketing Agent™. You have successfully moved beyond where most (if not all) of your competitors are today! CONGRATULATIONS...not many make it here. Not many competitors will have many customers (and others in their audience) saying this about them. Sure, they might have a few, but not many. You will have many...this is an incredible competitive advantage in any market. Our goal is to get everyone in our audience (especially our customers) to trust us completely. Take it one step at a time by keeping the Promises you make. It is a Journey, not a sprint.

Before we leave the topic of "Promises," let's take a minute to talk about your "**Brand Promise Guarantee.**" It is what you are committing to delivering every time to your customers in everything you do. It is your DNA. It is how you tell people you are different and unique. It carries a commitment to a value proposition you promise to fulfill by delivering on your Brand Promise. You "guarantee" it in everything you do.

Do you have a Brand Promise Guarantee? Often companies talk about it but have a hard time articulating it consistently to their customers (and employees). If it is a bit vague and elusive, it will be confusing in your audience's mind. What is your Brand Promise? It's easy to find out. Simply ask 25 of your customers to tell what they think your Brand Promise is to them. If you get 25 different answers, you probably don't have a single Brand Promise. If you 25 saying essentially the same thing, congratulations...you have a consistent Brand Promise.

If you need to focus more on this entire Brand Promise Guarantee topic, it is worth investing some leadership time in developing one for your organization.

While it takes some effort, it is absolutely worth it. Brand Promise starts with your Values and works its way up into your culture and who you are. If you desire to be a Customer Obsessed organization, you have a good start if you follow the recipe I am giving you in this book. It will define "who you are," and it will become a part of your DNA and culture.

For example, remember Sewell Automotive and their Brand Promise of "Customers for Life?" They promise their customers they will do whatever it takes to keep them as a customer forever...and their children's children. They will give you an experience unlike anyone else in the car business and do what they need to do to keep you as a loyal customer and Advocate for their dealership. They have a Brand Promise you can really sink your teeth into and bring to life. What is your Brand Promise?

I hope I have given you a deeper insight and understanding of WHY it is absolutely critical to keep the promises you make to build more Trust. I can't emphasize enough what an **INCREDIBLE OPPORTUNITY** this represents for any organization (large or small, for-profit, or non-profit). The opportunity is sitting here today, waiting for you to grab it. Every organization can make it happen if they are committed and put the horsepower behind executing it every day in every part of their organization. And if you have been paying attention throughout the book, you can see how this literally **kills commoditization**.

While I'm shocked at how few organizations have taken advantage of this opportunity, I'm also not. It isn't obvious until it's obvious. It may be the first time you have seen a process for how you can actually, and effectively build Trust throughout your organization. When it hit me years ago, it was like a light went on in my head. It was COMMON SENSE. It was a massive wake-up call for me and changed my thinking forever.

So, I built a process that everyone could easily understand. That is how the Advocacy Architecture™ was born. It is a fantastic opportunity for those who want to **STOP MARKETING** and build an army of Advocates and Marketing Agents™ **DYING TO DO IT FOR THEM.** Is that going to be you?

I sincerely hope so. Let's keep going and put more pieces of the puzzle (the formula) together for you if it is. Because when the three cornerstones of **The "*REMARK*"able Triangle™** are working together, you will be unstoppable...and completely differentiated. You will become "*REMARK*"able™.

Now let's look at the second cornerstone in The "*REMARK*"able Triangle™...

CUSTOMER EXPERIENCE

But How Did It Make You "FEEL"

I've learned that people will forget what you said, people will forget what you did, but people will never forget how you made them feel.

MAYA ANGELOU

If I asked your customers HOW you MADE THEM FEEL, what would they tell me? How do you think your customers feel with each interaction with your organization? Do you even know?

Now it's time to turn our attention to the area most people think about when they hear the words "Customer Obsessed"...the **Customer Experience.** And if we're honest about it, it is the one thing we all think about when interacting with an organization. How did we feel about the "experience" we had? As customers ourselves, we are continually evaluating how a business made us "feel" during the experience.

Customer Experience runs a close second (in importance) to Trust, which is why it is the second point on The *"REMARK"*able Triangle™

Our customer's experience is the one area we can make a significant impression...almost immediately. It is powerful and impactful. But the single most crucial question we need to be continually asking is...

How does our customer "FEEL" when they interact with our organization?

Wait...before you run off thinking this is some squishy, touchy-feely type of discussion, let me assure you it isn't. Designing an incredibly awesome and amazing Customer Experience is both an "art and a science." It is, as they say, combining the "head and the heart" to deliver an "experience" rather than just providing a "transaction." The "science" part of the experience is a specific process the organization's employees need to follow to create "consistency." The "art" side is tapping into the customers' emotions (how they feel) to create a deeper bond with them. It's the combination of the two that makes it something special. Many books and theories choose one or the other, either the "art" or the "science." The "Magic" happens when we focus on both!

When I talk to leaders in companies of all sizes and various industries, I don't find much commitment to fully understanding how the customer feels. I will often ask how they think their customer feels when interacting with their company. A typical response is usually something like this...

> ***"Well, I think our customers feel pretty good and are generally happy when they interact with us. We help them as quickly as possible, and I don't think we intentionally upset them or cause them any issues. I would say we do a pretty good job of giving them a good experience."***

If you were a customer of this company and heard the Business Owner, CEO, President, or any C-suite leader say this to you, how would it make you feel? My guess is not very special. I know I wouldn't feel like I was all that important to them, other than giving them my money.

You wouldn't get this type of response from a Customer Obsessed organization. Customer Obsessed organizations leaders (and employees) would give you an answer more like this...

> *"Well, I believe our customers would tell you they love working with us...let me tell you why. We go out of our way to make every one of them, regardless of size or volume, feel like they are the most important customer to us anytime time we are working with them. We have mapped out a precise process we follow for every interaction we have with them, even online. Our goal is to have them tell us how awesome we make them feel, and we go out of our way to help them get what they need on time. And more often than not, they tell us we have "made their day" and given them a very memorable experience. That's what I believe you would hear them say if you talked to them."*

Now ask yourself, which conversation is one that would be indicative of what your customers would say if I interviewed them today? How would they describe the experience they had with your company? It is the real "gut check" for where you are today. And it will tell you how much you would benefit from being Customed Obsessed.

Without repeating all the benefits (and opportunities) we talked about at the beginning of the book, I would ask you to think about your answers to the following questions...

- *How would our business change if we had our customers telling us they feel like the statement I shared from a Customer Obsessed company?*
- *How much more Trust and Advocacy could we build if our customers were raving about the experience they have with us?*
- *How much more Profitable and Differentiated, just to name a couple of benefits, do you think you would become?*

Let me be crystal clear about something right upfront concerning the "emotional side" of Customer Experiences. What doesn't work (and never lasts) is telling your employees to "be friendlier, smile more, and make your customers happy." It never works...it has no substance behind it. It is left to the individual to figure out what it even means. And there is zero chance of the experience being consistent across the organizations.

What does work is when you deliver a very precise, consistent, and repeatable incredible experience every time...that works. Having a "**Customer Experience Process**" is part of the formula for being Customer Obsessed. You deliver it in a way that continually WOW's your customer with every interaction. It is what your customers truly want, and it is what they deserve when they part with their money. Having a consistent and repeatable experience will also give you an extraordinarily strong ROI as well. Let me share with you an example I'm sure almost all of you can relate to, which demonstrates why this is both an art and a science...not random.

Think about one of your visits to "the happiest place on earth." You guessed it, Disneyland or Disneyworld. It didn't get branded "the happiest place on earth" for no reason...they earned it. It is, after all, their Brand Promise...the Happiest Place on Earth. Disney is an excellent example of a company that lives and executes on its Brand Promise. And their customers know it and talk about it to everyone else...we have become Advocates and Marketing Agents™ for the Happiest Place on Earth.

Take a minute and transport yourself back to one of your visits. From the time you booked the tickets, you (and your kids) were getting a bit giddy about the trip. You probably had to peel your kids off the wall when you told them you were going. They probably started watching lots of Disney movies and talking about their favorite character they wanted to meet. The excitement was building each day until the big day came. Some of you might have even had a "Disney calendar" to count down the days.

Then the big day came when you walked through the entrance, and everyone in your group was beyond excited...guaranteed. You couldn't wait to have your "dreams come true." There were probably a few characters waiting to greet you when you went in...maybe even one your kids (and you) were dying to meet...maybe even Mickey or Minnie. You immediately were transformed into kids again, regardless of your age. And whatever cares and worries you had melted when you crossed into the "Magic Kingdom." You had a slice of heaven, and you didn't want to leave.

You wandered around, went on some rides, ate some food, bought some souvenirs, and met some more characters. And if you weren't totally exhausted by the end of the day, you stayed for the nightly fireworks extravaganza. It was a day of bliss, and you probably slept better that night than you had for a long time with all those happy thoughts still racing through your head. Disneyland is a Customer Obsessed organization. A business that delivers an incredibly awesome and amazing Customer Experience in everything they do...every day. It's who they are, their DNA, their culture, their purpose for being, and their Brand Promise Guarantee.

Let's analyze this brief time transport back in time to the Magic Kingdom. As you relate your latest experience to my Disneyland description, you probably saw how Disney made this an "**art and a science**." It is 100% about "**how Disney made you feel**" the entire time you were there. They did everything they could think of to make you feel welcomed, special, important, and that you mattered to them so you could thoroughly enjoy yourself and escape reality...at least for a day. That is their entire goal...and they execute it every day with every guest to perfection.

What you didn't focus on (and probably forgot about) were their "products and services." You didn't focus on their quality of rides, the food, or even the souvenirs...their products and services. It didn't matter if these weren't the very best or not...and they weren't the best. **Their real "Product and Service" was THEM.** Their "hard products and services" were inconsequential compared to the "experience" and "how they made you feel" while you were their guest. If you are honest with yourself, I bet you can recall most of the experience you and your family had but have forgotten most (if not all) of the details about the products and services you consumed. Test this for yourself. Can you even recall the food you ate while you were there? What about the souvenirs? And even though their rides are certainly not the best among amusement parks, did their "mediocrity" detract from you leaving there wanting to come back? I would venture to say that none of these things mattered when it came to making Disneyland "**memorable**." It was the experience they gave you while you were there, not their (commodity) products and services.

As you think about this example, ask yourself if the experience you are delivering to your customers is more focused on "**how they feel**" when they work with you or on your "products and services." If it is more about your product and services, then you may be acting more like a "**commodity**." But suppose it is about how you make them feel and their experience when they interact with you. In that case, you are differentiating yourself from a commodity and being more Customer Obsessed. You are standing out in their mind, just like Disneyland. The experience and how you make them feel is what your audience remembers the most. Tapping into their emotions and linking these to a consistent Customer Experience is how you create this memorable experience, just like Disneyland.

One of the most significant issues most organizations have is employee alignment.

I can almost guarantee the customer experience you deliver isn't consistent from one employee to another. Each employee provides what "they think" is the right experience...which is different from the experience other employees are giving. Try this simple exercise.

Pick ten employees at random and ask them to write down how they would describe an extraordinary customer experience. Tell them to be as descriptive as possible when writing down what they would deliver to your customers, giving them an incredible experience. After you read through them, I can guarantee you NO TWO will be the same. It isn't their fault...they are just doing the best they know. The issue is that there isn't a consistent and repeatable process for them all to follow...let's fix that.

Let me bring this back to where we started. Delivering a "Disney" Customer Experience is an **art and a science.** A consistent and repeatable awesome Customer Experience is designed, planned, and executed the same way by all employees. There is nowhere in the Disney Customer Experience manual that says, "*Just go out there and smile and be as friendly as you can*." Everything they do is designed and planned to create their Customer Experience Map, then executed to perfection. And, perhaps most importantly, it is always consistent, so it is always incredible!

Granted, they hire employees who are more "wired" to be friendlier and happier. However, they "create" their experience process first and then ask their employees to overlay the process they created with their friendly and cheerful personality. Here's an action you can do in your organization...

> **ACTION ITEM:** Pick ten employees and/or leaders (randomly) in your organization and have them write down the answer to this question, "*What do you think an extraordinary, awesome Customer Experience would look like for our customers, and how would you deliver it?*"

You'll most likely get ten different versions. They won't be in alignment with each other, just like we talked about earlier. Some will be much "richer" than others, but none of them will be the same. Now, put yourself in your customer's shoes. How do you think your customers would "feel" after they interacted with your organization? Would they be confused? Would they say they weren't quite sure what to expect when they interact with your company? Would they love some and not like others? Would they feel more special from some of your employees and like an annoyance to others?

The short (and accurate) answer is they would feel all of these things...**they would feel confused.** I can absolutely guarantee the customer wouldn't know what experience you were trying to deliver consistently. This is precisely what I hear from customers when I interview them and ask them about their experiences.

By focusing on the Customer Experience as an "art and a science," you can **eliminate this confusion** and **deliver a consistent, repeatable experience** to ALL your customers. It is precisely why the very best companies (like Disney) don't leave their Customer Experience to chance. It is the primary reason why my brother and I wrote a 285-page book, "**Creating and Delivering a Totally Awesome Customer Experience,**" over a decade ago on this very topic (revised edition due out in 2021). The best experiences aren't random...they are well planned and executed consistently.

Having a recipe or a formula allows companies to eclipse their competitors by delivering a Customer Experience that rocks their world. It is WOW, over the top, incredibly awesome. Having this recipe is what makes it an "art" and a "science."

The recipe and formula for delivering a "consistent and repeatable" awesome Customer Experience is **Customer Experience Mapping.** These are literally "maps" your employees can use as a guide with every customer interaction so they can deliver these fantastic experiences to your customers. The next chapter, "The MAP to the Treasure," will give you the essential highlights of what Customer Experience Mapping is all about and how to do it.

Customer Obsessed companies can deliver a consistently incredible experience with every interaction all the time...it's just what they do.

When combined with the first cornerstone, TRUST, you are well on your way to building more Advocates and Marketing Agents™. These are the two most important factors needed to become "*REMARK*"able™.

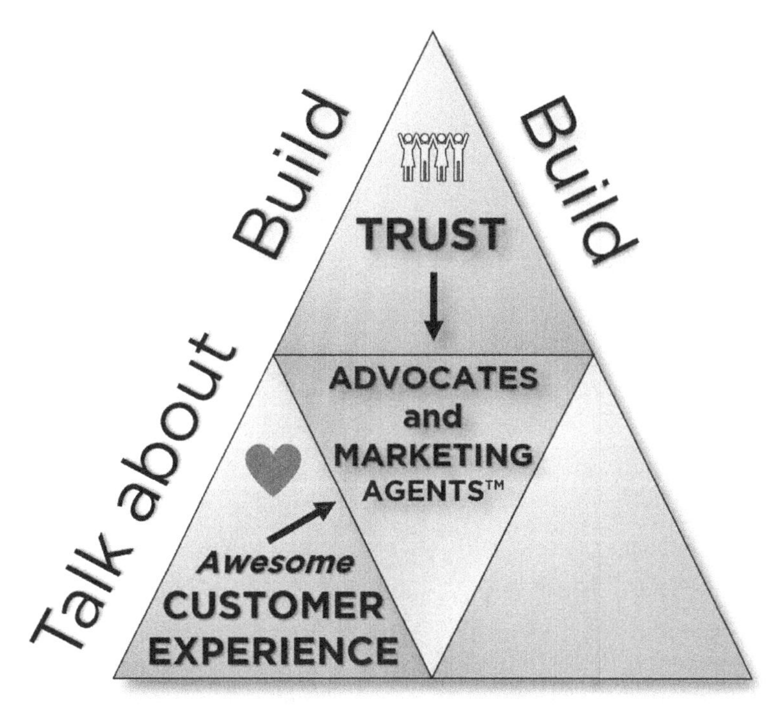

Customer Experience is an exciting and critical cornerstone of The "*REMARK*"able Triangle™...let's learn more about how to make this happen in your organization right now!

The MAP to The Treasure

In order to empathize with someone's Experience, you must be willing to believe them as they see it and not how you imagine their Experience to be.

BRENE BROWN

Do you have a "process map" for your Customer Experience, as you do for other processes in your business? If you had a treasure map to find a vast treasure, would you follow it?

In the majority of my conversations with top leaders, they believe their customer experience is already solid. In some cases, they think it rocks. Usually, they have a "lower bar" than I do when rating their customer experience. As they describe them, most are not very memorable, nor do they rock. They are not over the top amazing, and they don't truly delight their customers.

There are two easy ways to identify whether or not your customer experience rocks. **First**, find out what your customers say differentiates you from others. If they talk about price, terms, availability, or other such areas, you are a commodity to the customer. You know where you stand and can execute the plans I am sharing with you to change your position. **Second**, identify how you are getting most of your new customers. If it is through traditional marketing, as opposed to referrals, you are, once again, most likely operating with a commodity model. It's always better to know where you stand so you can see where you want to go from here. These are not uncommon places to be coming from...as evidenced by some outstanding research by Bain and Company. Sadly, their research bears out my claim that most customer experiences don't rock...they are usually well below that stage in the customer's mind. Here's the evidence...

There was a great (and famous) study by Bain and Company that specifically addresses delivering incredibly awesome and amazing customer experiences. Their study[10] asked the leaders of various companies if they gave a "superior experience" to their customers. The leaders from 80% of the companies said they did. From my experience, most leaders actually believe they do deliver a superior experience. But this is rarely the case, as demonstrated by Bain's research.

Bain and Company then asked these same companies' customers if they felt they were getting a "superior experience." Drum roll, please...**the ratings the leaders provided weren't even close to the results their customers gave**. Only 8% of the companies' customers said they were getting a superior customer experience, as opposed to 80% from the leaders. A gap of 72%...the gap between what leaders "think" they are delivering and what customers "say" they are providing. WOW...this is not only significant but demonstrates incredible misalignment on what customers actually feel. Once again, a tremendous OPPORTUNITY.

This gap between what the company thinks and what the customer tells us is what I refer to as the **Customer Reality Gap™**. You calculate it using two steps. **First**, you identify the number of customers the leadership team believes would rave about the customer experience currently being provided to the organization's customers. This is the number of customers you feel would say the experience "rocks" in their customers' eyes. It is an Experience your customers would rate much higher than what they get from your competitors...it is exceptional and superior to your competition.

Second, hire an outside individual or firm to talk (in-depth, no surveys) to your customers to learn more about how they truly feel. You identify the number of customers who feel your experience is extraordinary and superior...and well above the experience they receive from your competitors. **Third**, when you know both numbers (internal and external), you subtract the customer's view number from the leadership team's number. If they aren't in direct alignment (which is rarely the case), you have now identified your **Customer Reality Gap™**. You now know the gap between what you believe and reality. Now you can go to work to eliminate this gap. Your goal is to get the Gap to be zero.

I would challenge you, a leader in your organization, to take an active role in determining what your Customer Reality Gap™ is so you can develop the appropriate plans for getting them into alignment...get the gap to zero. This chapter will help you specifically do that...to get your actual customer experience in alignment with what you believe it to be.

The numbers Bain and Company discovered are similar to what I have seen as well...a significant misalignment between perceptions. It is very eye-opening and shocking. Yet even with this type of evidence available, leaders still tell me they are "already delivering" a really great customer experience. If you take the time to identify the Customer Reality Gap™ for your organization, you are one step closer to finding the "**Treasure.**"

> **Sidebar**: If you want to know how much your leadership team cares about your customers, just look at their calendars. They are the true tale of the tape, what is actually happening inside the organization. Often I see leaders spending minimal if any time with their customers. Talk to your customers...there is a world of opportunity sitting in front of you.

Leaders who honestly "want to improve" and "be the leader" in their industry always want to know how aligned they are (or aren't) with their customers. These are the leaders whose companies will dominate in their markets. These are the leaders who want to be Customer Obsessed and become "*REMARK*"able™.

One of the most valuable tools a company can embrace is Customer Experience Mapping...it is literally a "roadmap" for the experience you want your customer to have when interacting with your company.

The process of Customer Experience Mapping is straightforward and relatively easy to understand. However, creating "top quality" **Customer Experience Maps** takes a considerable amount of effort and focus. When you invest the time to develop these "Maps," you will have an experience that would actually "**rock your customer's world.**" You are designing an experience that is **over the top memorable and exciting** for your customers. Customer Experience Mapping gives you the specific process and scripts for how your employees would deliver this experience to your audience...consistently and repeatedly. These Maps are the magic that creates a **WOW** with your customers and gives them massive ammunition for telling others about you...**doing your marketing for you**.

Now I want to share with you how to develop Customer Experience Maps for your organization. Let me start by giving you some highlights and insights, tools, and actions to help get you headed in the right direction when designing a WOW Customer Experience. Once you see how these are constructed, you will have a better understanding of why this cornerstone will definitely help you be Customer Obsessed so you can become "*REMARK*"able™. Here are the **FOUR STEPS** to developing a Customer Experience Map of your own...

STEP ONE...determine the Customer Journey for your organization. There will be a separate Journey for each customer group you have chosen to serve. Once you have your Journey Maps, you can determine how many Customer

Experience Maps you will need to deliver the Journeys. I'll give you a hint...it's not as many as you might think, but more than just a few.

The average number of Maps needed for most organizations is between 20 - 30. The number of maps depends entirely on the size and complexity of your organization. If you have a small to medium-sized organization, this would be the total number of Maps for the entire organization. If you are a large organization, then you would break it down by your different companies, product lines, divisions, or however you measure your business units. If you have "profit centers, this is usually a pretty good place to start.

> **SIDE NOTE:** A "Journey Map" is simply a schematic that shows how a given customer group "moves through" your organization from the beginning stages, through the transaction, and ongoing follow-up. It shows where a particular customer group will interact with you and what you need along the way. It is truly a map of their Journey through the different parts of your organization.

Think of it as if you were planning a trip. You start with discovering where you want to go and then map out all the different places along the way you want to visit. Mapping these out in detail and the follow-up of the trip would be your Journey.

STEP TWO...as with everything strategic, it starts with the "end in mind." After you determine your Customer Journey and the "number of Journey Maps" you will need, you begin creating Customer Experience Maps (CEMs) based on your different customer groups. All CEMs start by identifying the Customer Experience you want your customer to receive. Think of this as a state of pure happiness. We need to determine what we would need to do to make our customers literally say, "***WOW, this is incredible...I've never been treated this way by anyone in this industry, you knocked it out of the park with how you treat me and me feel.***" We want this to be the "desired outcome" for every Map. In our book, **Creating and Delivering Totally Awesome Customer Experiences** (new revision due out in 2021), we call this the "**Experience Response Point**" or ERP.

There is a different ERP for each CEM. For example, the Map that describes how you first greet and interact with your customer will have a different ERP than how you deliver a particular service or how they interact with your accounting department. You get the idea...no two Maps have the same ERP because no two Maps interact with the customer exactly the same way.

STEP THREE...once you know the desired outcome (the ERP), you start to identify the individual steps needed to deliver this fantastic experience. This is where the rubber meets the road. Here is where you list out (in great detail) the exact process that needs to occur to deliver the desired outcome (ERP). These are not only descriptions of what you want to happen, but there are individual scripts of what you want your employees to say throughout this part of the customers' experience. These CEMs are quite detailed. When finished, you can actually use these CEMs as your training manual for all your employees. Like your organizational process maps, Customer Experience Maps are an integral and critical part of how you operate. They are vital to developing a Customer Obsessed culture.

Let's do a bit of a deep dive for a minute to give you some more detail on what exactly a Customer Experience Map looks entails. Let's analyze the CEM for the person "**Greeting someone who comes to visit your organization.**" This would be a single Map out of the entire group of Maps you identified as part of your Customer Journey. It starts by describing (in detail) the "desired outcome" (ERP) you want to have when someone comes to see you. An abridged version of the desired response we would want to hear from our customers might look like this...

> *"I can't believe how awesome they made me feel from the very beginning. When I first arrived, the person greeting me knew I was coming. They knew my name and greeted me as if they were waiting all day for me to arrive. They had my name on a reader board to welcome me when I arrived. And before I got to the door, a person was waiting to open it for me and greet me by name. Who does that these days? Then they offered me an assortment of great beverage choices (not just water or pop) and told me they had already notified the person I was going to see I had arrived. They said it would be less than 5 minutes. If I was hungry, they had an assortment of foods and snacks I could enjoy in their lounge (these were great items such as pastries, healthy trail mixes, and other such items). They offered me a seat in their lounge and proactively told me how to log into their WiFi while I was waiting. All I can say is WOW because I've never felt so important and cared about by anyone in this industry as I did today. I hope the rest of my experience goes the same way...this really made my day."*

The description above is what the "objective" looks like...our desired outcome, our ERP. Once we know this, we now work backward and design the TouchPoints, which will ensure we get this response, every time, from our customers. I can't emphasize how important it is to consistently and repeatedly deliver this experience with every interaction. We now have a starting point of knowing how we will make our customers feel special and important

STEP FOUR...this is where we start to design the specific details of the Customer Experience Map. We design and create the TouchPoints. TouchPoints are the way we take some type of action during their experience. TouchPoints can be an action we take, something we say, or a tool we might provide to help them reach our desired ERP. These TouchPoints are the heart and soul of a Customer Experience Map. They include the descriptions of what we want to accomplish and the necessary scripts for what to say. The easiest way to understand this is to look at an example of what a TouchPoint (or two) might look like for our above example of "Greeting someone who visits our organization."

One **TouchPoint** would be to have a way to know who was coming into the office on a particular day and make this available to the person who greets our guests. They could look up any information the company had on them and find a picture of them via social platforms like LinkedIn or Facebook. Now they would be prepared to greet them by name and know something about them before they arrived.

Another **TouchPoint** would be to develop the script for how we would greet our guests. It might go something like this, "*Greetings Sally, we are so happy to see you. I hope the trip to our office was easy for you. Welcome to (your company name). We've been expecting you. I have already notified Carl (company employee) you are here, and he said he would be right with you within 5 minutes. While you are waiting, please take advantage of our assortment of beverages. Here's a little list you can choose from. Please follow me to the lounge area to see some of the snacks we have available to enjoy while you are waiting. And feel free to take some with you on the road when you leave. Just let me know what you would like, and I will have them ready to go when you leave. Please don't be shy about wanting more than one of anything on the list. They are here for your enjoyment.*"

There would be several other TouchPoints needed to deliver this Customer Experience Map. It would also include some "tools" necessary for the person to use when they greeted your guest. Tools such as access to information about the guest arriving. Or a tool that allowed other employees to let the greeter know who was coming in that day. All these would work together to help design this Customer Experience Map.

I know this is a firehose for you in getting your arms around Customer Experience Mapping. Now you can see why we decided to write a 285-page book on it several years ago. The more detailed you make your CEMs, the better and more memorable the experience will be for your customers. It's the details that make a CEM truly come to life.

Let me close this chapter on Customer Experience Mapping, the "Treasure," by giving you a few more items to think about with the CEM process. **First**, and maybe the most obvious one, is that your "operational processes" will need to be modified or changed. In almost every situation, some processes fight against delivering an incredibly awesome and amazing experience. It happens because most organizations aren't Customer Obsessed, where the customer is at the center of your business. Most organizations, probably like your own, have designed processes for operational efficiency being at the center instead of your customer. When this happens, you see more efficient processes that might not focus on giving the customer the absolute best experience.

Let me give you an example. In some cases, it might be more efficient for us to invoice the customer 30 days after they have purchased our product or services to make sure we have incorporated all the costs involved in this product and/or service. By the end of 30 days, we know with 100% accuracy, the invoice is correct. But what if the customer prefers to get the invoice within a week so they can process it against their revenue so they can invoice others in their own business? In this case, we are making them wait three weeks beyond what they would prefer. Here we are focusing on us rather than our customers when it comes to invoicing.

A Customer Obsessed organization would recognize this right away and know the right answer is to get it to them in 7 days, even though the industry standard is 30 days...demonstrating our commitment to "helping our customer improve their business." We might agree to send them a "pre-invoice" with our best estimate of the charges, maybe even a little higher, so our customer could process it and move forward. We would then send an adjusted invoice with applicable credits when we figured out the exact costs. The goal is to provide what the customer needs, even if it means modifying our processes. While it might be slightly less efficient for us, it would show our customers how we focus on them.

The **second** area you will want to create is what I call "**Cool Tools**." These are tools such as checklists, emails, reports, online apps or programs, or a host of other tools that will help us be more responsive in serving our customers. For example, in a financial institution we worked with, we created a "placemat" with all their services and how they could help their customers...all listed in one place. It was a plastic-coated placemat where the customer could circle or write on it whatever they thought was relevant to them. The advisor could then go through these areas and explain how they would or wouldn't be relevant. Now they could fully understand how they could help their customers in one easy tool.

There are lots of these Cool Tools waiting to be created in your organization to help you deliver a fantastic experience to your customers. And they are all born out of the creation of the Customer Experience Map. Some of these tools are specifically designed for customer interaction, while others simply help our employees give our customers a much better experience. A Customer Obsessed organization is always thinking of new Cool Tools to help them be more successful in serving its customers. The beauty of these Cool Tools is that none of your competitors have them. You own them and are the first to create them for your customers. Customers remember this...they have elephant memories and rarely forget, especially when you do something special just for them.

The **third** area you will want to keep in mind concerns your people. Sadly, and unfortunately, not all your employees are wired to serve your customers in a way that exemplifies what you want to demonstrate when you are Customer Obsessed. This just happens. In almost every Customer Obsessed company, some employees simply do not fit. They cannot deliver an over the top, incredibly awesome and amazing experience...they just can't. As Jim Collins points out in his classic book, **Built to Last**, he says, "*There are only so many seats on the bus, and it's important that everyone is in the right seat doing the right things correctly.*" Sometimes you have the wrong person on the bus, and sometimes you have the right person in the wrong seat. These are all adjustments you need to make to help you deliver a WOW experience. If an employee is fighting this transformation, it is potentially a sign they are on the wrong bus.

For example, a manager in a distribution company did everything he could to avoid being Customer Obsessed. He found fault with all the Customer Experience Maps yet didn't offer any alternatives. He was just a "Negative Nelly" when it came to Customer Obsession. The other members of the team were excited, but he did his best to bring them down. It was a struggle...one we shouldn't have had to deal with in the process. But he had clout in the organization...he was an exceptional operations manager.

The only way for the organization to move forward was to eliminate him from the team. The CEO couldn't do it...he had allowed the employee to hold the organization “hostage” with his knowledge (something that happens often). He won. The CEO stopped the movement toward being Customer Obsessed until he could make sure he had transferred the knowledge to other people, so he wasn't held hostage. Then he could continue his Journey to be Customer Obsessed.

As you have probably figured out by now, the Customer Experience is an essential cornerstone in The “*REMARK*”able Triangle™. There is a lot that goes into creating an incredibly awesome and amazing Customer Experience. But it is well worth it. It will drive incredible Loyalty and build some great Relationships with your customers.

An incredibly awesome and amazing Customer Experience is the fuel that moves closer to creating Advocates and Marketing Agents™.

Let me sum it all up by going back to the purpose of this book...**to get others doing your marketing for you**. Everyone loves to talk about their incredibly awesome and amazing Customer Experience, just like we saw in the story about Disneyland. Are they talking about yours? If they are, what are they saying? If your audience isn’t raving about you, telling everyone they know how delighted and happy they are every time they work with your organization, WHY NOT? Changing your Customer Experience is a powerful cornerstone to helping you be Customer Obsessed so you can become "*REMARK*"able™ in the eyes of your customers.

And Customer Experience Mapping is an integral part of creating an incredibly awesome and amazing Customer Experience. It is the lifeblood of a Customer Obsessed organization. It gives your customers something tangible to tell others how you make them feel special and important.

And there is one crucial thing to always keep in mind...

While a customer can't talk about your products and services with complete knowledge and understanding (only you can do that since you create and use them), what customers can talk about, with 100% accuracy and with 100% certainty, is the experience they had with your company...every time. No one can challenge their knowledge of their experience...no one. They own it because they experienced it.

And they can talk about it with passion, commitment, and enthusiasm. If your customers can talk about their experience with this degree of confidence, wouldn't you want an army of them out there telling others about you? That is why creating an incredibly awesome and amazing Customer Experience is such a critical component of The "*REMARK*"able Triangle™.

We have now discussed two of the three cornerstones of The "*REMARK*"able Triangle™. Now let's dive into the third and final cornerstone needed to become a "*REMARK*"able™ company...

CONSISTENTLY HELPING

"Truly" Helping Changes the Game

You can get everything in life you want if you help enough other people get what they want.

ZIG ZIGLAR

How do you specifically "help" your audience improve their life and/or their business? What do you do that endears them to you because of how you helped them?

The third and final "cornerstone" to The "*REMARK*"able Triangle™ is one that is incredibly powerful yet missed by most organizations, even though it is obvious and straightforward. If you are aware of it, it will differentiate you almost immediately! It's what we all want as a customer.

Companies that are willing to Consistently Help their audience improve their life and/or their business stand out above all their competitors.

What exactly does **Consistently Helping** mean? It means that your organization's culture's primary focus is to find ways to help your audience make their life and/or their business better than it is today. It uses the information and knowledge your people possess (or can find) and helps your audience be better at whatever they do. You are doing things they would want to do for themselves to improve their life...but YOU are doing it for them, so they don't have to invest the time to do it themselves.

A client of mine routinely worked with Becky, a particular manager, at one of their customers who wanted to become a group leader for a specific product line. While she managed the product line, her goal was to become the leader of the entire team in the next year or two. My client felt she would be an excellent leader and would enjoy working with her in that role.

My client was working on being Customer Obsessed, so they focused on finding ways to "Consistently Help" their audience. Since they had extensive knowledge of both the industry and leadership, they decided to step in and help Becky in her quest to become a team leader. They put together a strategy to share some specific articles and other content they thought would be helpful and could help her learn more about what it takes to be a leader. They also shared specific stories of other people in their industry (and in other industries) who became leaders. They also found some online courses to help her understand and learn more about certain aspects of the role. They also gave her some books and highlighted the critical parts to read since they were familiar with them. Finally, they offered to mentor her along the way and coach her with their experiences as she continued to learn more about the role and leadership. They also gave her other industry-specific information since they had extensive knowledge in the industry.

You get the point of what they were doing. My client "invested" in Becky in a big way to help her reach her goal. And it worked. She got the new role and was incredibly appreciative of all the help she received from my client. They lived the third cornerstone for her...and she noticed.

Here's the essential part to take away from this example...none of this had anything to do with selling more of their products or services...nothing. They did it because they genuinely wanted to help Becky progress in her career. They didn't do it to get Becky into a higher position to sell more of their stuff. They truly cared about her and wanted to "help" her out. They had the knowledge and experience to help her out. They were putting their customers at the center of their business...they were acting Customer Obsessed. **It was now their culture...their DNA.**

My client became someone Becky could "trust completely" and who was deeply committed to helping her achieve her goals. She saw this and, like we would all do, sincerely appreciated the assistance. Remember the issue of **TIME**? Besides providing her with very helpful content, they saved her countless hours. They gave her back more of her most valuable asset, Time, and helped her get further using less of it.

Think back to the story of my grandfather buying his cows. He ultimately bought them from Joe, who he **trusted** completely, where he got an incredible **experience**, and received lots of **help** with his cattle. But what about Bob, the guy who "referred" my grandfather to Joe? Don't you think Bob benefited from this exchange as well? Bob was also a winner in this deal. He became even more trusted by my grandfather (and many others) because he gave them great advice and was an Advocate for Joe. Bob was an integral part of helping them improve their ranches. He was "helping" them, just as Joe was "helping" all of his customers.

It is pretty amazing what actually happens when you **Consistently Help** your audience. When you help your audience improve their lives and/or their business, you also generate massive trust. It is easy to see why your audience is more than happy to be your Advocate and Marketing Agent™, **doing your marketing for you,** when coupled with an incredible customer experience. Let me give you an exercise to help you understand this point even better...

> **EXERCISE:** I have a three-part exercise that will give you phenomenal insight into your own business. In **Part One**, write down the answer to this one question...

"What are the specific ways we sincerely and truly help our customers improve their lives and/or their businesses?"

Leave space below each answer as we will ask a follow-up question to each of your answers. Start writing...

Now that you have your list, **the second thing** to do is to put a checkmark next to each statement you believe you are genuinely doing to "help" your customer improve their life and/or their business. But only put a checkmark by an item if your customers would agree with your assessment. If you don't know what your customers would say or aren't confident they would say it is helping, leave it blank...no checkmark.

You have probably figured out by now that when I help companies develop this list out, we actually ask customers if they agree or not. Let me give you a Hint...this process is significantly better than asking your customers to fill out another survey that they hate filling out.

Now for the **third part** of the exercise. Remember the space you left underneath your answers? In the room you left, answer the final question...

"*WHY would your customer think/feel this truly helps improve their lives and/or their business?*"

It is actually the most vital question to answer. If your customer knows why you help them improve their life or business, they are far more committed and loyal to you...period. And if they truly believe you are helping them, they will "Advocate" for you to others because they believe it with their heart and mind. It is what allows you to be "remarked" about...and become "*REMARK*"able™.

When your customer clearly sees how you are helping them improve their own life, they have moved beyond being satisfied and have become loyal. And once they become loyal, then, and only then, are they willing to Advocate for you and your company. It is the position you want all your top customers to occupy. These are the customers singing your praises in the market. You are recognized as genuinely differentiated...and your customers are excited to tell others about it.

The answers to the Exercise questions above will give you tremendous insight into how much you "Consistently Help" your customers as a company. If the list is relatively short and there aren't many "why's" to support the list, there's an OPPORTUNITY for your organization. If the list is long and supported by some incredible "why's," you are well on your way to solidifying the third cornerstone of The "*REMARK*"able Triangle™...Consistently Helping.

Having a solid list from the Exercise above will dramatically improve your differentiation, your profitability, and build more trust with your audience. And most importantly, it will become part of your culture, your DNA. It is "why" you do what you do that others don't do. And it generates massive Word-of-Mouth for your company. It is a significant component to helping you become "*REMARK*"able™.

When people see you Consistently Helping your audience, customers (and others) are happy to do your marketing for you. And you pay them nothing! They do it because they Trust you, love the way you treat them, and know you are committed to improving their life and/or business.

You are now one step closer to building a Customer Obsessed culture. You are demonstrating through your actions that you are "investing" in your customers instead of spending countless dollars trying to "market" to them. You have changed your strategy from **PUSH to PULL**. No longer do you have to "push" marketing at them and hope they buy something from you. Now they are happy to "pull" you into their world and share what you are doing to help them with others. You have created happy customers who are your Advocates and Marketing Agents™...**dying to do your marketing for you**.

Showing your audience how much you want to help them when you aren't selling them a product or service is not the norm for businesses today. Most of the time, a company only wants to help you when they think you will buy something from them...you have changed the game. Think about how happy your employees will be when they can help your audience in areas they are knowledgeable about and isn't focused on something you sell. They will love working for a differentiated company...your culture will set you apart from your competitors.

Now you have all three of the cornerstones working together to complete The "*REMARK*"able Trianble™. Each cornerstone has its strength and power to help improve your organization to be more Customer Obsessed. While you can implement each cornerstone on its own, you can only maximize the benefits of becoming "*REMARK*"able™ when they are all working together.

Each cornerstone feeds off the other cornerstones. Their real LEVERAGE happens when the organization is doing all three together. This intertwining of the three is what gives an organization the multiplier of benefits. For example, it's great to share lots of information with your audience to Consistently Help them improve their lives and/or business. There is tremendous benefit in doing this one cornerstone. However, when you combine this with an incredibly awesome and amazing customer experience, you have two ways the customer knows how much you care about them and how important they are to you.

Now, combine these two cornerstones with a strategy of always keeping your promises, and you will build massive amounts of Trust, Relationships, and Loyalty. When your audience trusts you completely, you get even more leverage. All three cornerstones are now combined, leveraging each other, and this is what creates Advocates and Marketing Agents™. You are now getting the maximum value from The "*REMARK*"able Triangle™ and have a solid foundation for becoming "*REMARK*"able™. Below is what it looks like when you have all three cornerstones working together. Now you can start to realize all the benefits I talked about at the beginning in the section, The Opportunities.

In the next chapter, "**How YOU Can Help THEM,**" I will give you some very detailed and specific exercises and examples of what you can specifically do in this area. You won't want to miss this one...it is one of the most valuable aspects of this book. I can't wait until you read this chapter...it's a game-changer for any organization.

How YOU Can Help THEM

Build your reputation by helping other people build theirs.

ANTHONY J. D'ANGELO

Do you have a way to capture ideas and tap into your employees' creativity for the hundreds of ways you can help your audience and customers? How do you come up with ways to best help your audience?

Now that you have a better understanding of how powerful "**helping your audience improve their life and/or their business**" can be for your organization, let me cut to the chase. I want to dive into giving you some concrete (and detailed) actions you can take...today. These actions are tactical and something you can start doing immediately. I suggest you start small and then go all in to get the maximum benefit.

Tapping into your employees' creative and innovative minds for ways you can truly help your audience will change your business forever.

Let me give you a valuable exercise that will generate significant insights into ways you can truly help your audience improve their lives and/or their businesses. And whether you do it now or later, doing the exercise (and other action items) will give you a solid foundation for WHY Consistently Helping is such a "game-changer" for organizations.

I recommend you take a "3-year Approach" to this exercise. Meaning, you would do a total of 7 of these exercises over the next three years. Year one, you will do the exercise quarterly. In year two, you will do it semi-annually. And by year three (and beyond), you will do it annually. Here's how the exercise works...

Break your company up into teams. You can organize them in any way that makes sense for your organization...such as interdepartmental teams (my preference). Cross-pollination is always helpful when it comes to generating innovative ideas and insights. Assign a team leader for each group to orchestrate this exercise within their team and capture the information. The output will be shared and compiled later. Each team will meet for an "**Insight and Idea Session**." Here's the question I want them to answer...

> ***"Knowing who our customers are today, by persona, what ideas do you have, which you feel could help them improve their personal life and/or their business?"***
>
> **SIDE NOTE**: A Persona is a detailed description of your customers. It is a combination of demographics, psychographics, likes, habits, buying behaviors, and various other defining characteristics. There has been a lot of writing on Personas and how to create them...I would recommend reading this before doing the exercise.

Teams will meet for a few hours...some may need more time than others. They will most likely need to meet more than once to capture all their ideas. The goal is simple. We want to capture the creative thinking from every employee on how to "help" your audience of customers and others. We want your employees to think creatively about specific ways to truly help their customers improve their lives and/or business. These don't have to be monumental changes...simple ideas work just as well, if not better in some cases. In fact, a large group of smaller ideas can often times have more impact than one big idea that might be hard to implement.

The goal is to capture these ideas without judgment...THERE ARE NO BAD IDEAS. We want to capture ideas from everyone individually and then combine them with the other groups to create a "bucket of ideas." These are "brainstorming" or "creativity" sessions designed to capture wild and crazy ideas from all your employees. We want to capture "raw and unfiltered" thinking and ideas from everyone.

Once each group has captured as many ideas as possible, someone needs to compile them together. I recommend having an overall "**Idea Lead.**" They are responsible for collecting all the ideas and presenting them to a group, an **Idea Team**, for further refinement. The Idea Team will evaluate the ideas and "**prioritize" them based on "what they feel" would have the most impact**. You can determine the grading scale you are most comfortable with...I like a scale from 1 - 5.

Once the Idea Team has compiled and prioritized the ideas, the lists are presented to the leadership team for review. They will then go through this long list of ideas and do their final prioritization. The two areas the leadership team would use as their criteria would be...

Degree of impact the idea could have on our audience

Time frame by which we could execute a particular idea

Once each idea is labeled, we would create a "Prioritization Matrix" to determine which ideas will get executed...similar to the one shown below.

Now that we know where each idea fits in the matrix, we move from planning

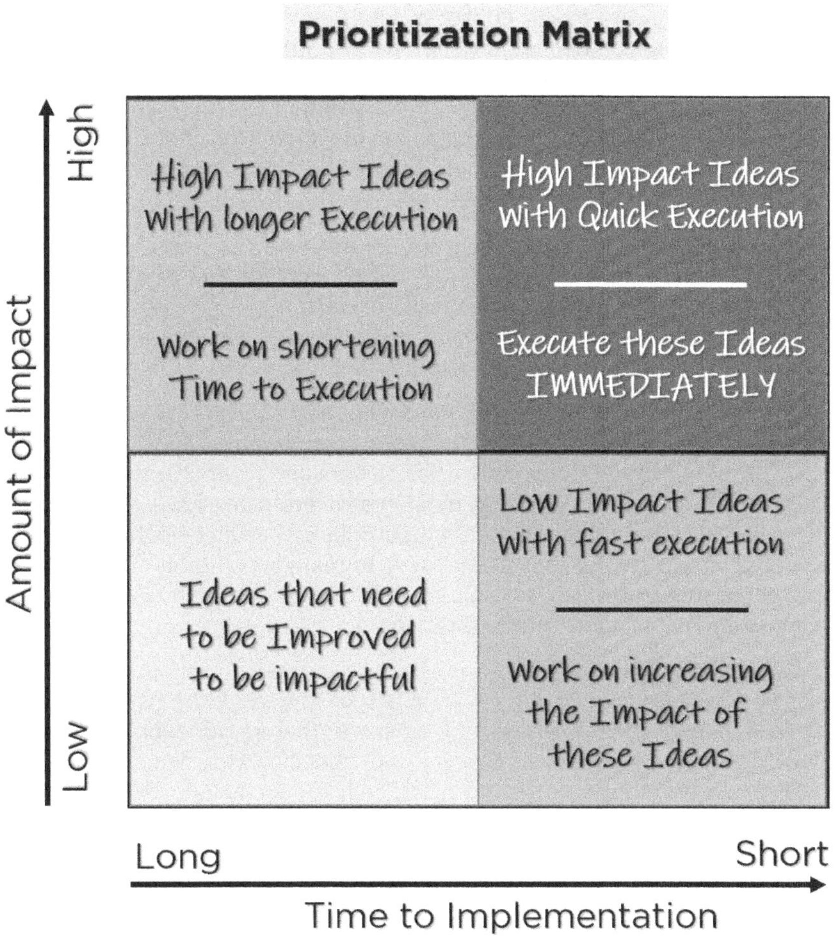

Prioritization Matrix

High	High Impact Ideas With longer Execution — Work on shortening Time to Execution	High Impact Ideas With Quick Execution — Execute these Ideas IMMEDIATELY
Low	Ideas that need to be Improved to be impactful	Low Impact Ideas With fast execution — Work on increasing the Impact of these Ideas
	Long	Short

Amount of Impact

Time to Implementation

to execution. We first look at the "Ideas we can execute today" by Persona, and then assign these to people (or groups) to develop specific execution plans. Next, we would look at the ideas we could implement quickly but might not have as much impact. We evaluate these to see if we can get some immediate value from implementing them now or if it will be better to wait on their implementation. While they may happen quicker, we also want ideas that will significantly impact our audience. No mediocrity allowed...we want exceptional...and so does our audience.

After looking at these two bins of ideas, we focus on the ones that will significantly impact our audience and take us longer to execute. Is there a way to shorten the time frame for implementing these ideas? If so, let's get these high impact ideas down into a quicker execution mode so we can make them happen sooner than we initially thought. These are fantastic ideas...we just need to find a way to make them happen sooner.

Finally, we see the fourth bucket of ideas...low impact and a long time to execute. From my perspective, I recommend putting these in a "holding bin" and review them somewhere down the road. Maybe they improve over time, or perhaps they don't. But when you see all the other three bins' ideas, you won't need to worry about these other ideas anytime soon. Now that we know where all the ideas fit and when we should execute them, let's dive deeper into what some of these ideas might look like.

One of the most powerful and quickest ideas we can implement would be **articles** on "**Ways to get the most out of our product for your particular position or business.**" It is a comfortable place to start since you already know the information. Yet, it is incredibly helpful since many of your customers may only be thinking of one or two uses for your products/services.

For example, we did a project for a financial services company, a credit union, several years back, which illustrates how powerful this simple idea can be for an organization. They had a lot of services (over 30) they offered to customers. The problem was that most customers didn't know about all their services (over 75% actually). It meant that while they could help their customers improve their life and/or their businesses in many ways, their audience didn't know about these services. And most of them were free and available to use. Their customers just didn't know about them.

We embarked on an effort to create some exciting tools their employees could use to help educate their customers so they could be used to improve their lives and/or their businesses. It wasn't a "feature, function, benefit" type of tool. Those are sales tools. It was a tool specifically designed to "help you improve your life." It was designed specifically for each customer Persona. For example, for the younger, more technologically savvy customers who were always in a hurry to get things done, they created a "cheat sheet" for using online resources so they would never have to go into the branches. It allowed them to do things with less time and effort.

Another Persona, their older, mostly retired audience, wanted a tool where they came into the branch and allowed the representative to show them better ways to use what they already had...no selling, just helping. They had plenty of time on their hands and welcomed the opportunity to sit down with someone for an hour and just talk about life and learn more. They loved it.

We created other such tools, all with the idea of "helping" their existing customer audience learn more about how to be better at managing their money. It focused entirely on "helping" them learn rather than "selling" to them and discouraging them from wanting to learn more and get more from their existing relationship. The result was a significant increase in customer acceptance and loyalty shot up. Customers actually came to them and wanted to use more services they didn't even know about before. They started moving more money over to their institution and building a better and deeper relationship with them.

Ultimately, what ended up happening was an increase in loyalty, and that these customers were so impressed, they started TELLING OTHERS.

They told their friends about how well they were treated and how "helpful" they were to them. And since they weren't getting this from their institution, they switched. The result was the following...

- Significant increase in the use of their products and services by existing customers (more revenue)
- Increased loyalty by the existing customer base (increased profitability, lower acquisition costs)
- More Word-of-Mouth and Advocacy from their existing customers (adding more customers with no added cost for customer acquisition...more revenue and higher profitability)
- Happier customers and happier employees (now they knew how they could genuinely help their customers)

The exercise I just shared with you is incredibly powerful. But, it is only powerful if leadership (and the employees) take it seriously. I use this often with any organization that feels they lack ways to "truly help" their audience. It's incredibly powerful...and it always works.

I just gave you complimentary consulting...no charge (other than the price of the book). I just gave you a gold mine if you choose to tap into it. I just gave you more money and ROI. And I just gave you something that works every time to differentiate you from your competitors. Will you use it? It is one of the ways I can "truly help" YOU.

What you just experienced in this chapter is exactly what this chapter is all about...**truly helping my audience**. You just experienced it for yourself! There was no selling, no marketing, no gimmicks, no manipulation of any kind...just helping my audience...YOU!

And if we follow this through the model I have shared with you throughout this book, you will most likely "share it" with someone else if you found it to be helpful and valuable. You might mention it to someone in person, share it, tweet it, or email it. When you do, you just DID MY MARKETING FOR ME! I hope this drives home the point about how powerful "**truly and consistently helping**" your audience can be for you and your organization.

When you do this over and over and over again, you build TRUST. And if you also have the opportunity to give your audience an incredible EXPERIENCE, we have just demonstrated, to our audience, The "*REMARK*"able Triangle™!! I hope you take a minute and just think about what you have read in this chapter. It is a live example of what I am encouraging you to do in your own company. It is walking the talk.

Now that we're in the groove, let me share several other ways you can genuinely help (not sell or pimp) your customers that will pay many dividends. And these benefits continue to grow as you get better and better at "helping" your customers.

There are many ways you can help your customers. To help you get started thinking in the right direction, let me give you some ideas...

- Create **articles** on how best to use your products and services, by Persona, product, or service
- Create a **blog** to discuss current trends, issues, questions, and areas of need within your audience
- Create "**how-to**" videos to help your audience to "visually" understand and use your product or service better
- Create a **podcast** for interviews with customers using your products and services to showcase their businesses
- Identify those you want to help move their careers forward and start providing them with **position and industry-relevant information**
- Share **business improvement** ideas
- Connect your audience with **partners** and others who could genuinely help them in certain situations and share their stories
- Connect them with others who you know that have **solved a specific business issue** they are struggling with and tell their story
- Create a "**mastermind**" group with other people in a similar position as you and have non-competing companies participate

There are so many more creative ways to help your customers and audience as a whole...but remember, you never "pay it forward" with the intent to "sell or pimp"

As you can see, there is a litany of ways you can **CONSISTENTLY TRULY HELP** your customers and general audience...you just need to add some creative juices to figuring them out. Many of the ones I listed above would work for most organizations...but there are others that would be specific to your business, industry, customer base, and other factors.

If you follow the directions on the exercise I shared with you, I can guarantee you will be blown away by the creativity sitting around in your organization. I guarantee it will change the way your audience feels about you and your company. And when this exercise becomes part of your DNA, where you do this all the time, you are well on your way to being Customer Obsessed. **Only Customer Obsessed companies have a culture that "wants" to do this and "looks forward" to helping their customers and others.** When this becomes "who you are" as an organization, you have added the third and final cornerstone to The *"REMARK"*able Triangle™. You are well on your way to becoming "*REMARK*"able™ and creating an army of Advocates and Marketing Agents™ anxious to spread the word about how incredibly awesome and amazing you are to work with and why others should work with you as well. The ultimate goal of this entire book.

Now you have all the cornerstones to be a Customer Obsessed company. What are you going to do next? How about learning some specific way to execute all this to become "*REMARK*"able™. The remaining chapters are all about how to help you implement what you have just learned...I call it "**LIFT OFF**." I want every company to catapult forward from where they are today and leap ahead of their competitors...not by a little, but by a massive amount. You can only make it happen through EXECUTION. When you execute what you have just learned, you will eclipse your competitors and start to realize and enjoy all the benefits (OPPORTUNITIES) I shared with you at the beginning of the book.

Let's do this...are you ready to **LIFT OFF** and get started?

RESULT

The Range Fire

If you do build a great experience, Customers tell each other about that. Word-of-mouth is very powerful.

JEFF BEZOS

”

How fast does word-of-mouth spread about your company? Does your audience tell their friends and colleagues about you regularly and frequently?

Range fires, by definition, spread fast and furious. Is your Word-of-Mouth spreading fast and furious? There is nothing more rewarding than to see tons of people buzzing about you and telling everyone they know. When others talk a lot about your business, this says something about you. It means you are someone others want to work with. It has always been the reward of being a successful company.

While one-on-one recommendations are better than nothing, we can do better? Leveraging your Advocates and Marketing Agents™ is the best way to get **Trusted Word-of-Mouth** spreading at the speed of a range fire...swift, consistent, and relentless.

Before the Internet Revolution, we couldn't leverage our Advocates as we can today. Today, we can actively **leverage** our audience of loyal, trusted Advocates to reach hundreds or thousands of people in seconds. Now you can too. Now you can take the oldest (and most powerful) form of authentic and credible communication (Word-of-Mouth) and leverage it...**put it on steroids**!

The "*REMARK*"able Triangle™ gives you the formula, the recipe, the roadmap for how to create this type of leverage, and get massive Word-of-Mouth...consistently and frequently. I hope you will take advantage of it and start your own "Range Fire." It is how you get to become "*REMARK*"able™.

Now that you know the master formula and recipe for becoming "*REMARK*"able™, let me share some additional formulas to help you move forward in being Customer Obsessed. Please use these formulas consistently on your Journey to becoming "*REMARK*"able™. They are simple and common sense, which makes them easy to remember and execute.

Let's start with an easy one...

> **Being Customer Obsessed leads to you becoming "*REMARK*"able™. "*REMARK*"able™ = Free Marketing**

As you become more and more "*REMARK*"able™, your customers, referral partners, friends, colleagues, and others will be your Advocates and Marketing Agents™..."**doing your marketing for you**" and telling others about you.

Free marketing comes from not having to spend more monies on attracting more customers...new customers will come to you. As I discussed in the marketing section earlier, you want to continue marketing, just not how you may be doing it today. Change it up and **invest in your customers.** This investment in your customers is what pays off for creating Advocates and Marketing Agents™ that are happily doing it for you...without any additional cost. It is free marketing...and it happens for companies who become "*REMARK*"able™.

Here's the second formula to think about...

> **Awesome Customer Experience + Relevant (helpful) Content = Word-of-Mouth**

When these two cornerstones are combined, you create Advocates and Marketing Agents™ out of your audience. It starts with an Awesome Customer Experience...not a great one and certainly not a good one...an incredibly awesome and amazing experience. Anything short of this is "ordinary," a commodity that others can easily deliver without much effort. It isn't about "satisfying" your customers. It is about dazzling your customers with an incredibly awesome and amazing experience.

In my first book, the definition for a satisfied customer was, "***Someone who is satisfied at the moment while continuing to look for the "next best deal.***" They will buy from a company until something better comes along, then they leave to work/purchase from the other company. These "**satisfied**" customers are merely in a "**holding pattern**" at the moment...not raving and certainly aren't loyal. They don't go out of their way to tell anyone anything about you...but they are satisfied. This doesn't work for a Customer Obsessed company. We want the Customer Experience to ROCK!

Satisfied Customers are "Mediocre Customers" in today's heavily competitive and commoditized market.

To create Word-of-Mouth for your company, you have to do something that causes them to say, "*WOW, how you treat me is amazing and incredible. No one else makes me feel the way your company does. No one else goes to the extent you do to help me in my life and/or my business.*" When your customers feel this way, you have checked off the first part of the formula...you have created and delivered an "**Awesome Customer Experience.**" It is an experience they can't wait to tell others about because it is so different and unique compared to what other organizations (inside or outside your industry) are giving to them.

The second part of the formula, "**Relevant (and helpful) Content,**" focuses on "what" they will be sharing when they talk about you. It is content so valuable that it positively impacts your audience's life and/or business. It's content they "look forward" to regularly getting because it positively impacts them. It is content that causes them to say, "*Whenever I get "content" from you, I always know it will be very relevant and helpful to me and allow me to be a better person or run my company better than I could without it.*"

When you create this level of content for your audience, they quickly recognize its value and want more of it. But they also find it valuable enough to **share with others** who they think it could help. By nature, humans have an innate desire to help others. Your audience essentially becomes your "**Marketing Agent for content**" in the market because they believe it will be of help to you...because it is valuable and helpful to them.

When you combine these two cornerstones (Awesome Customer Experience + Relevant and helpful Content), you have the two critical ingredients for creating Word-of-Mouth for your organization. This allows you to elevate yourself well above your competitors. But, most importantly, when you have Word-of-Mouth, you are building an army of Advocates and Marketing Agents™ who are out there doing your marketing for you...you're getting **FREE MARKETING**!

> **Disclaimer:** Creating content isn't free...it takes time and resources to create it. However, when you "redirect" the resources spent on low ROI marketing and reallocate it to creating something your audience finds incredibly valuable and wants to share, this is "**Customer Marketing,**" which has a much higher return. The ROI on Word-of-Mouth is always going up and carries the highest rate of return.

The "Granddaddy" formula...

> **Awesome Customer Experience + Relevant (helpful) Content + Trust = Advocacy**

Here is the formula which delivers the ultimate brass ring...**creating Advocates and Marketing Agents™** in the market. Since this is what the book's entire purpose is about, it's one I hope you (and all your employees) commit to memory and challenge yourselves daily. It is the formula that creates Customer Obsessed companies who become "*REMARK*"able™.

It's the same formula for creating "Word-of-Mouth" you read about above but with one very vital (and necessary) ingredient added to it...**TRUST**. Trust is an essential ingredient to creating Advocates and Marketing Agents™. **No one will put their character and reputation on the line if they don't Trust you...no one.** So, TRUST is not just a critical part of the formula. It is an essential part. It is the "magic ingredient" that will accelerate advocacy faster than any other ingredient. It's the **catalyst** to leverage the other cornerstones of The "*REMARK*"able Triangle™.

The formula for Leverage...

Advocates + Leveraged Marketing = Word-of-Mouth *on Steroids*

Advocates are your "vocal fans." When you combine Advocates with a "new way" of marketing, **Leveraged Customer Marketing**, you get massive amounts of Word-of-Mouth. You get the accelerator effect on your Word-of-Mouth. You are taking your organization to a significantly higher level in your industry...one where no one else may exist. A place you can own all by yourself. A place where customers (and others in your audience) see you as truly different and unique. I like that place...

Companies like Zappos (at the time I met with them) were getting over 75% of their business from repeat customers (loyalty) and word-of-mouth (from their Advocates). I can't think of a better model to follow for any business. Their CLV (Customer Lifetime Value) and incredibly low investment in traditional marketing (if any) creates a model that should be the envy of everyone. Or look at Nordstrom, who built their business solely on the way they treated their customers. They charged more than their competitors but demonstrated how treating the customer special and important created tremendous loyalty among their customers. They created countless Advocates to spread word-of-mouth about how awesome they treated you. Or what about Sewell Automotive, where their entire focus is on keeping you as a "customer for life?" If you are a "customer for life," you are loyal, and you tell others...you've also become an Advocate for how they treat you. Why not you?

The second part of this formula is "**Leveraged Marketing.**" Leveraged Marketing creates a marketing process that "feeds" your Advocate's "content" they can share. Most marketing merely pushes out information that tells your audience how wonderful you are or telling them (or guilting them) to buy your products and services. This is pimping. No one wants to be pimped today. Leveraged marketing gives your audience something helpful, useful, and valuable to them.

This entire book is about helping you convert your audience into your **Trusted Advocates and Marketing Agents™**, who go out of their way to tell others how incredibly awesome and amazing you are. There is no reason this can't happen with your audience...all the time. Customers become your Advocates and

Marketing Agents™ instead of a transaction. They are happy to do your marketing for you.

The ultimate "**Range Fire**" is getting more and more Advocates and Marketing Agents™ to spread word-of-mouth fast and frequently. Companies who create their own "Range Fires" eclipse their competitors and elevate themselves to the ultimate position of being the "**Loner**" in their industry. I want you to be the Loner...here's how to get there...

LIFT OFF

Burn The Ships

Whatever your purpose is that leads you to the point of no return, that's where you go.

BJ THE CHICAGO KID

Burn the Ships is one of the most critical chapters in this book. It is vital to helping you become "*REMARK*"able™. It is all about **GETTING STARTED.**

As with everything great, Customer Obsession requires your undying commitment...from the beginning and throughout the entire Journey. It is a "Journey," not a destination. Being Customer Obsessed doesn't have an end...it just continually gets better and better and better. If you want to have a successful Journey, there is one action you, as the top leader of leaders, absolutely, positively need to take.

BURN THE SHIPS!!

The concept of "**Burn the Ships**" is critically important. If you aren't familiar with the term, it originated with Hernando Cortez, a Spanish explorer who landed in what is now known as Mexico in 1519. Upon landing, he instructed his men to "burn the ships" that carried them across the Atlantic from Spain. When one poor soul complained, Cortez had him executed. As a result, his men were well motivated to continue to serve Cortez in his efforts to explore the new world.

Retreating is easy. If you want to be Customer Obsessed and become "*REMARK*"able™, retreating is not an option. "**Burn the Ships**" means you are all-in, 100% engaged, completely committed to the Journey...there is **no going back**.

Having worked with leaders over the past 30+ years, burning the ships is one of my favorite analogies in business and life. When you are willing to do it, you create situations such as...

- The "**flavor of the month**" – things are always changing...something new happens all the time so let's not get too committed to this new initiative...it also will pass like all the others
- "**Shiny Objects**" – there is always something new and exciting coming along to catch your eye and pursue, so all we have to do is wait for the new shiny object...there is always a new shiny object
- "**Don't get wedded to the change**" – don't get married to the new changes since we want to go back to the old way of doing things that we know and understand...just date so you can go back
- "**The latest brainstorm**" – when leadership comes up with a new idea and wants to implement it...if we come up with enough objections or issues, we know we can delay it until the next brainstorm idea and not have to implement this one

These mindsets kill innovation, momentum, and changes inside an organization. Do any of these sound familiar in your organization? If so, it might be time to reevaluate why initiatives "don't stick" and get scrapped. Now might be the perfect time to take a stand on something you are passionate about, such as Customer Obsession. Time to "burn the ships."

Employees will generally follow what their leader is committed to doing. It is up to you, as a leader, to demonstrate your commitment to becoming Customer Obsessed. **"Burning the Ships"** definitely communicates a different message to your employees. It says, "***We aren't going back to the old way of doing things so let's all work together to make this be a phenomenal success***." And, as you've already heard, Customer Obsession is all about your culture and DNA. It's "who" you are going forward, no going back. We aren't changing our culture back to what it was. We're all in on being Customer Obsessed. We want to become "*REMARK*"able™.

Customer Obsession isn't something we are going to "try and see how it goes." It requires the leadership team and employees to be ALL IN, or it will fail. I know this sounds a little harsh, but it's the only way your employees and customers will see you are committed to making this your new DNA.

Customer Obsession isn't something you can do half-way or part of the way...it has to be all the way to make it successful. It will be awkward and confusing...to both customers and employees. Your employees will not know what they are supposed to do if they don't believe you are completely committed to the Journey. Without 100% commitment, the Journey will die a slow (or maybe more rapid) death, and the organization will revert to where it was before...leaving your customers confused.

If you are not going to "burn the ships," my recommendation is not to start until you are ready to light the fire and set the ships ablaze.

CUSTOMER OBSESSION IS WHO YOU ARE, NOT WHAT YOU DO.

As I discussed in the chapter on what Customer Obsession is all about, being Customer Obsessed is who you are, your culture, and your DNA. It gives you purpose and answers the WHY question of "***Why are we in business?"*** Now you can answer it by saying, ***"We are in business to obsess over our customers, treat them better than anyone else, so they feel special and important, and to help improve their lives and/or their businesses***." This is being Customer Obsessed. This is how you become "*REMARK*"able™.

You can only change your culture or DNA when there isn't a "ship" to run back to...the old way of doing things. If the employees feel like this is an "initiative" or a "project" or something that has a "start and a finish," it will fail. You might get better as a company by focusing more on your customer, but you won't reap all the many rewards of becoming "*REMARK*"able™. And you won't build an army of Advocates and Marketing Agents™.

But when you "burn the ships," you have just set your company apart from your competitors. In the eyes of your customers and employees, you stand alone, "head and shoulders" above everyone else. You will become the "**Loner**" you want to become (more on that in the next chapter).

"Burning the Ships" lets you maximize the benefits and rewards (lower marketing costs, higher profitability, more customer retention/loyalty, greater word-of-mouth, and stronger advocacy) from the investments you have made (time, resources, and capital). And I believe you should always get the appropriate benefits from the investments you make.

If you want to be ALL ABOUT YOUR CUSTOMERS, then BURN THE SHIPS and go ALL IN and OBSESS over your customers.

Now that you have "Burned the Ships," let's look at some other things you can specifically do to make all this happen for you and your organization...

Become a Loner

> *When Jack Welch was the CEO of General Electric, he was able to produce record growth year after year by using a few simple principles relentlessly. The system of management he used was called DIFFERENTIATION.*
>
> CLAY CLARK

As you begin to think about your Journey to becoming *"REMARK"*able™ by being a Customer Obsessed organization, you need to change your MINDSET. You need to...

BECOME A LONER!

A "Loner" is, well, someone who stands alone and apart from everyone else. In most contexts, it's a negative term...describing someone who is "not included" in a group. That is precisely how I want your organization to be viewed. You don't want to be included in a group of your competitors. You will want to stand alone, unique, and different.

A group is a "herd" of like individuals or companies. You will be the one who escaped the herd. You are the one who decided not to follow the herd of other companies in your industry doing the same thing and delivering the same experience and getting the same results.

When you think of being a Loner as a positive term, it works really well to motivate you and your organization to achieve "**Lonership**" (a new word for you). You own it...it becomes your rally cry. Lonership is an exclusive membership...we don't want to allow others into our private club...the club of differentiation and standing alone in the eyes of our customers.

When you become a Loner, you start asking different questions. You no longer want to ask the questions "the herd" would ask, or you end up looking like you are part of the herd. You have to ask "loner questions" of your leadership team and all your employees. You change the language inside your organization, so your customer sees you differently...you aren't part of the herd any longer. For example, asking the question, "*How are we doing against our competition*," is a herd question.

Why would you measure yourself against criteria that you weren't trying to meet, such as the measurements your competitors are using? Measuring yourself against the herd is futile because these measurements are irrelevant to what you are trying to achieve...the status of being completely differentiated in the eyes of your customers and employees.

For example, if you choose to market in the same way as your competitors, you will look like your competitors...you are looking like the herd. If you decide to market differently, changing the language to something new and innovative to your audience, you will look and feel different to them...you won't look like the herd. To achieve this status of Lonership, your customers need to see you acting in different ways from your competitors.

When you do unique and different things that truly benefit your audience, they see you as entirely different from those who aren't doing the things you are doing. When you are viewed differently, your customers are more motivated to follow you and ignore the herd. They have seen something that is unique and different...and they like it.

For example, I get to work with several professional service firms, including attorneys, financial planners, wealth management companies, and others. What does the herd do to attract new clients? They offer free steak and seafood dinners at excellent restaurants to entice you to come in and hear their "pitch." They hope to either "scare" you or "strong-arm" you into working with them ...this is what the herd does. They all do the same thing. I could probably eat free for the rest of my life if I just decided to accept all the invitations I receive for these “free” high-pressure meals. Everyone in the herd does this, and they do it the same way with the same intentions.

A “Loner” firm does it differently...they do precisely the opposite of what the herd is doing, so they are viewed as being completely different. For example, they might overtly take a unique approach to look and act differently. If they do a seminar, they will do it entirely differently. They know exactly who their audience is and who they are trying to "help." They offer particular topics to help them learn more and take away some practical insights. But there is one huge difference...they approach it WITHOUT any type of pressure pitch or ask. They do it strictly based on helping their audience...not baiting them into scheduling a meeting.

Loners focus exclusively on "helping" their audience, not "selling" their audience. They let their audience sell themselves. I know you are saying to yourself, "*This never works. People need someone to move them along the sales process and help them get to the decision...if we don't push them, they won't make any decisions, and it will be a waste of time.*" I disagree.

You might get some people to buy because of coercion or fear or some other pressured emotion. But they will NEVER become your Advocate and Marketing Agent™ and tell anyone else to purchase from you...they will never do your marketing for you.

The best Advocates are the ones who sell themselves because they have done their analysis to prove this is the right decision for them...not because someone pressured them. Loners give them all the information and help with the research they need. But they need to get there on their own to be convinced this is the right decision. Customers rarely appreciate the product/service as much if they feel pressured to buy, even if it was the right decision for them. However, they will thoroughly enjoy it (and talk about it) if they came to this decision independently.

Without question, the best customers, in terms of happiness, loyalty, and advocacy, come from selling themselves...knowing this was the right decision for them and their situation. With your help, providing them the knowledge and insights, they make the final decision...without pressure. Most companies use the pressure tactic because they don't know how to help their audience. It isn't that the company can't do it. They just don't know how to do it.

Suppose you follow the recipe and formula I just shared with you on how to be Customer Obsessed. In that case, you will have given your audience enough information and assistance to make the right decision for themselves...even if it isn't working with you. They will remember this, and they will tell others about it...they will help do your marketing for you.

In the example above, the professional service firm model changed. Now they offer concrete and helpful insights into precisely the issues their audience needs to address. Their audience gets immensely useful, personalized information they can evaluate and see how this would impact their life...on their own. They present it in a way their audience can "connect" it to their own life. And they do it without any pressure.

The herd does not do this...they focus on the process of attracting lots of people, pressuring them, and pulling out the few weaker ones they can close and sell. It's the funnel...start with massive amounts of people and pressure them until a few buyers fall out. The conversion rate is low, and the unhappiness factor is high. You are not going to create any Advocates and Marketing Agents™ with this approach.

When you become a "Loner" because you are Customer Obsessed, it changes how you think and act. You desert the herd and build your own positive, helpful, and trusted approach your audience loves...and they talk about. This is just one of many ways they set themselves apart to become "*REMARK*"able™...and they get them to do their marketing for them.

The goal for Customer Obsessed companies is to make a comparison between themselves and their competitors dramatically different...show them they stand alone...Loners. When you become the "Loner" in your market, you have arrived. You are now seen as different and unique.

Change your mindset to seek loneliness. Seek to be unique and truly different in the eyes of your customers. You will see the impact of how your customers vote...and they always vote with their wallets.

The next chapter will give you some more specifics on how to lead your new Customer Obsessed Organization. These insights will provide you with a different way to think about your leadership role now that you have adopted the "Loner Mindset."

You are ready to break away from the herd...this is going to get exciting!

Not Your Average Leader

The task of the leader is to get his people from where they are to where they have not been.

HENRY KISSINGER

Leading a Customer Obsessed organization is going to be different for most Leaders. The art of leadership doesn't change, but how you lead will most likely be changing.

The primary area of change for Leaders is moving their customers to the center of their business and making them their primary FOCUS.

From my experience, most Leaders (business owners, CEOs, and C-suite executives) focus on the financial, product, or sometimes sales aspects of their business. They are trying to manage their financial risk and grow the business through new (or improved) products and services. They also have a strong emphasis on various sales activities. Leaders will often emerge from one of three areas...Finance, Sales, or Operations (product/service).

It's pretty rare to find a leader who was the Chief Customer Officer or Chief Experience Officer leading the company or driving most of the change...it's a pretty new area, and there isn't a vast inventory of people or skills available to most companies. While this is changing, it will take some time before these leaders become the top leader in their company

Now that we are firmly in the Customer Economy, we need to move from a product/service-centric approach to a Customer-Centric approach.

Often, the strongest Customer Obsessed leaders have been entrepreneurial...starting or growing a company focusing on the customer rather than on products or services. When you look at Zappos, or Amazon, or Nordstrom, or even Starbucks, you see that these have not been around an incredibly long time compared to General Motors, IBM, Dupont, and other companies. These relatively new companies came out of the blocks focusing on the customer and putting them in the center of their business.

And we can't ignore the commitment leaders like Jeff Bezos of Amazon makes to their customers. Jeff puts an empty chair at the table in all of his meetings. The empty chair represents the voice of the customer. It is a constant reminder of how the customer is at the "center of his business." Any decision that gets made always considers the "impact" it will have on their customers. This is Customer Obsession and a key component for why Amazon is as successful as they are today.

Customer Obsessed Leaders change their focus on what is at the center of their company. They move from being "Product/Service-Centric" to "Customer-Centric." They make decisions differently. They ask different questions, and their primary focus is on "**how it will impact their customers**" ahead of how a product will fit into their product line. Or they would ask, "*How would adding this product to our existing line benefit our customers?*" The questions change because the focus has changed.

As the questions change, so does everything else. The information they need to run the business changes (you'll hear more about this in the chapter on "**Measure What You Don't Measure**." The way they interact with their customers and employees changes. How they make decisions changes. And how they allocate resources (money, personnel, and equipment) changes.

Customer Obsessed leaders are 100% focused on their customers.

Leaders need to be more connected with how they treat their customers in all areas of the business. They focus on activities that allow them to grow and enhance the "Cornerstones" of The "*REMARK*"able Triangle™. Leaders focus on how they are doing concerning each Cornerstone. For example, they will now track the percentage of "promises being kept" as a new measurement in developing their culture and new DNA.

Let's say you run a distribution company. If you are like most distribution companies today, you focus on working with the best manufacturers to get the best products at the best prices. You also focus on logistics. You want to get these products into the end customer's hands as smoothly and as quickly as possible. Your systems and operations support making this happen. And if you do a great job of this, they will use you for more goods and services. You make money on the goods you carry and the efficiency of getting the goods to your customer.

What does it look like when this distribution company is Customer Obsessed? How do the priorities change? How does the traditional model change to put the customer at the center of everything you do?

As a leader, your meetings would start by asking several questions focused on your customers rather than products and logistics. They would include feedback you might have received (good or bad) and discussing "why" the customer felt this way and why they were saying these things. You would then talk about your products and services and any new ideas to enhance their business. You might create some teams to explore these further and see which ones have the most significant benefit to your customers, even if they didn't carry as high of margin as other products.

Then you might move on to employee recognition and rewarding those who the customers have been raving about. You might also be getting some financial updates on the Customer Lifetime Value (CLV) numbers and discuss strategies to keep your most valued customers. And you might even be talking about some specific customer appreciation programs you can put in place to recognize your customer's businesses for being so awesome. You might talk about how many new customers you got because your existing customers (and others) did your marketing for you and brought them to you. You would know just how much new business you got by becoming "*REMARK*"able™. And you might end by sharing how many new Advocates and Marketing Agents™ you have created.

This is what Customer Obsessed leaders do in their meetings. The focus has changed to how your business can make your customer's lives and/or businesses better tomorrow than they are today. What role can your business play in helping their business become the best it can be? What unique ideas would strictly benefit your customers? These are the types of questions and areas of focus Customer Obsessed leaders ask.

Customer Obsessed leaders are tremendous cheerleaders for their employees. After all, **Customer Obsession is all about culture**. It is who you have become and how you will act in everything you do. When this transition happens, and it will, leaders get a ton of ideas coming from their employees. The ideas will flow like a faucet. I'll warn you ahead of time...you will need a way to capture, evaluate, and implement them. And when you do, it will be a catalyst for generating even more ideas. It is fantastic...and the ideas you get will blow your mind...open the floodgates.

> **Sidebar/Cool Tool**: One way you can capture all of these incredibly creative and innovative ideas from your employees is to set up mailboxes where they can drop their ideas. You can use physical ones around your facility for those who might want to be anonymous. You can also set up email addresses they can send them to whenever they think of something. These emails are evaluated, prioritized, and rewarded by members of the leadership team. Try it...this works great and is easy to do.

Your employees will take more initiative and responsibility for how the customer feels. They will focus on building trust, treating them incredibly special, and will be creative in how they can help them improve their life and/or their business. Remember the Ritz Carlton story, where they allow each employee to spend up to $2,000 to fix a customer problem without getting anyone's authorization. They are entirely empowered to resolve an issue should it arise...right then, on the spot. How much do your employees have at their discretion to spend to fix a customer issue?

In the case of the Ritz Carlton, once the employee has resolved an issue for the customer, then they can talk about it and see what they can learn from it to prevent it from happening again or possibly build the new idea into their systems. Either way, it all starts with delighting the customer in a way your competitors don't. And since we are talking about leadership, I'll leave you with a question to think about as you continue to learn "WHAT" you can do to be Customer Obsessed.

> *"How would you lead your team of employees if your entire paycheck was based on what your customers said about your organization? What would you do differently if your paycheck was based on the percentage increase in Advocates and Marketing Agents™ at the end of the year?"*

Your perspective changes pretty quickly. It is the perspective your customer would love your company to have in place. Customer Obsession just allows you to be in direct alignment with your customers.

Now let me help you solve one of the most significant issues plaguing customers today...ANXIETY!

AKA

It is so much easier to be nice, to be respectful, to put yourself in your customers' shoes and try to understand how you might help, than it is to mend a broken customer relationship.

MARK CUBAN

There is an **INSTANT WIN** sitting in front of just about every organization right now...and most don't even see it...we miss it! It has the power to change your organization almost overnight.

Anxiety is the "**Silent Killer**" most organizations don't even know is happening inside their walls or out in the field. But since it is "Silent," it can be challenging to identify and eliminate. Customer Obsessed organizations are always on the hunt for where this "Silent Killer" may be hiding or where it is happening so they can flush it out and eliminate it.

If one of your primary strategies is to reduce (or eliminate) Customer Anxiety, your business will dramatically improve...guaranteed.

To help eliminate Anxiety from happening, at the source, I find it helpful to put yourself in your "customers shoes" as you think about how to stop it in your organization. The next time you are the customer, transacting with another company, ask yourself these questions...

- Do I feel any level of anxiety about "what is going to happen next?
- Do I understand what "the process" is going to be as a customer?
- Do I feel confident there will be "no surprises" along the way?
- Does the company I'm buying from have "the same outcome" in mind like me?

- Why am I feeling anxious or stressed?
- What would have to happen, so I don't feel anxious about any part of the experience I am about to have?

The answers to these questions will help you get your head around how your customers might be feeling when they interact with you. I can guarantee your customers are asking these same questions...formally or in their gut. These are the questions we all ask when we have an interaction with any organization.

The key is to "know in advance" what will eliminate your customer's anxiety. When you know, you can stop the "Silent Killer."

We are continually asking these questions whenever we embark on a new experience with a new (or existing) organization. Unfortunately, the answers (most of the time) tell us we are a bit anxious about an impending interaction. This is crazy. Why should I be spending any valuable "experience time" trying to figure out what will happen next when I should be enjoying the experience?

Customers can't concentrate on having (and enjoying) an incredibly awesome and amazing experience if they're anxious about what will happen next...no one can.

Customers are either enjoying the fantastic experience or worrying about what is going to happen next. They can't do both...and your customers can't either. What experience are they going to be having...the one where they are thoroughly enjoying the interaction or one where they are worrying and stressing over what will happen next?

Eliminating anxiety is solved by focusing on one word...ANTICIPATION. AKA stands for "ANTICIPATION KILLS ANXIETY."

ANTICIPATION is the key to changing the experience a customer has with your organization. It doesn't matter whether you are B2C, B2B, small business, large business, or not for profit...the **"Ability to Kill Anticipation"** will help you become a "*REMARK*"able™ organization. This one simple word has the potential to change the experience a customer has with an organization quickly and dramatically...almost immediately.

Anticipation is the missing ingredient for almost every organization that creates (unnecessary) anxiety with their customers. The question we need to answer is, "***Why aren't we communicating with our audience in a way that helps lower or eliminate their anxiety about their experience?***" It's the one question leadership (and everyone) should be asking (and answering) every day.

Our systems, procedures, and processes often create anxiety, not eliminate it. WHAT?!?

Unfortunately, Anxiety happens because of our processes and customer experience. Customer Obsessed companies change from being an "**anxiety-based system**" to an organization where they "**anticipate**" events before they happen to eliminate anxiety. Anxiety gets built into our processes...it's just how we conduct business today. So, while the concept of eliminating anxiety with anticipation sounds simple, making the necessary changes can be much more involved. Let's look at an example...

Think about your organization for a minute. You have specific ways of doing things (your processes) when you interact with your customers. It's how you do business. When you look deep and analyze the interactions you have with your customers, you will see areas where your employees are creating customer anxiety. And while it would be nice to change (or eliminate) these, changing these processes could wreak havoc inside the organization. You can't just tell someone (or a group) to stop doing certain things, flip a switch, and it's fixed. But you can take some specific actions to start reducing it reasonably quickly.

The first step, like most areas of change, starts with "recognizing" there is an issue. Recognizing and creating awareness is the starting line. Spend some time answering the questions at the beginning of the chapter. It is a great place to start. Become educated and knowledgeable about what is happening inside your organization that is creating customer anxiety.

The next step is to start analyzing where in your organization anxiety is being created. It might be pervasive throughout the organization (as it is for most organizations). That's OK. Once you have identified the areas, prioritize them based on the impact each area has on the overall customer interaction.

> **HINT**: **Ask your customers** about their experience and where they feel you are creating anxiety for them or where they don't know (or are confused about) what will happen next. Find out what surprises they experience along the way. Find out how they feel about the entire process of working with you (from the first interaction throughout their Journey) from an "experience" perspective. Ask them if they ever "feel" anxious, stressed, or confused with any of their interactions. I guarantee you will be shocked by what you will hear. If you aren't, they're probably lying to you...they aren't telling you what is really happening or how they truly feel. They're trying to be nice. We need to move beyond nice and get the facts. These insights are invaluable in helping eliminate their anxiety.

If you read my first book, ***Creating and Delivering Totally Awesome Customer Experiences***," hopefully you created your "Customer Experience Maps" for each area of your business. If so, you know what "should be happening" throughout your customer experience. If you haven't done this type of mapping yet, start by writing down the overall process you do today when interacting with your customers...this will be a great starting point.

Here's the critical question I want you to think about for a few minutes before continuing. **When you KNOW your processes, you KNOW what is going to happen next (most of the time)**. Ask yourself...

> ***"Why are we not COMMUNICATING all this information to our customer...in advance...so they know what will be happening next, and***

we can alleviate their anxiety about the process and the desired outcome?"

Answering this question is the heart of AKA...ANTICIPATION Kills Anxiety.

The word "**ANTICIPATION**" means "**knowing the information BEFORE your customer knows it.**" Then "**sharing it with them as early as possible**" so you can **ANTICIPATE** their concerns (and unknowns). Then you can put their mind at ease and relieve their anxiety. Anxiety gets created with the UNKNOWN. When we don't know what is going to happen next, we get anxious. When we don't know the outcome of something, we get a little more anxious. One of the most common causes of anxiety in customers is that they simply don't know what you know, and we aren't communicating it to them...we make them wait. **Why do we do this?**

It happens because we aren't a Customer Obsessed organization. We are thinking more about our own needs as a company, getting our work completed on a timely basis without errors, showing up on time, and focusing on product or process quality. For example, when I look at employee position descriptions, I never see a requirement for accountability to reduce customer anxiety. This needs to change. And if you make this change, I can guarantee that the company's focus will change from "internally focused" to "customer-focused." This is a massive step towards being Customer Obsessed and becoming "*REMARK*"able™.

When we know what will happen next and don't communicate it to our customers, we are feeding (and growing) our customers' anxiety. It's like watching your young child sledding down a hill, and you look ahead and see an obstacle in their way. When you see that the outcome will be harmful if they hit the obstacle, you jump up and either stop them or remove the obstacle...you don't let them hit it. We know the outcome in advance, and we remove it, so there is a much more positive outcome.

Knowing the potential outcome (with high probability) and not communicating this to our customer is like letting your kid hit the obstacle. You can fix this...and your customers will LOVE IT. Every time I talk about this in a speech or meeting, almost everyone starts nodding...everyone gets it. They are picturing this happening when they are a customer. They now realize they are "creating" anxiety in their customers. It is truly an ah-ha moment. They now see just how crazy this is...but they never thought about it this way.

Once leaders understand AKA's concept, they start writing AKA on their walls, on their computer screens, on their phones, and in other places throughout their business. They remind themselves always to be thinking "proactively" about communicating with their customers...sharing future outcomes.

For example, one client in the financial sector told me they put it on their computer screens. Now, whenever they get information their customer would want to know about, they immediately pass it along to them...well ahead of them asking for it. They would tell you this one simple change has gotten them more "atta boy's" and compliments than anything else they have recently done. It works...and it will work for you. Challenge your employees to try it and then have everyone share the results, the thank you's, and the positive comments they hear back from their customers. It's a game-changer for your employees and your culture.

There are lots of opportunities for us to improve on this throughout the organization. You know the obstacles or issues throughout the entire customer experience, and you usually know what will happen next in the process. You may also know the usual outcome. If you know all this with some degree of certainty, why not share it...proactively. AKA focuses on eliminating their stress and anxiety when working with your organization.

Now you know AKA...ANTICIPATION KILLS ANXIETY.

Here's another example you may be able to relate to in your business. In this particular company, a Cybersecurity company has customers who have common security issues. The customer is extremely anxious about these issues. And even as technology savvy as many of us are today, cybersecurity is still mysterious to most people. The customer is very fearful of what could happen because there are many "unknowns" in this area. They've been "surprised" with some bad things happening to their systems and possibly their data. They need an expert to help them get through this and put some corrective strategies in place to hopefully prevent or reduce this issue from happening in the future.

The cybersecurity company is Customer Obsessed...they help relieve their customer's anxiety from the initial call. A company representative calls you up and asks a series of questions to understand your issue fully...they listen really well. After you have answered all their questions, they instantly give you some "immediate relief" by letting you know the outcome they expect to get. They say something like this...

"Thank you for all the information, that was very helpful. Based on what you have told me, I want you to know I believe we can eliminate all of these issues, or at least the majority of them, and establish a plan to work on the few remaining ones. Let me share with you exactly what will happen as we work together, so you know what will be happening every step of the way. I don't want to leave you wondering what will happen next, and I don't want you to have any surprises. Essentially, you will know our desired outcome and what will be happening throughout the entire effort. Our goal is to do everything we can to give you an incredible experience and put your mind at ease. I want to get you back to doing what you do best without any anxiety or worry. How does that sound to you?"

As you can see from this powerful description, the cybersecurity company is preempting the customer's issues. They are the experts in this area and have done this many times before, so they know precisely what areas create customer anxiety and how to eliminate them before they occur. I would presume you have the same situation. You have been doing what you do for some time and know the process and outcomes very well. You've done this over and over again. If you have, why not devise a plan to communicate this in advance, proactively, and in detail to your customer? It will eliminate their anxiety...guaranteed.

We are all guilty of doing this to our customers. Here's why...

First, employees may not know what is going to happen next to the customer. They may know their job and their responsibility with the customer but not thoroughly educated on what will happen next when others get involved. It is a legitimate reason why an employee can't communicate the process and outcomes to a customer. However, you can easily correct this in several ways. First, document the process for how they interact with the customer. This is what Customer Experience Mapping is all about and the core of my first book, "*Creating and Delivering Totally Awesome Customer Experiences*." We talked briefly about how to do this in the chapter "**The MAP to the Treasure.**"

Second, employees feel like they don't want to "commit" to something they can't deliver on. Employees are very reluctant to talk about anything with a variable or go in a different direction than planned. They worry the customer would call them on it. It might make them look bad and not make the customer happy. So rather than committing to something they aren't entirely sure will happen, they say nothing. This situation is common and occurs when employees don't feel empowered or need approval before proceeding.

There is one crucial element to keep in mind when we talk about Customer Obsessed organizations. They are much "flatter" in organizational structure...giving their employees control to solve issues on the spot. Employees know the process and outcome and let the customer know there could be some bumps along the way. But they tell them not to worry since they will knock them down together. The key is to communicate with them with the intent of alleviating their anxiety in advance.

Confusion among your employees is a leading cause of Customer Anxiety.

Here are some questions I would encourage you to ask your leadership team about your organization...

- Do we "proactively" communicate (regularly) with our customers, so they have minimal (if any) anxiety with each interaction?
- Do we empower our employees to take care of any customer issue without delay?
- Do we have Customer Experience Maps to guide our employees through interactions as part of the overall customer experience?
- Do we have a "disaster plan" where our employees know what to do to resolve a problem on the spot?
- Do we "over-communicate" with our customers and keep them apprised of everything going on with their situation? Do we do this ahead of when things are going to happen?

When you have an "Anticipation Kills Anxiety" (AKA) strategy in place, you can answer these questions quickly. AKA is proactive and empowering...giving your employees the tools to anticipate and solve problems BEFORE they become known to your customers.

AKA relieves customer anxiety.

Education and communication are vital in reducing or eliminating Customer Anxiety. Once employees are comfortable delivering an incredibly awesome and amazing experience to the customer, they confidently "**anticipate**" what will happen next in the customer experience and Journey. When employees can anticipate something with a high degree of accuracy, **they willingly communicate this to the customer.**

Now picture how the AKA approach (and process) would work in your own business or organization. Envision a customer going through your ordering process, your dining process, your sky diving process, your purchasing process, your service process, or whatever process you have in place to deliver your desired experience. As you do, I hope you can start to see the opportunities available to your company if you were to use the **AKA (Anticipation Kills Anxiety)** strategy.

And here's the BIG BENEFIT to AKA. When your customers aren't stressed, aren't anxious, and aren't going to get surprised, they can sit back and enjoy their experience with your company. And when they can enjoy their experience (and Journey), they have more time (and ammunition) to share with others...**they have time to do your marketing for you**! They become your Advocates and Marketing Agents™!

When your customers talk about how stressful it is dealing with your competitors and how it is virtually stress-free interacting with you, YOU WIN. And who doesn't want to work with a company that purposefully helps lower their stress and anxiety? Everyone wants this...and now you are the one doing it. You will be the one they tell others about. It is just another reason why you can STOP MARKETING because your customers are now dying to do it for you. You're becoming "*REMARK*"able™.

When your customers aren't anxious about what will happen next and feel entirely confident that you will deliver the desired outcome, they can participate in the experience and enjoy themselves. When customers can stop focusing on their anxiety and start focusing on their feelings about the experience they are receiving, they can create very positive memories about their experience. It tells them you are different, memorable, and you have elevated your organization above your competitors. Congratulations!

I hope you have picked up throughout the book that **CUSTOMERS LOVE TO TALK ABOUT THEIR EXPERIENCES**. Creating and facilitating ways for your customer to tell others about how incredibly awesome and amazing you are is the primary goal for why you can STOP MARKETING...because your customers are "REMARKING" about YOU. Here's something to ponder...

When you think about AKA strategically, why wouldn't this be the mission of your company? To "ELIMINATE CUSTOMER ANXIETY!"

How incredible would your business (or organization) look to your customers if every employee rallied around this simple yet incredibly powerful Mission? And how differentiating would you look to your customers if they saw this from everyone inside your organization?

I don't know why any company wouldn't want this to be the focus of their business. It rallies and energizes your employees while delighting your customers. How about your company? Could it be your new Mission Statement? Something to think about. Now let's move to how we can measure our success...it isn't what you might think.

Measure What You Don't Measure

In business, the idea of measuring what you are doing, picking the measurements that count like customer satisfaction and performance...you thrive on that.

BILL GATES

Do you measure what truly drives your business? Do you measure your word-of-mouth free marketing? Do you measure the ROI of your Advocates?

Today, everyone wants to measure everything...more than I have ever seen in my career. The desire to measure is rising every day. Many new careers (and companies) started because of this quest for more data and more analytics to prove whatever it is we want to prove. There is no shortage of data in the world we live in today. But is it the right data?

Is it the "right data" to tell you how your business is really running? I'm sure you have fine-tuned the financial, product/service, and operational data. But what about your "**Customer data**?" Do you have any? If you do, is it mostly focused on the acquisition of new customers? Does it focus on churn and customer loyalty or retention? Does it track Customer Lifetime Value (CLV) and other measurements to show customer movement? Do you have in-depth customer data and analysis?

As you have read throughout this book, I prefer to keep things simple and straightforward so more people (rather than fewer) can understand and act upon it. The more people who understand the analytics and results, the easier it is to rally them around an area of focus or change their behavior.

The concept of "Big Data" never existed before the internet...or at least it wasn't that big. Today, we have so much data available it isn't just big. It's enormous! Much of it has to do with production and efficiency. Can we produce more without adding any additional time or cost? Can we make this process more efficient and not spend as much time on it as we have in the past? Can we eliminate some of the things we are doing because they are impeding our efficiency or adding more cost to the product or service? These types of questions get asked every day, and there are people (or systems) standing by to crunch the numbers and give us the answers. Efficiency. Cost Reduction. Throughput improvement. More efficient processes. And more.

Just because you can capture more data and produce more analytics (and reports) doesn't mean you should...unless they are the right analytics.

I would suggest you measure one more thing...perhaps the most critical.

Measure what your customers want you to measure...and improve upon.

Unfortunately, not much of what I have talked about throughout the book is measured today. Not because it isn't important or shouldn't be measured. It just isn't in the measurement mix today. It's hard to track and measure something that may not even be in existence today. How can you measure what isn't being tracked? You can't. I hope after reading this book, you are starting to think about some new areas you should be measuring.

For example, how many companies honestly measure the growth of their Advocates? Or, for that matter, how many even know what an Advocate is to them to measure it? The same goes for word-of-mouth...understood but not usually measured consistently.

When it comes to measuring, we need to have a common language that is well-defined and understood by everyone. We need to have a new language, just like we have for anything that is new and isn't part of our standard processes. Defining it is essential to act upon it.

The first step in this part of the Journey is defining certain areas where we want to start measuring and collecting data. Identifying these areas will be critically important as we build our Customer Obsessed organization. We will have **a common language** to talk about, and everyone will understand it so we can work to improve upon it.

What is this "new" language we need to learn?

I'm sure as you read through the book, you saw many opportunities to measure something different...most leaders do. Let's look at some of the most important Key Performance Indicators (KPIs) you might want to start incorporating into your leadership reports.

CUSTOMER SEGMENTATION...this is a big one but also one of the easier ones to figure out. Measuring customer segmentation focuses on identifying the customers who fit into specific segments based on various factors, such as revenue, longevity as a customer, frequency of purchasing, etc. Two more challenging aspects to quantify yet are incredibly important to identify are the "ease of working with" and "future opportunity." But these will give you much greater insight into which customers are the "right" customers to focus on as a company.

Once you have these various factors identified, it's essential to weigh them to determine their importance to your organization. Now you can create a "**Customer Opportunity Dashboard**" to give your customers a score within each area you identified. You now know a customer's relative importance to your business. The frequency you assess is based on the frequency by which your customers change or are added.

CUSTOMER OBSESSION ALIGNMENT...this is an exciting measurement because it aligns the customers you identified within your Customer Segmentation analysis with how well these customers fit within your Customer Obsession Journey. Let me explain with an example. Let's say you have identified ABC company as one at the top of your Customer Segmentation analysis. But as you identify more of your Customer Obsession Journey components, you realize they aren't aligned. The Customer Experience you offer and the ways you Consistently Help customers don't align with what it takes to serve the ABC company.

Now what? If you are out of alignment, one of two things is most likely occurring. You either have the wrong customer, or the cornerstone components of The "*REMARK*"able Triangle™ need to be modified to better serve this customer. ABC Company is an ideal customer for you based on your segmentation analysis...you would want more of these customers.

When this is the case, you need to reassess the elements of The "*REMARK*"able Triangle™ and see what areas need to be modified to align with what the ABC company wants or needs. When you identify these areas, you can adjust your promises, experience, and ways to help this new customer feel special and important during their experience. Tweaking the alignment will help you attract more ideal customers, based on your customer segmentation analysis. It's essential to regularly do this analysis to ensure your customers align with your Customer Obsession focus and Journey.

PROMISES...this area requires some ongoing analysis and measurement of a different nature. For example, do you have a formula like the one I shared in the chapter on "**Promises, Promises, Promises**?" If not, this is a new analytic and measurement you will want to inject into your leadership dashboard. As you may remember from that chapter, keeping the promises you make is an absolutely essential foundational element for building Trust, Relationships, Loyalty, and ultimately, Advocacy.

And since "**Trust is the currency of the Customer Economy,**" identifying your Promise Inventory™ and tracking the improvement in "Promises Kept" is vital to becoming "*REMARK*"able™. Trust is by far the most critical cornerstone you need to become "*REMARK*"able™. Without Trust, the engine has fallen off the boat...you're dead in the water. Developing a way to capture your promise data to feed your overall Promise Score is a linchpin for the organization. We always want Promises Made (PM) = Promises Kept (PK) to equal 100%.

There here are more elements of the Advocacy Architecture™ to measure...

TRUST. Once you measure the Promises (PM = PK) level in your organization, next up the ladder to Advocacy is Trust. Trust is a critical measurement with your customers since **NO ONE WILL EVER "REMARK" (OR TALK) ABOUT YOU IF THEY DON'T TRUST YOU.** Knowing this, wouldn't it behoove us to make this is one of our key areas of measurement?

Since you are already capturing Promises, how can you capture Trust? Trust is one of those "end result" measurements you can regularly see and see if it went up or down. You can get pretty sophisticated in how you want to measure trust, but there is one sure way to find out if this is moving up or down...**ask your customers.**

For example, when I interview customers, one of my primary questions is, "***Do you trust the ABC company? Completely and without hesitation?***" There are only two real answers to this question...yes or no. There is no "sort of" trust you. And there are two ways to figure this out easily...

> **First**, if the customer hesitates at all, they don't really trust you. Hesitation means they had to think about it, so they aren't 100% convinced they trust you...at least not in everything you do with every employee with every interaction. There is an underlying issue somewhere looming in the back of their mind. **Second**, if they "sort of" trust you...or they trust Bob or Sally, or the shipping department but not the sales department, then my response is the same, they don't trust you. Knowing why they don't trust you is incredibly important...it gives us a place to focus.

It is a gold mine for information when you ask them why they don't trust certain groups or people. They give you rich and helpful answers. If they trust you as a company, my next question is, "*Why do you trust them?*" Again, massive amounts of helpful information for you to analyze.

When it comes to analyzing and measuring Trust, it gets scored as "don't trust" or "trust." Measuring this number by customer is an excellent Customer Obsession Dashboard measurement.

CUSTOMER LOYALTY. Calculating customer Loyalty and Retention or Churn has been around for a while. Depending on your industry, measuring retention may have received the most attention. Having spent some time working in the communications industry, "churn" is the one word they focus on the most...how many customers did we lose today compared to how many we gained.

For example, if they run a particular marketing campaign, they look to see if they are picking up enough new customers to offset those leaving. Crazy game. Their customers are generally loyal to the price or "the deal" they are getting, not to the company or how well they are treated.

Measuring churn isn't the way to focus on Customer Loyalty.

Focusing on ways to create greater loyalty with your customer that does not involve "price" or other types of commodity elements is where companies find their most significant opportunity to become "*REMARK*"able™.

The most important place to start measuring Customer Loyalty is to determine your Client/Customer Lifetime Value (CLV)...especially for your top customers. What is the value they bring to your organization over the lifetime of their relationship? When you do the math, you get a completely different view of your customers and the real value they bring to your organization. Here's a simple formula to get you started (they get more complicated as you start capturing complex numbers in each area)...

> (Average Value of a Customer Transaction) x (Number of Recurring Transactions in Months/Years) x (Average Retention in Months/Years)...then subtract the cost of acquisition and ongoing support of this customer over the same period of time = the **LIFETIME VALUE OF THE CUSTOMER (CLV)**.

Looking at a simple example, if the average transaction for a particular customer was $500 and they purchased from you four times a year, this would give you a total revenue of $2,000 each year. If this customer stayed with you for five years, their estimated lifetime revenue for your company would be $10,000. However, to know the actual value (and profitability), you would need to subtract the cost to acquire and maintain this customer. Let's say it cost you $1,000 to initially acquire the customer and $250 per year to maintain them as a customer (your internal cost to support them). You would have a total cost of $2,000 (over the same 5-year period) to support this customer. When you subtract the revenues' costs, you end up netting $8,000 of gross profit for this particular customer...their "VALUE" over their "LIFETIME."

Looks like a pretty good customer, right? Absolutely! This analysis should be done "by customer" and shows each customer's return and value over a period of time. If you have thousands of customers, you may want to do this for a group of customers...a segment. Then you can compare the different segments to see which ones give you the greatest return. You can make some more strategic decisions based on some real metrics about your customers and their behaviors. There are two ways to really leverage this analysis.

First, figure out ways to increase the "average retention rate" of this customer segment. Every year you can keep them as a customer, you generate more profitability because the revenue will consistently exceed the costs to maintain them after their acquisition. CLV should be a very active strategy for leadership to incorporate into its Customer Obsession Strategic Plan and Dashboard.

Second, figure out ways to "get more" of these types of customers. The more customers you can get, who fit into this segment, will generate high CLV for all your customers...it is a great way to grow your profitability. Customer Obsessed organizations "attract" these customers "away from their competitors" because of how they treat them compared to their competitors. **Word spreads like a Range Fire.** The customers in these segments talk to other customers (just like them) and tell them they should work with you because of how awesome they are treated. The customers leave the competition and come over to you, the Customer Obsessed company. You can now reap the rewards of becoming "*REMARK*"able™ to your ideal segment's customers.

I don't know about you, but as a business leader (and owner), this makes a boatload of sense to me. Why would I not want as many customers as I could handle in the segment that makes me the most money...and then keep them for a very long time? Wouldn't you?

You can only do this if you are focused on CLV as a core measurement and metric in your business. It is powerful stuff...and it's sitting right in front of you. That's a formula for SUCCESS!

> **CAUTION:** This can really mess with your "marketing ROI" if you let it. For example, let's say you have high acquisition costs today...higher than your revenue for the customer. If marketing runs the ROI on this customer, it will look bad. The acquisition cost will exceed the revenue in the first year (and maybe the second year). If you do a "short-term ROI" on this customer, you will determine they are too expensive and look for other customers and segments. It could be an enormous mistake. You could be missing the gold mine because the vein of gold stopped just before you hit the big payday. Don't let marketing ROI stop you from getting all the gold possible from a critical customer segment.

Use some historical analysis to see what the "estimated CLV" could look like...this is a "long-tailed" view. When you do this analysis, you might just find this customer segment could be one of your biggest paydays and one you should be aggressively going after, despite the high initial acquisition costs.

Spend some time with this and put some hours of discussion and analysis into this model. I can guarantee you will come out with a better direction and have a much stronger game plan for which customer segments you should go after today and well into the future. Remember, if you are Customer Obsessed, you have a long-tail view of the world, and you know you can extend your ideal customers' lifetime because they will love working with you and want to stay much longer.

RETURN ON MARKETING...wait a minute, I thought we were supposed to "STOP MARKETING?" Great catch...if you caught this. You are correct. We aren't marketing in the old, more traditional "pimping" ways...we are doing "Customer Marketing," where we are focused on "helping" our customers, not shoving promotion after promotion down their throat and wondering why we have a .001% return. When you market with a different mentality and focus, marketing can deliver outstanding results and support for your organization. Let's look at this in a bit more detail...

> **"Customer Marketing" is explicitly focused on "how can you help your customer improve their life and/or their business.**

As you may remember from our discussion on The *"REMARK"*able Triangle™ model, the Triangle's third area is "Consistently Helping" your audience. Customer Obsession focuses on helping your customers improve their lives and/or their business. Customer Obsessed organizations create a Marketing Plan concentrated on ways to be "helpful to their segments" of customers. The Plan focuses on each segment, their needs, desires, and what will help them in their life and/or business.

When you know this level of detail about your audiences, you can truly help them in their life and/or their business. You can design a "**Consistently Helping Marketing Plan.**" You can measure how they respond to your content and other ways to improve their life and/or their business. This is the only "**Customer Obsessed Marketing Plan**" you need...do more of what they appreciate and find of value and less (or eliminate) what they don't value. Sounds too simple? "**Why make something that is simple more complex?**" The goal of this book is to keep things simple, so everyone gets it and can work towards the common goal of being Customer Obsessed. Simple gets executed...complicated doesn't.

Measuring all the "return on the content" you share with your audience will give you tremendous insight into what they want and don't want from you. Evaluate all the materials you share with them to learn what consistently helps your audience.

Now you can STOP MARKETING for "your benefit" and START MARKETING for "your customer's benefit." Now you are on the path to Customer Obsession and becoming "*REMARK*"able™.

As you have probably figured out by now, the best place to start identifying what to measure is by analyzing the Customer Journey and The *"REMARK"*able Triangle™. Let these two be your guide on what to measure and what metrics to capture. The key is to start measuring the components and elements that help you become Customer Obsessed. These are the areas of most importance (and value) to your customer. And when you measure what's important to your customer, it is enlightening how much information they are willing to share.

Most feedback collected from our customers is garbage...it doesn't tell us what they really feel or think...it just checks off some boxes.

I am continually asked how to get the best feedback from customers. Everyone wants to do surveys and use other "easy" data capture tools. I disagree with this approach. They are great for "checking off" that you asked your customers for some feedback but are a waste of time in providing in-depth and insightful information about how your customer "feels" or what is "important" and of "value" to them. The audience that fills them out is generally not an ideal sampling of how your overall customer audience feels about you and how you treat them. They don't provide any competitive differentiators or what you can do to improve to beat your competition...they can't.

If you really want to get deep and rich information from your customer, talk to them. Ask them directly. Or better yet, have someone on the outside ask them for you. You'll get even better information. It is like tapping into the vein of gold!

When an organization gets lazy (and cheap), they do surveys. If you want information quick and cheap, stick to surveys. If you want information that is "actionable and insightful," then design a plan to talk to your customers. I know the survey companies will be all over this and tell me how off course I am...I'm not...and they know it as well.

Talking to customers takes time and is more expensive. But when done correctly, the information is worth so much more than whatever you paid to collect it. Having someone from the outside doing this for you will get much more in-depth and honest information than your employees (or leadership) can ever get. Customers just open up more if they feel it is "anonymous" and are captured as "part of the overall population" than when someone internal asks them these questions.

Look at the "Content" you are producing for your audience. Are you doing blogs, or videos, or podcasts? If you aren't, start. Find out which format(s) your respective segments enjoy and put together a "library" of content they can view whenever they want. They will find it valuable and will consume it. They will quickly see you genuinely care about them and want more...and they will tell you what they want! They won't be telling this to your competitors. They will be asking them why they don't do the same...score one for you! Measure the content that works...do more of it.

Let me give you a specific example. A service company that did repairs on physical systems did things differently. They found customers had short memories. The customer forgot what they had done and would call them back to refresh their memory...a big "time suck" for both the company and the customer. As a Customer Obsessed organization, they brainstormed and came up with a way to start videoing the service call and sharing it with their customers. They made these available so their customers could easily access them whenever they needed a refresher. They loved this added service. They were able to acquire some "free" customers because their customers were telling others...they became "*REMARK*"able™.

Measuring Customer Obsession may be more in-depth than you might have first imagined, yet it is actually much more straightforward than most realize. It is an incredibly fun area to spend time in, and you'll begin to know more about your customers than you ever dreamed possible. It is a great way to differentiate your company in the marketplace. Rest assured, your competitors are not thinking this way. Start measuring...

The "First Stop" on The Customer Journey

The vast majority of small business owners want nothing to do with figuring out a website. They are neck-deep in their business trying to keep it going.

ANDREW YANG

For many, the search for your company or learning more about who you are begins at your website. Does yours "speak at" your audience or "speak to" your audience? Does it immediately start telling them who you are and what you do, or does it help them identify who they are and guide them to what they need?

Customer Obsessed websites are different...they focus on your audience. Does your site immediately tell them you are there to "help them," or does it immediately try to "sell them?" Does it have a blog (or other areas) designed to "help" them, whether they buy from you or not? Does it "start a relationship" or merely "give them information?" Does it cause them to say, "*WOW, this site is speaking directly to me,*" or does it say, "*Here's another site that is just like all the others I've seen...trying to sell me stuff.*"

Your website is often your first introduction to your audience...and you may never know they were there...or they stay and see you as different.

For many companies, websites have become just another "online brochure" that tells them who you are and what you do. They don't speak to the audience in a way and in a language that will cause them to feel like you are different...like you care...and most of all, you genuinely want to help them...whether they buy from you or not. Regardless of how someone got to your website, it is usually the first exposure they have to your company. **What does yours say to them?**

Here's a simple illustration that might help. When someone comes to your office or business, what is the first thing you do? Would you give them the catalog for all your products and services and tell them to look through them, figure out what they want, and then come back to the counter to place their order? Of course not. But this is exactly what happens with many websites. We don't ask "who they arc" or "what is their need" or "what can we do to help them in their life and/or their business," we just give them our product catalog and tell them to figure it out.

Your web presence shouldn't be any different than if you were greeting someone in person...which essentially you are...only virtually. We can't build a relationship when we act like a commodity...either in person or via our web presence.

Here are some quick ways which will help you change this dynamic. My **first recommendation** is to not start with a web designer. They are experts at putting things together that work well for the site's efficiency and the way it looks and flows. They have a role...but it's not in the beginning. The beginning should be you designing what you want to communicate...to whom...and with appropriate messaging, which will resonate well beyond your sales pitch. Your website should start with "**Why.**"

My **second recommendation** is to identify the Personas of your desired customer segments, as we have discussed in the last few chapters. Who is it you want to be marketing to, selling to, and WOWing? When you know the audience, you are well on your way to understanding your communication strategy. The audience is critically important. We can't be all things to all people. We must know our audience in everything we do, and our web presence isn't any different.

My **third recommendation** is to create a list of how you can truly help these Personas (just follow the recipe in the chapters on The "*REMARK*"able™ Triangle™). If you create a detailed list of how you can help them improve their life and/or their business, you are well on your way to creating a Customer Obsessed web presence.

For example, if I am one of your chosen Personas and you specifically know how you can help improve my business (or my life), you are "speaking my language" when visiting your site. I see myself very clearly on your site and know that you are indeed talking to me and my needs. When I see you care about me,

I'm far more interested in exploring the content you have available. I quickly realize you care about me.

The **fourth recommendation** is to show me "HOW" your products and services will help improve my life and/or my business. Now you can take your products and services and personalize them to help me solve my issue or question. You share what clearly demonstrates you understand me, my problems, and the "tailored solution" you have for me. Even though your products and services may be the same across all segments, you show me how they specifically help me, not someone else.

I now know you care. I now know you understand my issues and problems. I now realize you have solutions that specifically address my needs. When you know your "**why**" and "**how,**" you can easily communicate it through online tools, such as a website. Starting with your WHY and HOW, not the design, will allow you to bring your story (and your web presence) to life.

The **fifth and final recommendation** is to call in the web designer. Now is when they should enter the picture. You will lay out all the work you have done in the first four recommendations and ask them to put this together in a very current, pleasing, and beautiful website. Now they have all the information they need to design your site.

Your website will now be Customer Obsessed. It will be a place your audience looks forward to visiting because it speaks specifically to them in a way they can easily relate to. It will also a "helping site" where they can get assistance and answers, not just be sold or do a transaction. It will become a valuable resource your audience will want to visit often, not only when they want to buy something from you.

Most importantly, your web presence will help you become "*REMARK*"able™. It will be a place where your audience gets the information they can't wait to "share" with their friends and colleagues.

Your audience can now refer their friends and colleagues to your site because it is so helpful. They can grab your content they found relevant and send it (or share it via social channels) to others. They can become your Advocate and Marketing Agent™. This is the ultimate goal for your web presence...create something so helpful and useful your audience can't wait to share it with others...others just like them.

Let's say I see something on your site that I find particularly interesting and helpful regarding how to plan for my financial future (The ten things I need to have in place before I retire). It is a very insightful, helpful, and non-selling article. If I am your Advocate and trust you and your organization, I will happily post this on my social accounts, such as Twitter or Facebook. **I just did your marketing for you**...I became your Advocate and Marketing Agent™. It cost you nothing beyond the cost to prepare the material. And I marketed it for you with high credibility since my audience trusts me.

Here's why becoming "*REMARK*"able™ is so critically important for an organization. I'm just one person...but I have the potential to reach 10,000 people with who I'm connected online. If only 1% of my audience (a very tiny percentage) acted on this and checked it (and your business) out, you would get 100 free visitors. And they would be coming in with a level of trust for you already established because they got it from me, someone they trust.

But here's the kicker...I'm just one person in your audience. Let's say that out of your audience, ten people, just like me, shared this content the same way. When this happens, you just picked up 1000 new visitors to check you out...for free. And this is just the first level of sharing. If this new group of 1000 people shared this with their audiences (assuming they have only 1000 people in their audiences), you just reached 1,000,000 people! Now let's say only 1% of these new people check you out. You just picked up 10,000 new people checking you out...who trust you more than any promotion you could ever run yourself...and all this benefit came for free.

How can you NOT get excited about this? How can you NOT want to create a website and presence that generates this "sharing machine" for your company? How can you NOT want all this free marketing?

When you have a website that supports your overall Customer Obsessed culture and strategy, you get these kinds of benefits...for free. You now have a website that supports your goal to become "*REMARK*"able™, and it's returning great benefits to you. It's a website I'm excited to visit and share...and help you promote. And it doesn't shove an online brochure or "sign up today box" in my face every time I come to visit you. This is a Customer Obsessed web presence. When you create this type of site, you can STOP MARKETING because your audience uses your website to help do your marketing for you!

Are you getting excited and anxious to get started? If so, let's get things put into motion...let's LAUNCH it!

Are you READY??

The way to get started is to quit talking and begin doing.

WALT DISNEY

OK, you're done reading the book. Now you have two choices. Are you ready to LAUNCH, or do you need more time to digest all this and figure out your action plan? Either way works. My goal was to accomplish three things for you throughout the book...

First, to help you understand WHY becoming "*REMARK*"able™ by being Customer Obsessed is so critically important for your success as a business or organization given today's Customer Economy.

Second, to help give you a RECIPE and FORMULA for HOW you can be Customer Obsessed and become "*REMARK*"able™...and STOP MARKETING.

Third, to help answer your questions for WHY WOULDN'T YOU DO IT...and give you the motivation and information to GET STARTED!

I hope you have learned something and now feel more empowered to make this happen in your organization. I also hope you can see all the benefits, besides just the financial ones, of being Customer Obsessed and becoming "*REMARK*"able™. But what I really hope you see is how this can move your CULTURE and DNA (and your entire organization) to one that is **truly differentiated** in the eyes of your customer.

There were some primary (and underlying) goals I set out to accomplish when I wrote this book. Without question, my number one goal was to expose business leaders to the model of Customer Obsession and how you can truly differentiate your business. Because, when you are totally and completely differentiated and loved by your customers, you get your audience of Advocates and Marketing Agents™ telling everyone they know how incredibly awesome and amazing you are to work with...becoming "*REMARK*"able™.

My goal to help you **STOP MARKETING** and start "**INVESTING**" in your customer is equally powerful...I hope this caught your attention. You don't need to do all this "pimping" in the marketplace if your audience tells everyone they know how much they TRUST you and that you are the only one to work with and buy from. Investing in your customers using **The "*REMARK*"able Triangle™** has significantly more benefit (financial and otherwise) than any marketing campaign you could ever generate.

When your audience of TRUSTED customers (and others) are out there throwing your name around (proactively) for free, it's a tough formula to beat...it simply works and delivers a high return. If you take nothing else away from this book, **adopt the Advocacy Architecture™** as a core foundation for your organization. While it won't make you Customer Obsessed, it will definitely improve your business...and quickly.

Keep the Promises you make, and the difference will be almost immediately noticeable to your customers (and employees).

The "*REMARK*"able Triangle™ is a very specific recipe and formula any organization can use. It's "dirt simple." I designed it so literally every organization on the planet could use it. I didn't want it to be complex...I just wanted it to get used. I want every employee in your organization to understand it and use it.

Simple = Execution.

I hope you saw that The "*REMARK*"able Triangle™ model is "common sense" and just makes sense. The model is easy to grasp and understand. Everyone gets it because it is what we, as customers, want. There isn't any part of the model you can't easily describe to someone. This makes it executable. It puts it in terms that every employee in any industry can easily grasp and execute.

I was giving a speech at a company retreat not that long ago, and as I talked about each component of The "*REMARK*"able Triangle™, you could see all the heads nodding. So, I asked them, "*I know by the nodding of your head this makes sense to you. The real question is whether it is simple and straightforward enough that every employee in your organization can change how they work to incorporate the Triangle's three elements?*" They unanimously said it was the first time they had seen a model they could literally explain to any employee using one sheet of paper. Employees would get this model...immediately!" I smiled...they got it.

I hope everyone reading this book will want to be a Customer Obsessed organization. And somewhere along your Journey become "*REMARK*"able™ so you, too, can reap all the benefits from having an army of Trusted Advocates and Marketing Agents™ doing your marketing for you. Every one of us would be better off (and happier) if this happened...we are all customers as well.

There are four levels where you could begin your Journey to being Customer Obsessed and becoming *"REMARK"*able™...

Level One...you take The *"REMARK"*able Triangle™ model and develop a strategy for transforming your organization into being Customer Obsessed. You feel comfortable and knowledgeable enough to move forward. If this sounds like where you are, and you feel comfortable enough at this point to make this happen from concept to implementation, CONGRATULATIONS!

If you are truly here and ready to dive in and start your Customer Obsession Journey, please check in with me from time to time and let me know how you are doing. This Level usually happens when an organization has already decided they want to be Customer Obsessed but just didn't have a recipe and formula for getting there. That's why it was so vital for me to keep the Promise I made you at the beginning of the book...to give you the exact formula you could follow to make it happen. Now you have it...go make it happen!

I would encourage you to become a regular reader of my blogs, check out the courses that I will be releasing soon, and plug into my other medium of podcasting and/or video to continually get updates on more stories, thinking, and ideas in this area. They will help you continually refine what you are doing so you can stay ahead of your competitors.

You may also want me to come in at some point early in the process and speak to your employees and answer some of their more in-depth questions about being Customer Obsessed. And if you ever need a bit more assistance from time to time or just want to bounce some ideas off me, we can chat.

Level Two...leaders will understand and get excited about the information and want to make it happen, but don't feel entirely comfortable how they should proceed to be successful at being Customer Obsessed. **This is the most common response**. Most of you will feel this way after reading the book. You get it, are excited about it, and see the benefits of being Customer Obsessed, but just aren't quite sure how to make it happen. If this is where you are, CONGRATULATIONS!

You are at a great juncture...you've decided you want to climb the mountain but just need some guidance to get the Journey started and get going. That's smart. Understanding the Journey before you just dive in always gets better results than "Ready, Fire, Aim." If this describes you, I recommend you create a strategy and a plan.

Shoot me a message or give me a call. You will find my contact information in the back of the book or on my website, WOM10.com. I can give you some more insights into how to get your Journey started for your particular organization. Not all organizations are the same, and so not every strategy is the same. Think of your strategy and plan as a "custom made suit" where one size does not fit everyone. You want it designed to fit your individual needs and situation...I can help you understand how you can make this happen.

Level Three...you really like the idea of becoming Customer Obsessed, but the timing might be off for making this happen. You could be in the middle of a significant acquisition, moving locations, or other issues that might need to be taken care of before getting started. I get it...and it makes perfect sense. Or you "get it" but feel like you need some additional information and knowledge before you begin your Journey. This is also very common among leaders who are first learning about Customer Obsession.

I have an easy way to continue moving forward but not committing the company to a transformation process right now. I created **The Customer Obsession Council** specifically for leaders just like you. It is a group where leaders, like yourself, come together to learn more about Customer Obsession. These Councils are packed with education and information to help you learn more. They are also full of tips and actions you can use today to help your organization move closer to the starting line of beginning your Journey.

The Council is an easy way to "dip your toe in the water" with Customer Obsession before undertaking the Journey. It's for those who want to be Customer Obsessed but just aren't sure how to make the leap. It's an excellent opportunity to explore Customer Obsession in more detail with other leaders in a similar situation. It's a low-risk way to further explore Customer Obsession before committing to "Burn the Ships." You can learn about The Customer Obsession Council on my website at WOM10.com.

The Final Level...Level Four...this is the most difficult one for me to hear and experience. This is where leaders feel Customer Obsession isn't for them. They haven't come to grips with the entire concept of commoditization and the power of differentiation. Or their industry is a significant laggard and hasn't yet experienced the dire consequences of commoditization.

If this is where you are, no worries. Thank you for reading through the book and gaining a better understanding of Customer Obsession and how to become "*REMARK*"able™. I would encourage you to keep an open mind. Now that you understand it better, you can hopefully see what others are doing in Customer Obsession. Stay in touch with the concept and read my blog. At some point, you might even want to join The Customer Obsession Council to start doing a deeper dive into how it might work for your organization.

Regardless of which Level you are at currently, **THANK YOU**. Thank you for taking the time to read the book. Thank you for taking the time to learn more about what becoming "*REMARK*"able™ is all about. **And most of all, thank you for your TIME**. I know how valuable this is, and I sincerely appreciate you investing some of it with me.

I hope I have opened up your mind to a new (or expanded) way of thinking about your customers. If I was successful, I consider the investment it took to write this a huge success. As I mentioned early in the book, my passion is simply to get your audience telling others how incredibly awesome and amazing you are, so they buy from you, not your competition. My close second goal is that you pick up some things from the book you would want to incorporate into your organization. Such as...

Adopt the **Advocacy Architecture™.** Start keeping all (or at least more) of the promises you and your employees make to your customers. Put together a **Promise Inventory™** so you can improve and build more **Trust**.

Focus on building **TRUST**. It will never let you down. Remember, no one on the planet will ever recommend you or be your Advocate unless they trust you.

Improve your **Customer Experience** and see how your "customers feel" about every interaction they have with you and your employees. You can change a lot by creating and delivering an incredibly awesome and amazing Customer Experience.

Find lots of ways to **Consistently Help** your audience of customers (and others) to improve their life and/or their business. They will reward you with more loyalty and share it with others.

Implement **AKA** and **Kill the Anxiety**. Do some investigation to see how much anxiety you might be creating and create some specific plans to eliminate it...immediately. This, alone, will help differentiate you from all your competitors.

Finally, continually evaluate your business to see if Customer Obsessed benefits and becoming "*REMARK*"able™ can help your business grow. Whether you want to avoid **commoditization** or simply build a more **profitable** business, Customer Obsession will change this equation. Or maybe having **happier employees** or creating more **Customer Loyalty** and **Advocacy** is of interest. Being Customer Obsessed will get you there.

Always focus on just how powerful "**true Differentiation**" is in our world economy and highly competitive marketplace. And please, **STOP MARKETING,** and start investing in your customers in new and unique ways so they can become your **Trusted Advocates and Marketing Agents™**. Because, at the end of the day, they are "**dying to do it for you!**"

Being **CUSTOMER OBSESSED** and **becoming "*REMARK*"able™** can make all this a reality. Now, make it happen...

THANK YOU...

Ongoing Encouragement

> "*If you are a leader, you should never forget that everyone needs encouragement. And everyone who receives it - young or old, successful or less-than-successful, unknown or famous is changed by it.*
>
> JOHN C. MAXWELL"

CONGRATULATIONS...you finished the book and stretched your mind in some new ways. You have some new ideas about growing your business in various areas by being Customer Obsessed. And you are well on your way to becoming "*REMARK*"able™...this is AWESOME!

I don't want to mislead you either...you're going to hit some speed bumps. You might even find yourself in the "Valley of Despair" along the way to being Customer Obsessed. And you might find some "pockets of resistance" you never knew existed inside your organization. Don't despair...you can (and will) get through all of these...but you might need a little extra help along the way. If you do, I'm here.

Just because you read my book doesn't mean I will leave you behind to fend for yourself. Sure, you can hire me to guide you through the entire process and increase your odds of success, but you might just need some guidance instead. I want to see you succeed...that is my passion, remember? So, I have put together a list of some resources that might help you along the way that are either no cost to you or certainly less than hiring me to be your guide.

Here are some resources (and ideas) I would offer to you. These will get you through many of these valleys or through the bumps along the way...

Read or skim through this book again, and you will gain a better (and deeper) understanding of some of the areas you are stuck in. Spend some time working through these areas in more detail. You want to go as deep as you can in certain areas to feel comfortable executing them and staying the course. For example, one area that everyone absolutely loves but gets stuck on is Promises. Super simple to grasp but a bit more challenging to analyze and change inside an organization. More in-depth reading and studying in this area can help. I plan to write another book on Trust and the Advocacy Architecture™ specifically for this purpose. Stay tuned and check back on my website (WOM10.com) for more updates on this release's timing.

Pass the book along (or pick up some additional copies) and give them to your leadership team to read over the next couple of weeks (set a deadline) so they can better understand what you are excited about and talking about. There is strength in numbers. If you have your leadership team on board, then move to your management team. The more of your leaders who are knowledgeable about Customer Obsession, the easier it is to create the Strategy and build the plans for transforming your organization. Allies are wonderful to have during initial startup and during difficult times.

Book me to come into your organization (or association) and speak. My speeches are always customized and tailored for a specific group. It works great in getting a more extensive group excited about Customer Obsession concepts in a short time. Without a doubt, these are the most effective ways to get a larger group excited and involved in the desire to become "*REMARK*"able™. They are also a lot of fun for the audience, and when I'm around, we get a lot of questions answered. These events are always a winner and can move your efforts along faster than most other activities we could do. There is more information about these different speaking options on my website, WOM10.com.

Go to my website, WOM10.com, and read through the process it takes to start your Journey. There are some specific steps to help you get started. There are other resources that can help you through your Journey. Check back often or subscribe since I will be adding a lot of additional handy insights and tools to help you be successful in your Journey of being Customer Obsessed and becoming "*REMARK*"able™.

Pick up a copy of my first book, "**Creating and Delivering Totally Awesome Customer Experiences,**" so you have a better understanding of what it takes to create a foundation of an extraordinary customer experience (you can probably snag a copy in the library if you don't want to buy one). Sadly, there is a limited supply of this original book left, and when they're gone, they're gone...until I rewrite the book. I plan to rewrite this sometime in 2021, so stay tuned for this release. If you want to dive into this now, I would strongly recommend you jump on Amazon and order one before they are gone.

Read my blog...I share lots of insights and stories on how you can start thinking differently, why you should, how you can begin to transition your company, and some specifics of things that will help you along your Journey. My blog is a "deep content" blog, so each post is pretty hearty with information. I have almost 500 posts on the site currently and add more all the time. Subscribe to the blog, so you can get the latest posts when they come out. You can also check many of these out on LinkedIn and Ezinearticles.com as well.

Let's meet (or talk)...not so I can "pimp" you to buy something, but so I can give you some direction and guidance for how you might want to move forward. I never charge for this initial discussion. As you read initially, it's simply my gift to you as a reader and devotee of Customer Obsession. The bottom line is that I'm here to help you along your Journey, whether you ever hire me or not.

Start to sketch out your Customer Obsession Journey so you can start to see how it could be incorporated into your company. It will take several revisions before you get this down, but it's worth the time invested. You need to spend some quality time creating a solid, actionable plan. Just get started!

Keep your eye out for some new online courses I am developing for all aspects of Customer Obsession...these will serve as guides for you and your teams and give you the structure, motivation, and roadmap to get through the different components. These will help you through all areas of Customer Obsession.

If you ever need some input, insights, or encouragement, shoot me a message. You can find my email address on my website (WOM10.com)...just shoot me a note. Even if you think you shouldn't, do it...it might just get you over a bump you're stuck on and allow you to continue on your Journey to becoming "*REMARK*"able™.

Again, CONGRATULATIONS, you have just entered the elite of the elite...companies who will become "*REMARK*"able™ in their industry. It will be an incredible Journey and one you will never forget. If there is ever anything I can do for you, please, please, please, don't hesitate to ask.

Blaine W. Millet

My "Other" Passion for ALL of US

With our brains and our smarts and our altruistic capability, we can do a lot of good.

JULIE PAYETTE

”

I want to close by sharing another "passion" I have with my Customer Obsession work and becoming *"REMARK"*able™. While somewhat related to the business side, it is more from a personal goal and objective. I think it will give you a slightly different way of thinking about all of this.

Spend the next 5 minutes thinking about YOU, being a customer. It might just change the way you think about the world around you and how we can help each other.

There is an altruistic advantage to all of us if we embrace the core of Customer Obsession. What would our world be like if more companies were obsessed with their customers? Would it be a safer, more trusted way to shop and buy? Would it ultimately save you time, anxiety, and other stresses if you knew every organization you dealt with was "all in" on treating you like you were special and important? I believe it would be a much better place. We would feel better about interacting with each other (not just from the buying experience) and have a much more positive attitude regarding how we treat people.

We could spend our time and energy exploring better solutions and options to help each other in our lives and/or our businesses...instead of playing all these marketing games. As you have read, a big part of this is understanding which organizations will serve us the way we desire to be served and work with those organizations. Similarly, it's also finding the right group of people we want to serve and going all-in on serving them the way they appreciate. This misalignment causes more grief than we can imagine. We could significantly reduce this...and all our experiences would be a hundred times more delightful.

A crucial part of being Customer Obsessed is "helping" others. But if we use the concepts I shared earlier with everyone in everything we do, how could this change our overall perspective on life? How can we help each other? What if we were "**People Obsessed**"? I know...sounds a bit creepy when you say it, but when you understand what it means, it makes total sense.

Suppose we, as people, were obsessed over how we could help each other feel incredible after each interaction with us (the way we want to obsess over our customers to make them feel incredible). How would that change all of our interactions? Wouldn't they be much more positive and exciting if we knew we were the center of their business? Wouldn't it be amazing if every time we interacted with someone, they left saying, "*WOW, that was an amazing person, and I feel like they truly cared about me and my situation.*" And if this happened, wouldn't you, in turn, say, *"I can't wait to tell others about this person*." What would that world look like?

It isn't any different for our customers...we want them to leave saying the same thing, "*WOW, this is an amazing company, and I love working with them because of how they make me feel*." There really isn't any difference...other than we carry it beyond the walls of our companies or outside of the internet...we make it personal about who we are and how we want people to remember us.

I have **one simple goal** in every meeting I have...**to leave the meeting with the person feeling like they got more than they gave**. I always want them to feel like they got some real value from investing their time to meet with me...even if the meeting was requested by them and not me. I want to help people do better because of meeting with me. After all, TIME is our most valuable asset, so I want to make sure they get the most out of the time we spend together.

> **SIDE NOTE:** I believe we have too many meetings. We meet to discuss the meeting we just had and plan the next meeting to discuss it in another meeting...lots of meetings. No wonder we have "**meeting anxiety**" and go into most of them, expecting to waste our precious time. Let's stop meeting just to meet where we don't add value to the other person or group.

My personal goal...I don't ever want the person (or group) I am meeting with to feel they wasted their time after our meeting!

Years ago, I made a conscious decision not to waste anyone's time. I had to give them something of "value" during the meeting to feel they hadn't wasted their time meeting with me. And I live by that with every encounter I have...I MUST give more than I get.

I also want to do this in my speeches as well...give the audience something they can take away and actually do something with so they feel like it was a great use of their "time." If my audience can leave feeling like they got something new, or a different way to think about their business, or some actionable things they can start to do immediately, I have succeeded.

Often, I ask a particular question as a part of my discussions with groups, "***Why is it we are willing to treat our customers in a way that we, as customers, would not personally feel good about if we were treated that way?***" Think about this question from both a personal perspective and with your business in mind. Ask yourself one question, as if you were a customer of your own business, "***Would I be raving to others about how incredibly awesome and amazing I was treated? And did they make me feel special and valued?***" Yes or no? Then ask why or why not?

That's my passion...to change this answer. I want every person that works in a business to say, ***"I would love being one of our customers because of how we care about them, treat them, and how we make them feel."***

What would our world look like if every business could execute this? How would our buying habits change, and how much more trust and caring would we see developing with businesses? How much more time would we save that we could use for better things than fighting with customers or companies?

When this happens, we are **Customer (People) Obsessed**. Why can't this happen in all aspects of our life? Why can't we answer this question in the affirmative in EVERY interaction we have with people, not just customers. When we meet someone new, why don't we all want them to leave the conversation feeling like they got a lot more out of it than they gave? Why wouldn't we want to have them leave feeling this was a great use of their time? Why wouldn't we want them to feel like they want to meet again because this discussion was so helpful?

If everyone moved their mindset to this type of thinking...WOW...this would be a pretty fantastic planet. I know...a bit out there and farfetched. Or is it...to be continued.

Thank you again for your TIME. I know you invested a lot of it to read this book. I sincerely hope it was worth it to you, and you received much more value than the price of the book and the time invested. If you did, then all my years of writing this book were well spent.

Drop me a note and let me know about your company...Customer Obsessed or not. I would love to visit or interact with you in some way and see if I can offer you some insights or thoughts along your Journey. It's what I do. I wish you nothing but incredibly awesome and amazing success in whatever you do.

All my best...

Acknowledgments

Where do you start when you want to thank everyone who has contributed something or had an influence on my writing? It is a massive list that spans many decades of work. Let me share some highlights...

Although I dedicated the book to my wife, Lorrie, she is also someone who needs to be acknowledged. She, like Mike, was always encouraging me to "get it done." She knew how important this was to me and that it needed to be written...so it got done. She also helped edit the book and provided invaluable feedback on its readability. Thank you Lorrie...

Similarly, my family (Krystal, JB, Katrina, Tyler, Kyle, little Jackson and Ollie, Joyce, and Gary) also need to be recognized for their constant support and encouragement along the way. Their massive support through my time with cancer was incredible. But they knew all along I needed to write this book and kept encouraging me to get it done. Thank you family...

One person, Mike Langhout, deserves to be at the top of my list. Not only did Mike strongly encourage me to write the book, but he has also been a constant cheerleader for me to get it done. He is that "thorn in your side" that you can't get rid of, but I am so thankful and blessed that he was there. Mike also provided some great feedback and helped edit the book. When he told me, "This is a really great book that is a game-changer for anyone who chooses the path to become "REMARK"able™," I knew it was time to publish. I can't thank him enough for all he did to bring this to print. Thanks Mike...

I want to thank Rick and Laura Smith for their undying support and encouragement and for spending time reading through the book. As the ex-CEO of a very successful company, his opinion was invaluable. Hearing him tell me, "This is a great book every business leader needs to read and adopt," was both comforting and encouraging. Thank you Rick and Laura.

Dave Carroll is a constant cheerleader for me and this book. He has introduced me to some fantastic people over the years...it's what he does. He is the consummate connector of people. He was also quite helpful in the final edits of this book. And when Dave tells me he uses my methodology every day in his business, that is a tremendous vote of confidence. Thanks Dave.

I also want to thank the hundreds of supporters who have been a constant encouragement over the years to get this written. My sincere thanks to each of you for keeping me focused and motivated throughout this journey. You know who you are. While this list is certainly not complete, here's a start (in alphabetical order)...

Thank you... Jessica and Bryce Arnett, Sundar Balakrishnan, Beth Baska, Scott Becker, Steve Bean, Earl Bell, Kevin Blair, Roger Blier, Michelle Bomberger, Walter Boos, Jeff Boyer, Dennis Brislawn, Richard Brune, Marianne and Darrel Brunner, Jeff and Pam Campbell, Joe Castleberry, Pedro Castro, John Dammarell, Scott Dowling, Phil Eaton, Greg Endicott, Craig Engelbrecht, Tod Fiscus, Denise Foster, Eric Fry, Craig Gaudry, Elizabeth Harris, John Hartman, Cathi Hatch, Mike Hendrickson, Barry Horn, Mike Howerton, Jim Jamison, Jim Johnson, Peter and Judy Kapsales, Tim Knapp, Sandeep Krishnamurthy, Wendy Kristek, Jeff Levy, Stacy Lill, Stu Linscott, Tom Lofton, Janis Machala, Amanda Mayo, Pete McDowell, Brian McKenzie, Alex Millet, David Millet, Marilyn Milne, Mark Mitchell, George Myers, Arti O'Brien, JP O'Donnell, Nancy Truitt Pierce, Alan Pratt, Bill Price, Mike Prospeck, Gabe Pyle, Mark and Georgianne Rasmussen, Roger Reynolds, Liz Richards, Detlef Schrempf, David Shapiro, Cary Sholer, Tom Silver, Rick and Laura Smith, Larry Stout, Matt Swank, Samantha Theaumont, Carla Thompson, Jim and Ellen Walker, Tom Walker, Rob Watson, John Wilkinson, Jeanene Williams, Scott Winston, Bruce Worrall, Walt Yeager, and many, many others.

THANK YOU! You have all been an inspiration to me in some way along this journey, and I sincerely thank you for your support and encouragement.

About the Author

BLAINE MILLET

This book happened because of God and Cancer. And it's the right place to start to tell you about myself. Here is my story...

Let me step back and give you a brief "historical" background...my career that led me to write this book. If you allow me a few minutes to read about my journey, I think you'll appreciate the book even more.

I grew up with my dad owning his own business. He designed and installed kitchens and all the things that go into making them beautiful. He was an entrepreneur. I worked in that business until I graduated from the University of Utah with a B.S. in Biology and an MBA focused on finance and marketing. Working for my dad taught me many things that worked and didn't work for a small business owner. Fast forward to the end...his business ended up closing its doors because an employee embezzled a substantial sum of money from him. It was a sad way to end a lifelong enterprise.

On the good side of what worked was his ability to interact with his customers. They loved him. He was over the top helpful and went out of his way to help them out. I can still remember delivering appliances on Christmas Eve for our customers so they could enjoy them on Christmas Day. He was Customer Obsessed and "*REMARK*"able™. And his customers went out of their way to do his marketing for him. I was fortunate enough to see how this worked firsthand at an early age. I learned a lot about customers from him.

When I graduated from college, I started my new career in sales for IBM in Seattle. This was eye-opening. I spent my entire life in a small business and was immediately thrust into a Fortune 100 company. My MBA prepared me well for how to understand and work in such a behemoth organization. I learned a ton and was quite successful. I learned from my mentors the same thing I learned from my dad...putting the customer first rewarded you nicely.

Since I didn't want to move from Seattle (IBM meant "I've Been Moved" in those days), I took a position running a regional practice for a national search firm. It was eye-opening for me with regard to the customer. In the search business, you have two customers...the employee and the employer. It was a tough business. But if you were Customer focused, you did well. You got great candidates telling their friends, while at the same time, hiring managers were telling others to work with you. Being Customer-focused was key to success.

As it turns out, after being in the search business for several years, Arthur Andersen recruited me to help them build a national sales organization. It was the first of its kind in large public accounting firms. I was part of an initial team of 5 people focused on this new opportunity. Boy do I have some stories to tell about this role, but time and space are too precious...ask me sometime.

I stayed with Andersen for eight years. Four years in the sales organization and four years were starting up and running a small-midsize business consulting practice. The four years spent consulting were at warp speed. I loved it. Helping companies get better at what they do was exhilarating and very rewarding. Taking care of your customers is (or should be) the lifeblood of any consultant or advisor. It is a perfect opportunity to be Customer Obsessed and excel.

One of the areas I introduced into my consulting practice was "Customer Satisfaction Analysis." Believe it or not, it didn't exist in our strategic planning methodology. To me, it was (and is) where everything starts. Incorporating this was a real differentiator for us. We started with the customer and built everything else around helping the customer. It was my first opportunity to create a formal process for incorporating everything I had learned throughout my career and building a methodology. It was a breakthrough time for me.

I left Andersen and joined my brother in an international dotcom startup focused on marketing systems. We worked together for a couple of years before we both left. Truth be told, it was a mess. Great software and applications, but definitely not a Customer Obsessed company.

But there is always a hidden lining in everything. It led my brother, Gary, and I to write a book about how powerful Customer Experiences can be for an organization. And, we developed a specific formula for how any company could do it consistently. Our book "**Creating and Delivering Totally Awesome Customer Experiences**" was a landmark. We didn't see any other book like it at the time, so we created a methodology to make the Customer Experience a business process. It was also my first taste of being an author.

The book changed everything for me. It gave me a solid foundation to guide and help companies understand how compelling being Customer Obsessed could be for their business. We wrote this book while I was a Partner at Grant Thornton, another public accounting firm. Unfortunately, I didn't get to use this groundbreaking methodology in the firm. As my brother and I continued to develop it further, I was recruited to help start-up a new role inside Sprint. A few of us came in to create a Strategic Client Advisory position. While the role was interesting, the company wasn't. It wasn't Customer Obsessed, and it soon became evident it wasn't where I belonged.

It was time for me to take this out on my own and start my own company...which I did in 2007. It began, appropriately named, as Customer Experiences Inc. It evolved over the years to become WOM^{10} (Word-of-Mouth on Steroids). It had (and still has) one simple focus...

> ***To Inspire and help Businesses become "REMARK"able™ by being Customer Obsessed, creating an army of Advocates and Marketing Agents™ who happily and excitedly do their marketing for them.***

WOM^{10} started around the same time as the Internet Revolution and the introduction of Social Media. I spent several years helping companies see how powerful Social Media could be when used with their customers. For those leaders who "got it," it was compelling. They could "help" their audiences, which got them the attention they deserved and needed. During this time, I became an author again and co-authored an e-book, ***"Business Tools – What Executives need to know about Social Media."*** This book focused on the "mind shift" needed to successfully leverage social media to be a powerful tool in helping an organization become "*REMARK*"able™.

My goal was to get companies to STOP MARKETING and START LEVERAGING the most powerful marketing engine available...their audience and customers. As you can see by now, it has been a constant theme with me my entire life and was the genesis behind starting WOM^{10}...and it hasn't changed. It has always been in my background. WOM^{10} allowed me to put it all together into a straightforward and easy to use methodology...The "*REMARK*"able Triangle™.

Today, I get introduced as a Nationally Recognized Speaker, which gives me an excellent platform to share this incredible opportunity with thousands of people. Besides my speaking and this book, I also write a lot about how and why you would want to become "*REMARK*"able™ on my blog. It has been around for a long time and has some gold nuggets you might also enjoy. That's it. It's where I am today.

But now, back to where I started in the beginning...God and Cancer.

Let's start with the cancer portion. In January of 2017, I got the call none of us want from our doctor. The one that says the CT scan showed a mass the size of an orange in my bladder...cancer. That word put just about everything on hold, including my book. I had three surgeries, several immunotherapy treatments throughout the rest of the year, and battled a blood clot in my leg. It was a memorable year. But I got through it with the help of my family and God. Today, almost four years later, I am still cancer-free. I'm truly blessed. Now for the God component...

While I have always been a "Christian," I wasn't what I would call a fully committed one. I can admit it today. During my cancer, I saw, felt, and heard from God in many ways, more than I can share here. Hit me up sometime if you would like to hear my story...it's pretty exciting. During this time, God showed up for me...a lot. He guided me through the most challenging time in my life. And I am eternally committed to him and Jesus Christ for giving me so many gifts.

But there is one other big part of the God story. I know now that he wanted me to put my book on hold. He didn't want me to finish it...at least not yet. It wasn't the right time, even though I was ready to get it published. He was right. It wasn't ready for primetime. The extra time he gave me during my cancer allowed me to create a more straightforward, concise structure to encapsulate this powerful, game-changing methodology. He showed me what was missing and gave me extra time to create what you are reading today. He literally gave me The "*REMARK*"able Triangle™...the simple and straightforward structure for how anyone can become "*REMARK*"able™.

It was exactly what I needed to finish the book and give you, the reader, a simple and straightforward formula and recipe any company can execute. It was the answer I needed to pull everything together.

If I hadn't gotten cancer, you wouldn't be getting this powerful formula. With this break from writing, God led me to the structure of The "*REMARK*"able Triangle™ and the centerpiece any company can use to become "*REMARK*"able™. I can't describe the feeling of how incredible this was for me...I'm still in shock today.

So, without God, my cancer, and the unbelievable support from my wife and family, you wouldn't have gotten the most powerful model I have ever created (or seen) to help an organization truly differentiate themselves. And I have God to thank for guiding me to create what will change your business...forever.

That's my story. That's who I am. I appreciate you reading through it and taking the time to understand how all this came about. It wasn't quick, haphazard, or something trendy. It is a lifetime of learning and experiences that allowed me to write this book. I'm incredibly proud of it. I know it is the right book at the right time for the right reasons. And it is something that can genuinely and honestly change your business forever. It can help you be truly unique and differentiated in the eyes of your customers (and audience), so they can be your Advocates and Marketing Agents™.

I hope this book can help change your story. I hope you can look back and say this helped you become incredibly awesome and amazing...and that you became "*REMARK*"able™. I wish you nothing but the very best, and if I can ever be of help to you, or you just want to chat, give me a shout.

Research and References

1) Forrester Research: **2018 Customer Service Trends: How Operations Become Faster, Cheaper — And Yet, More Human Vision: The Contact Centers For Customer Service Playbook** by Kate Leggett January 24, 2018
2) Salesforce.com: **Customer Expectations Hit All-Time Highs** from State of the Connected Customer 2018.
3) Watermark Consulting Group: **2019 Customer Experience ROI Study**
4) Neil Patel: **Fastest Way to Lose Customers** from Kissmetrics research data
5) Econsultancy: **Marketers more focused on acquisition than retention** by Christopher Ratcliff August 19, 2014
6) Invesp research - Convince & Convert: **Why you should be focusing on Customer Retention, not Acquisition**, by Chris Marr
7) Amazon: **The Fourth Industrial Revolution** by Klaus Schwab, January 13, 2017
8) Forrester Research: **Competitive Strategy In The Age Of The Customer** by Josh Bernoff, June 6, 2011
9) Edelman Research: **2018 Edelman Trust Barometer Reveals Record-breaking Drop in Trust in the U.S.** by Edelman, January 22, 2018
10) Bain and Company, **Focus on the Customer** by Mark Gottfredson and Rob Markey, August 13, 2014

Made in the USA
Monee, IL
07 April 2021

65046830R00163